"After reading *The Mystery of the Divine Paternal Heart of God Our Father*, I can't begin to estimate or envision the many years Dr. Thomas W. Petrisko dedicated to researching, verifying and organizing the immense, diverse and intriguing contents of this Holy Spirit inspired book. From renowned Scripture scholar, retreat master and author, Father William McCarthy's Foreword to Catholic author extraordinariness's spellbinding writing in each chapter, this book is "literately addictive" and will surely create a huge number of "I can't put this book down" evangelists of its important mission.

Indeed, Dr. Thomas W. Petrisko's classic is truly the work of the Holy Spirit as the inspired words and themes of centuries of Popes, Saints, renowned theologians and Doctors of the Church, and their encyclicals, books, documents and articles are brought together in a way that I foresee will quickly become required reading for Catholic hierarchy, priests, religious and laity.

This gift from Heaven, so brilliantly assembled by Dr. Petrisko, allows us to easily recognize the knowledge and wisdom of the wisest of the wise throughout the history of the Church regarding the essence of God Our Father's merciful love for his children. Thus, as *The Mystery of the Divine Paternal Heart of God Our Father* so wonderfully, irresistibly and convincingly reveals, we all are called to become acutely aware of Our Father's plan for us, His children, His Church and the world in this extremely unpredictable and unprecedented times-for it is a plan that was born in His Divine Paternal Heart, the Abyss of His great Love for all mankind!

—Bud MacFarlane, M.I.
International renowned Catholic Evangelist
Militia Immaculata of St. Maximilian Kolbe

"Dr. Petrisko's new book on God the Father is a theological gem. Moreover, his doctrinal development of the Father is presented in the guidelines described by Cardinal John Henry Newman in the nineteenth century. Adhering to Newman rules, Petrisko's treatise on the Father is not only in consistent continuity with past doctrine and not contradictory, but also a natural and logical outgrowth of the truth of who God our Father is according to the Fathers' and Doctors' of the Church. Petrisko shows us the truth of our Father's love existed in seed form in the earlier writing and that his development of the doctrine on the Father is a consolidation, not a destruction of "old truth". The love of the Father, as seen in Jesus Christ, is and has always been the key to the great hope our faith offers the world. Now, this hope is even more visible in the truth of the invisible reality of the Heart of God the Father, the great wellspring of love and mercy that Mankind today, more than ever, is searching for.

—Dr. Raymond Badzik
Catholic Lay Leader and Eucharistic Minister

Praise for *The Mystery of the Divine Paternal Heart of God Our Father*

"One of the most *significantly* and *accurately* written historical accounts ever of the Father's Love for His children. This is a gifted book for all ages of time, perhaps revealing the key that unlocks the doorway to the "*Kingdom on earth as it is in Heaven*:" The *Divine Paternal Heart of God our Father*!

—Mary Lou Sokol
Catholic Educator and Youth Minister

"Not many have made such a thorough researched study of our Eternal Father as Dr. Petrisko has done. It opens for us a much deeper understanding and devotion to our loving Father, especially for this age." May our Father be praised even more by this book!"

—Sister Agnes McCormick
Catholic Administrator and
President of the Marian Resource Center

"A *ground breaking* work on an area I knew little about, but enjoyed reading and learning. An easy to read book for clergy and lay people alike, on the least understood Person of the Most Holy Trinity – the Eternal Father. We know a lot about Jesus and the workings of the Holy Spirit, but as Jesus said, "I and the Father are one."

—Ted Flynn
MaxKol Communications
Author of *The Thunder of Justice* and *Hope of the Wicked*

"As I have seen, the whole life and ministry of Dr. Petrisko is directed to God the Father. And now, he is calling the *Catholic Church* to have a special devotion to the Father and to set up a special Feast to bring honor, praise and worship to the Father. In this book, I believe the great apostle of God the Father, Thomas Petrisko, has written a masterful theological and spiritual treatise to promote the devotion needed to the *Paternal Heart of the Father* that will hopefully lead up to this special Feast Day for God the Father – **The Solemnity of the Divine Paternal Heart: The Feast of the Father of All Mankind!**"

—Rev. William J. McCarthy, MSA
October 16, 2013
Feast of St. Mary Margaret Alcoque

"Dr. Thomas Petrisko sheds light on this infinite desire of the Father to be known, loved and honored by each of His children, now in this grace-filled 'Era of Time.' He foresees Mary, leading her children to bring about the long awaited Triumph of her Immaculate Heart in order to usher in that promised 'Era of Peace,' a time when the Church will know the Father intimately and live in the Kingdom of His Divine Will.

Furthermore, Dr. Petrisko calls for a *Feast* in honor of the *Divine Paternal Heart* of the Father. This Feast will help us to see with 'the Eyes of our Souls' – to experience the Love of our Father in the depths of our spiritual heart and to return to Him as His prodigal children. But more importantly, this Feast would bring about the unification of all God's children that there might be: "One body and one Spirit, as you were also called to the one hope of your call; one Lord, one faith, one baptism; one God and Father of all, Who is over all and through all and in all" (Eph 4:4-6).

—Father David Tourville
New York

"Our hearts are created out of love. This love is the *Heart of the Father*. If we listen, if we act on His Love, then we can bring His Love to the world. Dr. Petrisko's insights in this book on the Father's Love will bring you straight to the "Heart" of why you exist and how to share our Father's *Heart*, His Love, with all you meet!"

—Marty Rotella
Catholic Contemporary Music Artist
and Speaker

"Words *cannot* describe the importance of Dr. Petrisko's book to our contemporary world. In a time when the "culture of death" prevails in the world, God the Father is truly the answer. He is the great remedy for darkness and evil and the great means of healing that is needed for the world. In union with His Son Jesus and the Holy Spirit, our Father represents the hope that all of His prodigal sons and daughters desperately need to seek and find, a hope contained in the Love and Mercy emanating from His *Divine Paternal Heart*!"

—Dr. Frank Novasack, Jr.,
Catholic Author and Music Artist
Nova Productions, LLC

The Mystery of the
Divine Paternal Heart
of God Our Father

Why the Time Has Come to Honor the Love
of the Father of All Mankind with a Feast

DR. THOMAS W. PETRISKO

ST. ANDREW'S
PRODUCTIONS

Special thanks to Ignatius Press, Alba House, Queenship Publishing, Random House and all other publishers for permission to quote from their works.

© 2015 St. Andrew's Productions

All rights reserved. No part of this book may be produced in any manner without permission in writing from the publisher.

ISBN: 978-1-891903-44-1

Published by:
St. Andrew's Productions
5168 Campbells Run Road, Ste 203
Pittsburgh, PA 15205

Tel: 412-787-9735
Fax: 412-787-5204
Web: Saintandrew.com
Email: standrewsproductions@yahoo.com

The author and publisher are grateful to those publishers of others whose materials, whether in the public domain or protected by copyright laws, have been used in one form or another in this book. Every reasonable effort has been made to determine copyright holders of excerpted materials and photographs and to secure permissions as needed. If any copyrighted materials have been inadvertently used in this work without proper credit being given in one form or another, please notify the Publisher in writing so that future printings of this work may be corrected accordingly.

PRINTED IN THE UNITED STATES OF AMERICA

Available to Speak

Dr. Thomas W. Petrisko is available to come to your Church or organization to speak about God the Father's great love for mankind and His call for His children to return to Him. He is also available for radio, television, internet and print media interviews. If you desire to contact him, please call: (412)-787-9735 or contact St. Andrew's Productions at www.saintandrew.com

IN APPRECIATION

I am deeply indebted to my mother, Mary Petrisko, who departed for her eternal reward shortly before this book was undertaken. I believe the Lord used her life of sacrifice and suffering to birth this work. I am especially appreciative of my wife, Emily, and to my six children, Maria, Sarah, Joshua, Natasha, Dominique and Jesse. Their sacrifice and support of me cannot be minimized as I failed them often to answer God's call in my life.

I wish to thank my editors, Dr. Frank Novasack, Jr., Erica Rankin and Michael Fontecchio. I am also grateful to Fr. William McCarthy, Fr. Peter Murphy, and Fr. David Tourville for their invaluable prayers, spiritual guidance, words and assistance. I also appreciate the support, advice and inspiration I received from Mary Lou Sokol, Dr. Raymond Badzik, Amanda DeFazio, and the Petrisko and Sanchez families.

Dedication

This book is dedicated to all the great souls that gave their fiat to the Divine Paternal Heart of God the Father. From Abraham, Moses, David and Elijah to John, Paul, Francis and Theresa; may all come to follow in their footsteps in seeking to answer the call of the Father's Heart.

Cover Artwork

The cover design is by Michael Fontecchio and John Elsman. The front cover image was provided by Mary Lou Sokol and used with permission. The image may not be altered or reproduced.

Scriptural Credits

Scriptural quotations are taken from the Holy Bible – RSV: Catholic Edition. Alternate translations from the Latin Vulgate Bible (Douay Rheims Version – DV) are indicated when used. Some of the Scriptural quotations are from the New American Bible, the New American Bible – St. Joseph Edition, the New American Bible – Fireside Family Edition 1984-1985, the Douay Rheims Bible, the New American Bible – Red Letter Edition 1986, the New Jerusalem Bible, the New Jerusalem Bible, 1966, The Douay Rheims Old Testament of the Holy Catholic Bible, 1992.

To

Emily Petrisko, my extraordinary wife and soulmate, and to my children, Maria, Sarah, Joshua, Natasha, Dominique and Jesse who have all come to feel and know the presence of the Love of the Father in their lives.

Contents

Foreword
Show Us the Father xiii

Introduction
Finding our Father 1

Part I
The Threshold of the Father

Chapter One
Original Separation 25

Chapter Two
The Rays of God's Fatherhood 33

Chapter Three
One With the Father 39

Chapter Four
The Threshold of the Father 49

Part II
Nearest to the Father's Heart

Chapter Five
Nearest to the Father's Heart 57

Chapter Six
The Mystery of the Father's Heart 65

Chapter Seven
A Crisis of Civilization 75

Part III
The Heart of God in Scripture and the Church

Chapter Eight
A Fatherly God 87

Chapter Nine
The Heart of God in the Old Testament 93

Chapter Ten
The Propriety of the Father 101

Part IV
The Divine Paternal Heart of God the Father

Capter Eleven
The Theology of God the Father. 113

Chapter Twelve
Christ Reveals the Father 121

Chapter Thirteen
The Heart of the Father in the New Testament 131

Chapter Fourteen
The Paternal Heart and the Bread of Life. 139

Chapter Fifteen
The Sacred Heart of Jesus 147

Chapter Sixteen
Divine Hearts. 157

Chapter Seventeen
The Right Hand of the Father 165

Chapter Eighteen
The Divine Paternal Heart of God Our Father 171

Part V
Triumph of the Living Father

Chapter Nineteen
The Paternal Heart of Life 185

Chapter Twenty
An Attack on God Himself 191

Chapter Twenty-One
The Grandeur of the Father's Love 197

Chapter Twenty-Two
The Living Father 203

Chapter Twenty-Three
Favored Daughter of the Father 209

Chapter Twenty-Four
Our Lady of the Paternal Heart 219

Chapter Twenty-Five
The Triumph of the Immaculate Heart. 225

Part VI
Temples of God

Chapter Twenty-Six
David: A Man After God's Own Heart. 237

Chapter Twenty-Seven
The Heart of Solomon 245

Chapter Twenty-Eight
"My Heart Shall Be There" 255

Chapter Twenty-Nine
Christ: The New Temple 263

Chapter Thirty
Temples of God 269

Part VII
The Coming of the Father

Chapter Thirty-One
The Ark of the Father 281

Chapter Thirty-Two
The Coming of the Father 287

Chapter Thirty-Three
The Our Father 295

Part VIII
To Know, Love and Honor God Our Father

Chapter Thirty-Four
Consecration to our Father 301

Chapter Thirty-Five
The Solemnity of the Divine Paternal Heart of God Our Father . 313

Chapter Thirty-Six
The Feast of the Father of All Mankind 317

Chapter Thirty-Seven
The Celebration of Life 325

Chapter Thirty-Eight
St. Philip and the Apostles of the Father 333

Epilogue
Back to the Garden 341

Notes 349

Appendix A 375

Appendix B 427

"Did not Christ say that our Father, who 'sees in secret,' is always waiting for us to have recourse to Him in every need and always waiting for us to study His mystery: the mystery of the Father and His love?"

—St. John Paul II, *Dives in Misericordia*

XIV *The Mystery of the Divine Paternal Heart of God Our Father*

Foreword

SHOW US THE FATHER

By Fr. William J. McCarthy, MSA

At the *Last Supper* Jesus revealed to His disciples the essence of God the Father: "In my Father's house there are many dwellings. I am going ahead to prepare a place for you so that where I am you also may be" (Jn 14:2), "I am the way, and the truth, and the life; no one comes to the Father except through me" (Jn 14:6). "'Lord,' Philip said to him, 'Show us the Father and that will be enough for us.' Jesus replied, 'After I have been with you for all this time, you still do not know me? Whoever has seen me has seen the Father'" (Jn 14:9).

In his book, Dr. Petrisko has shown us the essence of the Father too; the Father's *Divine Paternal Heart* – full of love and mercy for all His children. Indeed, all life, all holiness, all wisdom flows from the Father through the Son in the power of the Holy Spirit. And the great plan of the Father's Heart is to share this *Divine Trinitarian Life* with us as His children.

Jesus is that plan – incarnate. Yes, in following Jesus we come to know the Father's love for us: "The Son can do nothing by himself, he can do only what he sees the Father doing" (Jn 5:9).

The spirituality of Jesus, as Dr. Petrisko shows us, is to do nothing except what the Father wishes and thereby we enter into the Heart of the Father to receive His love and mercy, for Jesus always listened to and obeyed the Father (cf. Jn 5:19).

The Church teaches us that God the Father loves us so much that He sent His Son to form us into a *Mystical Body* – His Church; and also to dwell in our spirits so that we, like Him, may love tenderly and obey always the Father. True spirituality, therefore, does not begin with the *Law* on down – we are not legalists – nor with the *Bible* on down – we are not fundamentalists; but with the Father on down! In showing us the Heart of the Father, Dr. Petrisko shows us the *plan* of the Father, which is to create His *divine family* on earth. And, he says, in turning to the Father's Paternal Heart, in honoring His love for mankind with a Feast Day in the *Catholic Church* – we can further make this happen.

As we read in the *Prologue* of the Gospel of St. John, the revelation of Jesus being *"nearest to the Father's Heart"* (Jn 1:18) has stirred the curiosity of theologians for ages. As Dr. Petrisko writes, the union of the Father and Son, this union of life in the Heart of the Father, is a profound mystery of the faith. In their great writings, the Fathers and Doctors express their understanding of this inner domain of God's divine nature, often defined as His *Bosom*, His *Side* or His *Abyss*. The Father's Heart is inexpressibly described as the source of the infinite and infallible love and mercy of the Father.

Today's leaders of the Church have said the same. Pope Benedict XVI writes, "The saying at the end of the *Prologue* is the decisive key to the image of Jesus. 'No one has ever seen God; it is only the Son, who is nearest to the Father's Heart, who has made him known'" (Jn 1:18). Likewise, Pope John Paul II tells us that the Father's Heart is part of the great "mystery of the Father" that the Church is called to better understand, especially in the Father's intimate relationship with the Son. He writes, "Undoubtedly certain elements of the Old Testament revelation constituted a preparation for what we have in the Gospels. Nevertheless, only the Son was capable of introducing us to this mystery. Since no one has seen God, no one knew the mystery of his inner life, the Son alone knew it. It is only the Son, who is nearest to the Father's Heart, who has made him known."

And truly, our Father is the *greatest* mystery. All life has a beginning, and the Father is that beginning, "In the beginning…was God" (Jn 1:1). Therefore all life, holiness, wisdom, mercy and love flows from the Father, from the mystery of His love. St. Paul states, "It is for this reason that I kneel before the Father in whom every family in heaven and earth receives its name" (Eph 3:14). Indeed, we are made in the Father's image and likeness, not He in ours. He will never be like us. But we were willed to be like Him. The Father begets us by grace and adoption. We don't *invent* God as Freud and the intellectuals would say; He creates us. The Father creates us as male and female, although the Father is, in essence, both; yet transcending both. What does the Father give to us? Everything, including His Son, His Church, His wisdom, His love and His mercy; but most of all His very *Life* – the *Life* in His Paternal Heart. In this way, He makes us partakers in His divinity (cf. 2 Pt 1:4).

God becomes our Father, and we His children, at *Baptism*. Thus, the divine life in our God is a life in which we were made for and have our being. But we become sons and daughters, only insofar as we allow God to be our Father, as Jesus always did. This divine life that Jesus shares with us makes us the Father's children – brothers and sisters in the *family of God*. Yes, this God is therefore a *Family*: Father, Son and Holy Spirit, loving one another and delighting in one another. As Pope John Paul II states, 'God is a Family,' because in the Godhead are all the essence of family life; fatherhood, sonship, relationship and love. Moreover, what God is doing upon earth is creating a one, holy universal family because God is one holy Father who loves everyone. Thus, in Heaven, perhaps after Purgatory, in which all division will be healed, all sin will be cleansed and all heresy enlightened, we will be partakers of the one, holy Father who is God.

To see into the Heart of the Father, therefore, puts an end to all atheism, humanism, secularism, radical feminism, all legalism and all fundamentalism and puts into us an eternity of love and mercy. To image the Father's Heart tells us not only about origin and authority, but also about meaning and fulfillment.

Thank you Dr. Petrisko, who shows us the Theocentrism in which the Father is the absolute center of all reality and life. The Father is not up there or down here (*humanism*) or part of reality (*paganism*) or totally only imminent (*pantheism*) or total transcendent (*deism*); but the Father *is* all in *all*. Such Theocentricism is not abstract but totally personal, heartwarming, gentle, kind, and merciful.

As I have seen, the whole life and ministry of Dr. Petrisko is directed to the Father. And now, he is calling the *Catholic Church* to have a special devotion to the Father and to set up a special Feast to bring honor, praise and worship to the Father. In this book, I believe the great apostle of God the Father, Thomas Petrisko, has written a masterful theological and spiritual treatise to promote the devotion needed to the Paternal Heart of the Father that will hopefully lead up to this special Feast Day for God the Father – **The Solemnity of the Divine Paternal Heart: The Feast of the Father of All Mankind**!

Indeed, the time has come for us to acknowledge this role of God the Father, and to realize that he who has seen Jesus and His Sacred Heart, has also seen the Father and His Paternal Heart.

Rev. William J. McCarthy, MSA
October 16, 2013
Feast of St. Mary Margaret Alcoque

"The Church begins there, in the *Heart of the Father*, who had this idea…of love. So this love story began, a story that has gone on for so long and is yet not ended."
—Pope Francis

Introduction

FINDING OUR FATHER

"Not that anyone has seen the Father—only the one who is from God has seen the Father" (Jn 6:46).

Laid out in the scheme of mankind's salvation history is the end, the ultimate completion of the journey that holds the promise of a new beginning.

The process to the end is gradual, with every person playing a role in God's plan for mankind to return to Him. However, the hope of the Christian lies in the great finale. Life everlasting—life in a state of supreme and definitive happiness, and life dwelling with the Most Holy Trinity—awaits the tried and true.

This is the mystery of the blessed communion with God and Christ that Scripture speaks of in images: life, light, peace, wedding feasts, wine of the kingdom, the heavenly Jerusalem, and the new Paradise. It is to be, St. Paul writes, "what no eye has seen, nor ear heard, nor the human heart conceived, what God has prepared for those who love him" (1 Cor 2:9).

At the center of this mystery lies another great mystery: the reality of returning to God the Father. Scripture's words in this regard are powerful and incomprehensible: those who die in His grace and friendship will see Him "as he is," "face to face" (1 Jn 3:2, 1 Cor 13:12, cf. Rev 22:4). We will gaze upon Him with the *eyes of our soul*.

In this life, God cannot be seen as He is; He opens up His mystery to man's contemplation, gives him the capacity to understand, and then awaits us. He awaits us to draw near to Him in order for us to some day return to Him. Our Father awaits us whether we believe in Him or not, whether we are a sinner or a saint. From Adam to the last soul, He awaits all to seek His embrace and to one day arrive safely at His house. He waits in order to welcome His children home, and to reveal the love He poured upon our lives—from the first moment of conception to the last beat of our hearts.

And as all shall find to be true, no one has been left to journey without His watchful eye upon every step. The Bible conveys this promise, for our Father sees over His children. He guards them from the dangers of sin and eternal death, waiting to raise them up to eternal life in Him.

While the ancient Scriptures emphasize God as a loving Father of our first parents—Adam and Eve—of the Patriarchs—Abraham, Isaac, and Jacob—and of its heroes—Moses, David, and the prophets—God was no less of a Father to the controversial figures of Israel's ancestry and history, who struggled with sin or rebelled against His will. He was the Father of Cain and Ishmael, of Essau and Laban, of Dathan, Jezebel, Saul, and Absalom. He was Father to the many whose lives vividly portrayed the day-to-day struggles and failings of the human flesh.

Moreover, God's paternity extended beyond His chosen people. Although they could not hear His voice or know His words, the Ammonites, Moabites, Ishmaelites, and Canaanites were His children too, as were the Egyptians, Philistines, Assyrians, Babylonians, and many others. Thus, we need to remember that God was Father of the Pharaohs at the time of the *exodus*, and of the Kings of Babylon during the times of the *exile*. Scripture reveals He guided and used them. He aided them when in need. In their sleep He warned of approaching trouble, and helped them escape ruin. He was Father of *all* of the so-called *gentiles* in the Bible. While they were not His *First Born*, they were still His children who He loved and watched over, who He provided for and knew by name.

He was *Father of all* and His hand was *on all*.

The New Testament amplifies and illuminates this truth of the Father's love for every one of His children. While God sends Israel its promised *Savior* and establishes His Church through Jesus' chosen Apostles, He can be found blessing the Samaritans, Greeks, Cyrenians, Ethiopians, and even the hated Romans. From Herod to Caiaphas, from the Canaanite woman to the Roman centurion, we find God at work. He heals the sick, feeds the hungry, and tries to nudge souls out of darkness toward light.

Even Pilate, Christ's reluctant judge, seems to have been warned by the Father through his wife's dream, which had asked for the life of Jesus, "that holy man" (Mt 27:19), to be spared.

As in the Old Testament, we find a merciful Father leading back the misled, the lost, and the rebellious. We find Him healing the broken of body and converting the hard of heart, all the while calling His fallen, sinful children back to His loving arms through His patient, guiding, paternal will and His only beloved Son, Jesus Christ.

Our world today is no different. God is Father to not just Jews, Catholics, and Protestants, not only to Moslems, Buddhists, and Hindus, but to people of every faith and of no faith: to agnostics, atheists, and even satanists. He is Father to Americans and Europeans, Asians and Africans, to people of every land and nation, every island and country. Unfailingly, He loves and nurtures all, wishing to lose none of His sheep. He is Father to each and every person conceived, and each soul is precious in His eyes.

There is no mystery to this truth. The Gospels are clear how the Father sees (cf. Mt 6:18) and provides (cf. Mt 6:32) for all His children, that "his sun rises on the bad and the good" and He "causes rain to fall on the just and the unjust" (Mt. 5:45). More than that, He knows every need before spoken (cf. Mt 6:8), repays for good deeds (cf. Mt 6:4) and rescues those who call upon Him for deliverance from evil (cf. Mt 6:13). Because of His attentive love, He is always ready to answer prayers and give good things when asked, even to the "ungrateful and the wicked" (Lk 6:35), especially through His Son, Jesus Christ (cf. Mt 7:11), who reveals the Father to us (cf. Mt. 11:27).

And yes, Christ revealed the Father in the fullness of His Being. God our Father, Jesus established, is truth (cf. Jn 4:23) and power (cf. Mk 10:17-18). He is merciful and compassionate (cf. Lk 6:36). He is good (cf. Mk 10:17-18) and holy (cf. Jn 17:3). The Father is the one, true *Father of All Mankind*, who is a "living God" (Mt 16:16), who "*is* life" (cf. Jn 5:26) and "*gives* life" (Jn 6:33). He is a divine "Person" (cf. Mt 16:16, Jn 5:26), not a wooden statue or stone idol, not a wanton idea or cosmic force, and not "dead" as today's world rushes to declare Him. From the beginning, the Father has been forever real and present in the world, always serving His children in His hidden and humble way, always *Father* to all so none are *Fatherless*. In essence, He is a "perfect Father" (cf. Mt 5:48) to those of every race, color, religion, kingdom, and nation. He is Father because of His great *paternal love* for His children.

He is *Father*, Christ revealed, because He *is* Love (cf. Jn 3:35)!

Yes, God our Father *is* Love—infinite, unfathomable, and everlasting love! He is a love that flows from an abyss of love, His *Divine Paternal Heart*, the font of all love and life, and the mystical home every soul is invited to return to in the footsteps of Christ, the Redeemer.

✸✸✸✸✸✸✸

In 1856, Pope Pius IX established the *Feast of the Sacred Heart of Jesus* in the Universal Church.[1] This followed centuries of widespread devotion to the Sacred Heart that was promulgated by the popes and some of the great Saints of the Middle Ages, such as, St. Bonaventure, St. Catherine of Sienna, St. John Eudes, and St. Margaret Mary.

Pope Pius XI said that the Sacred Heart expressed the very summary of our faith, "*totus religionis summa*," for it symbolized the inexhaustible source of mercy and love poured out by God the Father through the pierced Heart of His only begotten Son, Jesus.[2]

Understood by the Church to be a great source of refuge for mankind during times of crises, the Sacred Heart of Jesus became viewed as a trusted, necessary, and reliable way to turn to God on behalf of struggling humanity. The Sacred Heart is intended to remind man that his heart, like the rest of him, is made in the image and likeness of Christ. In essence, the Sacred Heart conveys the understanding that man's heart needs the love of Christ's Heart—a Heart recognized by the Church to be *human* and *divine*—in order to be enlightened by God's truth and will, and in order to resist and overcome the evils of the world. Thus, moved by the Holy Spirit, the Sacred Heart of the Son, opened on the Cross by the will of the Father, redeems and repairs the sins of each generation as it remains the ultimate symbolic testimony of Christ's love for man.

With the advent of the modern world, along with the growing danger and unpredictability of the times, the popes turned even more to the Sacred Heart. From Pope Leo' XIII's encyclical letter, *Annum Sacrum,* which consecrated the world to the Sacred Heart – to Pope Pius XI's encyclical letter, *Miserentissimus Redemptor* – which called upon the mercy of Christ's Heart for the crimes and impurity of the age – every pope has looked to the Sacred Heart of Jesus to help the world find the true peace that, Scriptures' words attest, comes only from God. Through increased devotion and consecration to the Sacred Heart, the hope and prayer of the Church is that God will change the hearts of men, "that hearts of stone will turn to hearts of flesh,"[3] transforming humanity and forwarding the Kingdom of God on earth.

Now I believe the Holy Spirit leads the Church forward in a special way, helping to secure a safe passage through our unique and turbulent times. This time though, the Spirit uses the profound moment at hand to bring about a better understanding of the mystery of God our Father and the truth of His great love for mankind, a love best discovered and understood in the symbolism of His Divine Paternal Heart—the mysterious *Bosom* of all life – past, present and future.

As St. John Paul II writes in *Tertio Millennio Adveniente,* "God seeks man out moved by his *Fatherly Heart.*"[4]

THE DIVINE PATERNAL HEART OF GOD OUR FATHER

The mystery of the *Heart of the Father*—the divine enigmatic womb of all love and life—is an extraordinary, bountiful mystery of the faith that is waiting to be explored. According to theologians, the Father's Paternal Heart is, in essence, the furnace of all love itself; the absolute, unquestionable source of the fabric, the energy of *all* that is seen and unseen. In summation, it is the ultimate, infinite, and perfect core of divine reality; it is the unfathomable home of the sacred intimacy Christ shared with His Father before creation; it is for believers the mystical reward we are invited to return to forever, as Christ did.

Thus, in our time, our Father's Paternal Heart is the divine Heart that the Church and all humanity needs to come to see, to know, and to love; for in the mystery of the Father's Heart lies the peace, happiness, and joy the world has been searching for since our original separation from our Father in the beginning. Within the Father's Heart, we find the way – the way back to the *Garden*, to our full access to the *Tree of Life* (cf. Rv 22:14).

Unlike the Sacred Heart of Jesus and the Immaculate Heart of Mary, the Divine Paternal Heart of God the Father is not as well-known by the faithful—despite its veritable presence in Scripture and the writings of the Church Fathers, Saints and Popes. Perhaps like other mysteries of the faith, it has remained hidden for a reason and is now coming to be revealed in the timely way other divine truths have in the past. Nevertheless, in light of the perilous age we now live in, I believe the time has come for our Father's Paternal Heart to become better understood and loved, for His Heart to become the great source of divine assistance that the Church and the world seek. For we are living in unique, grave, and urgent times—times that call for mankind to turn to its heavenly Father, to His *steadfast* and *everlasting* love.

BUILDING A CIVILIZATION OF LOVE

As in the past, the needs of God's children often define the moment Heaven uses to bring a great truth of our faith to life.[5] A *"crisis of civilization"*[6] has descended upon the world and it must be countered and replaced by a new *"civilization of love"*[7]– one that will restore the hope and peace of God in hearts throughout the world and that will bring the "new springtime of Christian life."[8] It is to be a *civilization of love and life* in God, one that St. John Paul

II prayed would arise in his vision of a more *"definitive coming of the Kingdom of God."*[9] It is to be a civilization, Pope Benedict XVI wrote in his encyclical letter, *Caritas in Veritate*, "whose seed, God has planted in every people, in every culture."[10]

In *Dives in Misericordia*, St. John Paul II explained that this coming *civilization of love* is to emerge from the mercy of the Father. The Pope wrote that in responding to the words of His Son on the Cross, "Father, forgive them, for they know not what they do" (Lk 23:34), God the Father now gathers His people – "all men and women without exception or division: without difference of race, culture, language, or world outlook, without distinction between friends and enemies"[11]— to Himself, to He who is "Father." Our Father gathers His children together in hope of a better future, as He sees the multitude of threats that man has unleashed upon himself through his own hands – the many evils that man is now subdued, dominated and enslaved by – that man is suffering from even under the threat of his very existence. Within this framework of our present day world, God—the "Father of mercies"[12] revealed in Christ— guides the Church and the world back to Himself; back to the mystery of His mercy and love, which humanity needs in order to build a *civilization of love*.

Thus, this *civilization of love* that the Father gathers, that the Father calls to Himself, can find no greater symbol of His love in our times than in His Heart, the Divine Paternal Heart of the Creator, who is *Love*, who is *Life* itself.

THE PATERNAL HEART IN SCRIPTURE AND TRADITION

As with the Sacred Heart of Jesus, the theological roots of the Paternal Heart of God the Father are well-rooted in Scripture and in the writings and experiences of the great men and women of the Church over the past two thousand years. Foreshadowed in numerous passages of the Old Testament that speak of the "Heart of God," most memorably in the words that reveal God chose David because he was a man after "his own Heart" (1 Sm 13:14, Acts 13:22), the Heart of God is also viewed by theologians as synonymous in the Bible with His Abyss, His Bosom, His Side, or His Breast.

According to Scriptural scholars who apply the *Doctrine of Appropriation*, the passages that speak of the Heart of God in these ancient writings are understood as being most representative of the Person of God the Father. This is because the anthropomorphic language of the Old Testament that speaks of God's Heart is seen by theologians to be symbolizing God the Father's paternal love and mercy as revealed in both creation and in His Covenants with Israel— divine characteristics that are more *appropriately* associated with the Father than with Jesus or the Holy Spirit.[13]

In the New Testament, the writings of Sts. John and Paul help to unfold the mystery of God the Father's paternal love—the truth of His Fatherly Heart. The Gospels and Epistles present this truth as revealed by Christ in the Father's divine Personhood, in His inseparable unity in love and nature with His only begotten Son, and in Christ's call for mankind to come to know in spirit and in truth the love of its heavenly Father.

Beyond question, Patristic literature reveals the *Prologue* of St. John's Gospel contains and perfectly captures the most comprehensive synthesis of this truth.

THE WRITINGS OF THE FATHERS

By the second century, archival writings of the early Church were beginning to reveal that there was great interest in the Gospel of St. John and its revelation of Christ being "nearest to the Heart of the Father." Early theologians saw this as symbolizing the infinite wellspring of the Father's love for His Son and His adopted children. By this time, references to the Heart of the Father could be found in the ancient manuscripts of the bishops and theologians of this period. For example, St. Theophilus, the sixth Bishop of Antioch, had written that even "in Paradise the Son is residing within the Heart of the Father, conversing with the Father in the Garden over Adam."[14]

The symbolic reality of the Father's Heart is extensively present in the writings of the Eastern and Western Church Fathers. From Tertullian and St. Basil, to St. Ambrose and St. Athaniasus, the early Patristic writers dwelled on the love of God the Father, contemplating His Heart's sublime treasure of mysteries and its infinite repository of graces.

Regarded as the Father of Latin Theology and considered the first true-theologian of the West, Tertullian elaborated on the Father's Heart in his writings, "Alone begotten of God, in a way peculiar to himself, from the *womb* of his own Heart – even as the Father himself testifies, "My Heart, says he, has emitted my most excellent Word."[15] St. Basil, known as Basil the Great, is one of the three Cappadocian Fathers, with his brother St. Gregory of Nyssa and his friend St. Gregory of Nazianzus. He too explored this mystery, "A Father's Bosom is a fit and becoming seat for a Son."[16] One of the four great Fathers of the Latin Church, St. Ambrose, expounded on the Heart of the Father, "The Son lives by the Father, because he is the Word given forth from the Heart of the Father, because he comes forth from the Father, because he is begotten of the bowels of the Father, because the Father is the fountain and the root of the Son's Being."[17]

Known for his work in combating the *Arian Heresy*, St. Althaniasus was elected Bishop of Alexandria and promoted monasticism. He, too, identified the symbolic source of the Father's love – His Heart: "God, being without parts, is Father of the Son without partition or passion; for there is neither effluence of the immaterial, or influx from without, as among men; and being uncompounded in nature he is Father of one only Son. This is why he is only-begotten, and alone in the Father's Bosom, and alone is acknowledged by the Father to be from him, saying, 'This is my beloved Son, in whom I am well-pleased'" (Mt 3:17).[18]

THE MIDDLE AGES

Over the centuries, many prominent Church figures such as St. Gregory, St. John Damascene, St. Thomas Aquinas, and St. John Eudes have revealed in their writings the great paternal love of the Father they had come to understand while pondering His divine Heart.

The last of the Latin Fathers and founder of the medieval papacy, St. Gregory the Great, recommended that the faithful "learn the Heart of God in the words of God, that you may long more ardently for things eternal.[19] St. John Damascene, known also as St. John of Damascus and considered the last of the Eastern Fathers, writes in his acclaimed *De Fide Orthodoxa*, "No one has seen God at any time; the only begotten Son, who is in the Bosom of the Father, he has declared him. The Deity is, therefore, ineffable and incomprehensible."[20]

Considered by many to be one of the most brilliant minds ever in Christian thought, St. Thomas Aquinas asserted in his *Summa Theologica*, "But the Son possesses a position of singularity above others in having by nature what he receives, as Basil also declares; hence he is called only begotten; the only begotten who is in the Bosom of the Father, he hath declared unto us."[21]

St. John Eudes, who was known for his theology of the Sacred Heart of Jesus, wrote also of God the Father's Heart: "You have given us the Spirit and Heart of your Son, which is your own Spirit and your own Heart; and you have given them to be our

Spirit and our Heart according to the promise that you made by the mouth of your prophet in these words: 'I will give you a new heart and I will put a new spirit within you.'"[22] St. Eudes also visualized the mercy of the Father emanating from His Heart, "Return to that most loving Heart of your Father, which is full of love and mercy for you, which will receive you home, heaping upon you blessings. Return, you transgressors, to the Heart, 'which means to my Heart that is all yours, since I have given it entirely to you."[23]

Throughout the late Middle Ages, we find a host of the great voices of the Church contemplating the Father's Heart in their writings. St. Francis de Sales describes too the mercy of the Father's Paternal Heart in his classic work, *Introduction to the Devout Life*: "The chorus of the Church Triumphant and those of the Church Militant are united to our Lord in this divine action, so that with him, in him and through him, they may ravish the Heart of God the Father and make his mercy all our own."[24]

In his book, *The Incarnation, Birth and Infancy of Jesus Christ*, St. Alphonsus de Liguori examines the unity of the Father and the Son, especially in their being together in the Father's Heart: "The eternal Word descends on earth to save man; and whence does he descend? *His going out is from the end of Heaven.* He descends from the Bosom of his divine Father, where from eternity he was begotten in the brightness of the Saints. And where does he descend? He descends into the womb of a virgin, a child of Adam, which in comparison with the Bosom of God is an object of horror; wherefore the Church sings, 'Thou didst not abhor the Virgin's womb.' Yes, because the Word, being in the Bosom of the Father, is God like the Father—is immense, omnipotent, most blessed and supreme Lord, and equal in everything to the Father."[25]

St. Louis de Montfort was the founder of *The Company of Mary* and of *The Daughters of Wisdom*. Most known for his *True Devotion to Mary* treatise, he contemplated in his book, *The Love of Eternal Wisdom*, the Father's love, and envisioned how prayer reaches the Father's Heart: "It is not so much the length of a prayer, but the fervor with which it is said which pleases almighty God and touches his Heart." He also contemplated the unity of the Father and the Son in the Father's Heart before creation, "Eternal Wisdom began to manifest himself outside the Bosom of his Father where he dwelt from eternity, when he made light, heaven and earth."[26]

The writings of many of the great women of the Church also speak to us of the Heart of the Father. St. Catherine of Siena, whose sublime work, *The Dialogue* – a mystical conversation with God the Father – led souls to profoundly understand the Father and His Love, the love of His Heart. She wrote of how a soul is called to rest in, to be in union with the Heart of the Divine. St. Teresa Avila taught complete surrender to the love of God, to the "Heart of God," wrote her Jesuit biographer, Fr. Ribera. St. Margaret Mary Alacoque wrote, "I need nothing but God, and to lose myself in the Heart of God."

In their writings, St. Therese of Lisieux, the *Little Flower*, and St. Faustina Kowalska, of the *Divine Mercy in My Soul* revelations, both speak of their experiences with the Heart of their God. In her *Story of a Soul*, St. Theresa envisions the great love of God and speaks of Jesus plunging souls "into the Heart of the Trinity,"[27] while St. Faustina Kowalska confesses in *The Diary of M. Faustina Kowalska* that as a child "the Father lifted me from the ground up to his Heart."[28]

TODAY'S CHURCH

In more recent times, Popes Pius XII, John Paul II, Benedict XVI and Frances have written or spoken of the Father's Heart in their letters or public audiences. In his encyclical letter, *Haurietis Aquas*, Pope Pius XII writes that the way to "the Heart of God [*the Father*] was through the Heart of Christ," because Scripture tells us "no one cometh to the Father except through Christ."[29] St. John Paul II contemplated the Heart of the Father in many of his writings and addresses. In one of his weekly audiences, he examined the mystery of the Father as revealed in the Gospels, a mystery he tells us only Jesus could reveal because of His being *in* the Heart of His Father before all time: "Undoubtedly, certain elements of the Old Testament revelation constituted a preparation for what we have in the Gospels. Nevertheless, only the Son was capable of introducing us to this mystery. Since "no one has seen God" no one knew the mystery of his inner life, the Son alone knew it. It is only the Son, who is *nearest to the Father's Heart*, who has made him known."[30]

His successor, Pope Benedict XVI, writes in his book, *Jesus of Nazareth*, of the unity of the Father and the Son – a unity that he also explains began before creation in the Heart of the Father: "Jesus' teaching is not the product of human learning, of whatever kind. It originates from immediate contact with the Father, from 'face-to-face' dialogue—from the vision of the one who rests close to the Father's Heart. It is the Son's word. Without this inner grounding, his teaching would be pure presumption. That is just what the learned men of Jesus' time judged it to be, and they did so precisely because they could not accept its inner grounding: see and knowing face-to-face."[31]

At his morning Mass on April 24, 2013, in the Chapel of Casa Santa Marta, Pope Frances spoke of the great love of God the Father for the Church, a love he described as originating in the

Father's Heart: "The Church begins there, in the Heart of the Father, who had this idea...of love. So this love story began, a story that has gone on for so long and is yet not ended."[32]

Although we find considerable references to the Father's Heart in the writings and history of the Church, perhaps there is no greater testimony of the truth of the love of the Father than its definitive citation in the *Catechism of the Catholic Church*. Foreshadowed in the psalm, "the plan of the Lord stands forever, the design of his Heart" (Ps 33:11), we read in the *Catechism* that God's desire for His people is a **"mysterious design of his wisdom and goodness"** and a **"plan born in the Father's Heart."**[33]

A CRISIS OF CIVILIZATION

In our times, the mystery of the Father and His love – the mystery of His Paternal Heart – is a truth that the Church and the world need to contemplate, understand, and embrace, for His Heart holds a sure and safe way for mankind to ask its Father for the heavenly assistance that it seeks to free itself from the evils of our age.

As few can deny, mankind's troubles are many. A *crisis of civilization* has emerged as large cracks are appearing in the pillars of historic Judeo-Christian beliefs. In complete transparency, the *Modern Attack*, foreseen in Pope Pius XII's times, is in full force and advancing.[34]

Indeed, western culture has replaced the God of Revelation with different gods; some old, some new,[35] while science, government, and politics now contain the power to influence and destroy life as never before through human rights oppression, economic injustice, and population control methods, especially abortion. At the same time, in the hope of removing God from the conscience of the people, supporters of atheism, materialism, sensualism and other forms of secularism use the world's unbridled network of mass communication and entertainment to disfigure and dismantle all Christian morality and truth. Finally, and most concerning, the fragile atmosphere of peace on the planet is becoming of greater concern too. Wars, fratricidal struggles and spasmodic episodes of terrorism continue to be waged throughout the world – bringing to the forefront, according to experts, the subdued, yet very real and mounting danger of a nuclear event.[36]

In 1950, Pope Pius XII foresaw how these emerging difficulties would affect both the Church and the world, and likened it to "the eruption of a volcano whose incandescent lava yard by yard covers its slopes – a devastating attitude is presently disfiguring society, constantly advancing and threatening to afflict all areas of life."[37]

Pope Paul VI saw these same threats manifesting their presence "like waves of the ocean enveloping and agitating the Church herself."[38]

RETURNING TO THE FATHER

Consequently, in a world where the promise, the hope, the gift of life is removed from the hands of God, where social movements forward agendas to redefine marriage and the human family, where a multitude of international societal ills threaten peace and justice and where the potential for the annihilation of nations is now more than just prophecy and science fiction,[39] the time has come for us to turn back to He who is the *Author of life* – He who is the *Creator of heaven and earth* – He who awaits our return to His loving and merciful arms. It is time to turn to our Father!

For can there be peace in the world without the Father?

Can creation move forward without the Creator?

Yes, it is time to hurry to the Father, who is ready to *defend* and *protect* life, to *restore* and *uphold* the family, to *come down* and *deliver* His prodigal children from the dangerous consequences of their misspent choices.

Yes, it is time to turn to God our Father – to His Paternal Heart – a Heart overflowing with love for His lost children, a love that has been contained and reserved by our Father in trembling anticipation of His reunification with all creation in the way it was meant to be from the beginning.

WE ARE HIS PRODIGALS

This understanding of God the Father's great love for His children will be new for some; however, the theology of this truth has never been hidden, it just has not been fully explored and understood as the Holy Spirit now intends it to be.

Each of us is conceived in the Father's Heart and each is called—moreover, drawn—to return to His Heart. As the *Prodigal Son* hurried into the arms of his loving and forgiving father, so are we invited to seek and discover that moment of supreme joy, of supreme surrender to our Father's loving embrace—to His Paternal Heart. Indeed, we are called to that same spark of awareness, that epiphany the *Prodigal Son* experienced as he raced home into the arms of his onrushing father. In his heart, he knew and remembered his father's great love for him and set out to return to such an undying love – to return to his father's heart.

Returning to our heavenly Father, to the love of His Paternal Heart, is the most profound hunger of the human soul. Father Jean Galot, SJ, an eminent biblicist and theologian known for his work in the areas of Christology, taught at the Pontifical Gregorian University in Rome. In his book, *ABBA FATHER, We Long to See Your Face (Theological Insights Into the First Person of the Trini-*

ty), he writes that every human heart desires to know the Father, to penetrate His Paternal Heart,

> "'No one has ever seen God; the only begotten son of God—who is in the Bosom of the Father—he has revealed him' (Jn 1:18). The purpose of this revelation is to plunge us 'into the *Heart of the Father*,' into his intimacy. The only begotten Son shares with us his life and contemplation totally oriented to the Father. He enables us to penetrate with him into the unsearchable depths of the Father. The total intimacy he has established with us opens our way to total intimacy with the Father."[40]

Total intimacy with our Father, *with* and *in* His Paternal Heart: this is the truth that needs to be illuminated, so our Father's children realize their heritage and inheritance and the love our Father in heaven has for them and desires to pour out upon souls in a special way.

THE FEAST OF THE FATHER

But our Father's call is more than just an invitation for *some* of His children to experience a greater personal relationship with Him, more than just a call to the few. Rather, it is a call for *all* mankind to return to its Father and His merciful Heart, so that He can shower His love upon us all and heal our broken world, and so we can honor Him in a way that is long overdue.

Accordingly then, from the highest levels of the Church to the pulpits of every parish in every diocese, the call must go out to all the faithful – that their Father is anxiously awaiting His children to return to His Paternal Heart, so He can share with them the depths of the mysteries of His divine paternal love with them, and so that He can satisfy the deepest yearnings of their hearts – the yearning to know their Father. As St. Phillip said, "Lord, show us the Father, and we will be satisfied" (Jn 14:8). Yes, the time has come for God's children to return to their Father, in order to consecrate themselves to Him, in order to know, love, and honor in a greater way the One who Christ so desired all to know, love and honor – His Father and our Father—the Father of *all* mankind.

Moreover, the Catholic Church needs to hear the voice of God's children, their cry of love for their heavenly Father, by responding with a feast for our Father, the *Feast of Life*:

The Solemnity of the Divine Paternal Heart: The Feast of the Father of All Mankind

Throughout His life, Christ was aware that He came from the Father and was going to the Father (cf. Jn 3:13). The Church now must likewise deepen her awareness of having come from the Father and of advancing toward Him—towards *life* in Him. Such a feast would express this awareness with clarity.[41]

Father Raniero Cantalamessa, O.F.M. Cap., *The Preacher to the Papal Household* since 1980 under both Pope John Paul II and Pope Benedict XVI, is a professor, theologian and the author of numerous articles and books. In his writings, Fr. Cantalamessa calls for a feast in the Catholic Church dedicated to God the Father. Fr. Cantalamessa states:

> "It's sad that in the whole liturgical year there isn't a feast dedicated to the Father, that in the whole Missal there isn't even a votive Mass in his honour. Come to think of it, it's very strange; there are many feasts dedicated to Jesus the Son; there is a Feast of the Holy Spirit; there are many feasts dedicated to Mary…There isn't a single feast dedicated to the Father, "*source and origin of all divinity*"…Feasts are a living catechesis and today there is an urgent need for a catechesis on the Father. Besides its catechetic value, a feast dedicated to the Father would also have, like any other feast, the value of *homologesis*, that is of a public and joyful confession of faith…Christians would certainly give great joy to the risen Lord if they were able to

project "ecumenically," that is, reach an agreement with all the churches who accept it in order to celebrate, with one accord, the *Feast of the Father* on the same day.

While we look forward to this day, we can already celebrate the *Feast of the Father* "in Spirit and in truth" within the intimacy of our hearts. We can promote little spiritual initiatives to make the Father more known and to honour him; at the same time, we can express all our filial love for him in union with Jesus, who always celebrates his Father."[42]

FATHER OF THE NEW EVANGELIZATION

According to Fr. Galot, such a feast would allow Catholics and Christians of every denomination worldwide to relive the mystery of salvation in its various stages and in its most important events each year. He writes that our Father is at the beginning and at the conclusion of this mystery. Most significantly, the entire process of sanctification results from our Father's paternal love, His Paternal Heart—which is "primordial and decisive," therefore deserving to be recognized and honored through both individual consecration and a special feast.[43]

Such a feast would be more than a celebration on the Catholic liturgical calendar. The creation of a feast in honor of God our Father would espouse profound ecumenical implications. In association with the *New Evangelization*, it would be a basis for unity among all Christians and for all human beings. This is because our Father, the one and only Father – the *Father of the New Evangelization*—embraces the lives of all His children in His Fatherly love, in the life found in His Paternal Heart.[44] Therefore, like Christmas, Easter, and other common Christian celebrations, along with our common patrimony in the *Our Father* prayer, a feast for God our Father could not only come to be shared by all Christian denominations, but wherever the sanctity of human fatherhood is held in respect and honor. For truly, the joy of finding God, manifested in many religions as one common Father, would be an inspiration for every person.[45]

Finally, in pondering humanity's march through time since departing Eden, I believe a feast honoring our Father's Heart would mean God's prodigal children would be farther down the road and closer to home, closer to *finding our Father* – racing towards the coming of the Kingdom and the promised *Triumph of the Immaculate Heart* on earth.

It is to be Our Lady's long awaited triumph of love, peace, and joy—the *Triumph of Life*—so desired, so anticipated, and finally delivered from the Immaculate Heart of Mary to the Divine Paternal Heart of God Our Father.

Thomas W. Petrisko
October 13, 2013
Pittsburgh, PA

Part I

The Threshold of the Father

"When the Lord saw how great the wickedness of human beings was on earth, and how every desire that his heart conceived was ever anything but evil, the Lord regretted making human beings on the earth, and his *Heart* was grieved" (Gn 6:5-6).

Chapter One

ORIGINAL SEPARATION

*"When they heard the sound of the LORD God
moving about in the garden at the breezy time of the day,
the man and his wife hid themselves from the LORD
God among the trees of the garden" (Gn 3:8).*

From the beginning, God the Father created man for the sake of communion with His divine life.[1] This plan, "born in the Father's Heart,"[2] became marred by the decisions and actions of our first parents in the earthly paradise known as the Garden of Eden.

Filled with mystery, deceit, tragedy and redemption, the story of this drama is almost universally known, and incomparable in the enormity of its consequences.

As we read in the first book of the Bible, *The Book of Genesis*, a seductive voice lurks in the Garden, opposed to God, who deceives Adam and Eve into betraying their Creator.[3] Scripture and Tradition see in this being an evil angel, called Satan, or the devil,[4] who, along with other angels were created naturally good by God, but "became evil by their own doing."[5] While not explained in great detail, Scripture speaks of a "sin" of these angels.[6] This sin consists in a free choice of these created spirits who radically and irrevocably rejected God and His reign,[7] causing their "fall" and for them to be forever separated from the love of God.

In essence, our first parents do the same; through their free will they disobey God, in thought and deed, by choosing to "sin." Thus, because of the decision to listen to the Tempter and eat from the *Tree of the Knowledge of Good and Evil*, that is, because of *Original Sin,* man also experienced a "fall," and subsequently, "let his trust in his Creator die in his heart."[8]

After the *Fall*, man's perception of God was permanently altered in many ways. Rather than a God who is *Love*, He became seen as a God that could not be trusted. St. John Paul II writes that He was seen as a God in the sense of a master – slave relationship.[9]

Even worse, Pope Benedict XVI writes that God became associated with being "a vengeful God," despite Scripture's emphasis of His passionate, providential love for His people.[10]

THE MYSTERY OF ORIGINAL SIN

The Church teaches that with the Fall, the overwhelming misery which oppresses men, our inclination toward evil and death, cannot be understood apart from their connection with Adam's Original Sin – and the fact that he transmitted to us a *sin* in which we were born "afflicted,"[11] a "sin which is the death of the soul" and is a mystery that we cannot fully understand.[12]

We do know that the root of Original Sin is "pride" (Tb 4:14) and that pride is the "beginning of all sin" (cf. Sir 10:13). However, the gravity of Original Sin and the magnitude of its consequences are part of its mystery. The Fathers of the Church emphasized this truth. St. Augustine regarded Adam's Sin as an "inexpressibly great sin."[13]

Original Sin is called sin only in an analogical sense; it is a sin "contracted" and not "committed," a "state" and not an "act."[14] At its core, it is a deprivation of the *original holiness* given to our first parents from the very beginning when God invited them to intimate communion with Himself. Human nature, therefore, has not been totally corrupted by Original Sin; it is wounded in the natural powers to it. It is subject to guilt, ignorance, suffering, the dominion of death; and to an inclination to evil and sin called *concupiscence* – "the spark of sin" – that draws us, our hearts, away from God.[15]

It is noted that not only was man's harmony with God's will lost by the Fall, but harmony within creation was also broken.[16] Visible creation became alien and hostile to man. Because of man, because of death entering into the life of man, creation became subject "to its bondage to decay."[17] Inasmuch as can be understood, mankind and the earth were radically and forever changed with Original Sin and the aftermath of its generational effects.

After the first sin, the world became virtually inundated by sin and evil. Thus, the consequences of Original Sin and of all men's personal sins put the world as a whole in the sinful condition aptly described in St. John's expression, "the sin of the world" (Jn 1:29).[18]

This dramatic situation especially put man in constant battle with the Evil One and his powers of domination. The *Catechism* states:

> "The whole of man's history has been the story of dour combat with the powers of evil, stretching, so our Lord tells us, from the very dawn of history until the last day. Finding himself in the midst of the battlefield, man has to struggle to do what is right, and it is at great cost to himself, and aided by God's grace, that he succeeds in achieving his own inner integrity."[19]

SEPARATION FROM OUR FATHER

There is another element to the mystery surrounding the tragedy of Eden. Because of Original Sin, mankind became separated not just *from* God, but especially *from* the "Fatherhood of God," losing within himself the awareness in his heart of the everlasting love and guiding will of his Eternal Father and Creator.[20] This occurred because God was subject to the violation of *not* just the disobedience of man to His *command*, but also disobedience to His *divine will* as Father and Creator, as expressed in that command.[21]

In theological terms, this disobedience to God's will through Original Sin *immediately* brought upon man the loss of his "Sanctifying Grace." By definition, Sanctifying Grace is the abiding, interior, efficacious communication of the Father's Spirit in a human being that belongs to the whole soul, mind, will and affections, thereby granting participation in the *divine life*.[22] Before Original Sin, man possessed Sanctifying Grace, which contained all of the Spirit's gifts that make him righteous before God.[23] The Church teaches that man "was in friendship with God at the beginning" – a condition known as *Original Perfection* and *Original Righteousness*.[24] Consequently, the loss of this extraordinary grace left man's will in opposition to the Eternal Father's will.

The significance of the loss of Sanctifying Grace is best understood in relation to the Sacrament of Baptism.[25] The Council of Trent defined Original Sin as the death of the soul. The death of the soul is the absence of supernatural life in a soul, that is, of Sanctifying Grace.[26] In Baptism, Original Sin is eradicated through the infusion of Sanctifying Grace.[27] It follows from this, then, that Original Sin is a condition of being deprived of this grace.[28] This flows from the Pauline contrast between sin proceeding from Adam and justice proceeding from Jesus Christ (Rm 5:10).[29] Since justice from Christ consists formally *in* Sanctifying Grace, so the Sin inherited from Adam consists formally in the *lack of* Sanctifying Grace.[30] Accordingly then, it is the will of God that Sanctifying Grace should be present in man and, as a result of this truth, the *guilt* of Original Sin signifies that Adam and Eve turned away from the Father's will.[31]

"In the state of *Original Justice*, before sin," St. John Paul II said in his general audience of October 2, 1986, "Sanctifying Grace was like a 'supernatural endowment'[27] of human nature. The loss of this grace is contained in the inner 'logic' of sin, which is a rejection of the will of God, who bestows this gift."[32]

The Church teaches that Adam's descendants were stripped of Sanctifying Grace too,[33] except for Mary, who from the first instant of her conception was preserved from any stain of Original Sin. She was therefore conceived, "full of grace," as the Archangel Gabriel's words declare at the *Annunciation*.

And as we know, Mary did not "reject the will of the "Most High" (cf. Lk 1:35) and gave to God the Father her *fiat* in consenting to become the Mother of the Redeemer.

HIDING FROM OUR FATHER

In his book, *Crossing the Threshold of Hope*, St. John Paul II writes that Original Sin attempts to destroy and abolish God's *"rays of Fatherhood"* which are intended to permeate the created world and are contained in the trinitarian mystery of God Himself.[34] This, he says, is truly the key for interpreting reality.[35]

In other words, Original Sin, because of the loss of Sanctifying Grace, causes man to lose sight and understanding of God as *Father* in the true sense and full meaning of the word. It places in *doubt* the truth about God, who is love,[36] and about God *"as* Father,"[37] and denies His great "paternal love" for man. This, in turn, creates "fear" of God the Father and inclines man to battle Him – to take sides against its Father.[38]

As a result, man refuses the Father's will, the "truth and holiness of Him," especially His "Fatherly goodness."[39] Furthermore, as our first parents did in the Garden (Gn 3:15), Original Sin causes man to turn away from its Father, and in his guilt, to flee and hide from His love.[40]

Moreover, in his encyclical letter, *Dominum et Vivificatem*, St. John Paul II writes that Original Sin is not only a rejection of the Father and His sanctifying Spirit but also a rejection of Christ, the *Word of the Father*, who was "with the Father from the beginning"[41] (cf. Jn 1:1), who is "nearest to the Father's Heart" (cf. Jn 1:18). St. John Paul II writes, "According to the witness concerning the *beginning*, sin in its original reality takes place in man's will and conscience first of all as "disobedience," that is, as opposition of the will of man to the will of God. This *original disobedience* presupposes a rejection, or at least a turning away from the truth contained in the *Word of God*, who creates the world. This Word is the same Word who was "in the beginning with God," who "was God," and without whom "nothing has been made of all that is," since "the world was made through him…therefore, at the root of human sin is the lie, which is a radical rejection of the truth contained in the *Word of the Father*, through whom is expressed the loving omnipotence of the Creator: the omnipotence and also the love "of God the Father, Creator of heaven and earth."[42]

In essence, Adam and Eve's Original Sin permitted Satan to be able to deceive man into perceiving God the Father as a "threat to man."[43] He was able to "sow in man's soul a seed of opposition"[44] to the Father, His *Spirit* and His *Word*, who "from the beginning" would be considered as man's enemy, "not as his Father."[45]

"Man rejects the Father's love," St. John Paul II states, "as did the *Prodigal Son* in the first phase of his foolish adventure."[46]

The Bible reflects this reality of man's troubled walk through time without the guiding hand of its Father. It is a tearful and sorrowful journey of many deserts, trials, and deliverances. In truth, it is not hard to argue that the Bible is the *literal* unfolding of the *Parable of the Prodigal Son*. Through the lives and events of the people recorded in the Old and New Testaments, humanity is seen to be astray and mired in woe, often following misguided paths that are dark and far from the love and will of its heavenly Father.

Like in the parable, our loving Father can be found looking, calling and waiting for His wayward children to find their way back to Him. This has been the case in every epoch of history due to Original Sin.[47]

"...God therefore goes in search of man who is His special possession in a way unlike any other creature. Man is God's possession by virtue of a choice made in love: God seeks man out, moved by His *Fatherly Heart.*"
—St. John Paul II

Chapter Two

THE RAYS OF GOD'S FATHERHOOD

"I will put enmity between you and the woman, and between your offspring and hers; He will strike at your head, while you strike at his heel" (Gn 3:15).

We read in Scripture that God had no intent on giving up on man, for His love would not allow Him. The Church recalls mankind's *original separation* from its heavenly Father as well as His will to restore His fallen children.[1] The *Dogmatic Constitution of the Church* states,

> "The Eternal Father, in accordance with the utterly gratuitous and mysterious design of his wisdom and goodness, created the whole universe, and chose to raise up men to share in his own divine life; and when they had fallen in Adam, he did not abandon them..."[2]

Indeed, though man's heart was eclipsed, the *rays of God's Fatherhood* shined upon him and the world. From the opening pages of the Old Testament to the conclusion of the New Testament, the Eternal Father's desire to help overcome Original Sin and its effects, His interventions to illuminate the truth of His divine paternity in our minds, hearts and souls and to bring us back to communion in the divine life with Him, is ever visible.[3]

The origins of this drama, as every believer knows, are found in the *Book of Genesis.* Immediately after the Fall in Eden, God moves to rescue Adam and Eve from their dilemma. As He will do with every soul until the end of time, God takes the initiative and goes in search of our fallen parents, who in their guilt and shame are hiding from Him "among the trees" of the Garden (Gn 3:8). "Where are you?", the Lord asks Adam (Gn 3:9). Upon confronting them and receiving Adam and Eve's account of their actions, God immediately moves to begin to right the great error of Original Sin.

Promising to crush the Diabolical Tempter and to save the human race from the power of sin and death through a Messiah Redeemer (cf. Gn 3:15, known as the *Protoevangelium* or *First Gospel*), the paternal love of God is witnessed in His mercy for our disgraced parents. Though banished from the Garden, God clothes and resettles them. He then begins to instill within them a concept of *human fatherhood* in order for them to better understand *divine Fatherhood.*[4]

He does this first by blessing them with children, as Adam becomes a *father* to two sons, Cain and Abel. Adam then fathers a third son, Seth, who is "begotten in his (*Adam's*) likeness and after his image" (Gn 5:3), as man is "made in the image and likeness of God" (cf. Gn 1:26, 5:1).

Thus begins the Bible's *story of a family*, the human family.

FATHERHOOD: HUMAN AND DIVINE

It is a family that quickly experiences the greatest of tragedies; murder enters the world through Cain slaying the *just Abel*. But as with Adam and Eve, God is a forgiving Father and mercifully permits Cain to go on with his life. He even marks him with a sign for his protection and promises sevenfold vengeance if anyone kills Cain (cf. Gn 4:15). Cain and Seth become *fathers* too, as God's *rays of Fatherhood* guide forward the human race.

Further along in *Genesis*, we read that God's "Heart" is saddened by man's sinful ways (cf. Gn 6:5-6). Though grieved and compelled to take action, God works through Noah to reveal that as a Father He desires the salvation of His human family – just as Noah, a father, desires the salvation of his family from the impending storm of divine justice.[5] Through His *Covenant* with Noah, God institutes an agreement with man that continues to reveal the importance of *human fatherhood* and the unfolding truth of His *divine Fatherhood* in the generations after the flood, a truth He hopes man discovers not just in his intellect, but in his heart through *faith* and *love*.

While there are many chosen souls throughout Scripture, it is in the story of Abraham, called by God out of "his father's house" (cf. Gn 12:1), that we find the most revealing insight into God's plan for man to come to know Him as a Father. This is because Abraham's *obedient faith* is rooted in God's promises to him that *he* will be a "father,"[6] Abraham's deepest yearning, which was thought to be impossible because of old age.

For Abraham, the hope of becoming a father withstands time, ordeals and tests, as his irrepressible faith permits him to trust and wait for God to keep His word. It is a promise foretelling not only paternity for Abraham, but that his descendants are to be as countless as the "stars" (Gn 15:5) and that he is to be "the father of a host of nations" (Gn 17:5). These words become a promise fulfilled, for Abraham is acclaimed today to be the *father* of the three great monotheistic religions.

In a symbolic way, Abraham's desire to be a father represents God's desire, His desire to be known, loved and honored as mankind's heavenly Father, the true *Father of Nations*. This is seen in contrast to man's ambition to forge his own earthly unity as first witnessed at Babel (cf. Gn 11:1-9).[7] It also illuminates the Father's plan; through His long withstanding *faithfulness* to His children, like Abraham's faithfulness to Him, He will guide them back to Him.

These recurring themes prevail throughout the Old Testament. Through His covenants with His chosen people, a God who is a caring and protective Father emerges before the human race. The Second Vatican Council's *Dogmatic Constitution on Divine Revelation* states, "After the era of the Patriarchs, he taught this nation by Moses and the prophets to recognize him as the only living and true God, as a *provident Father* and just judge."[8]

Thus, from Moses – the great father figure of the Exodus, who was "raised in his father's house (Acts 7:2)" and "became the father of two sons (Acts 7:29)," and who God tells at the foot of Mt. Horeb", "I am the God of your *father*" (Ex 3:6) – to David – whose paternal lineage leads to the coming of the promised Messiah – the lives of Abraham's descendants keep the focus on *fatherhood*, and coming to truly know God as a *Father*.

Three aspects of fatherhood – paternal love, generation, and resemblance – affirm human paternity. However, God's Fatherhood is a Fatherhood that transcends human fatherhood, one that God hopes man sees is the origin, standard, and model (cf. Eph 3:14) of human fatherhood, although no one is father as *God is Father*.[9]

CALL ME "FATHER"

Although identifying God as a *Father* is found only fourteen times in the Old Testament, each time it is with significance. The Father is the Creator: "Is he not your Father, who created you, who made you and established you" (Dt 32:6). The Father is merciful: "As a father pities his children, so the Lord pities those who fear him. For he knows our name; he remembers that we are dust" (Ps 103:13f). The Father is the Father of all mankind: "Have we all not one Father? Has not one God created us? (Mal 2:10). And God's Fatherhood is especially towards Israel – who is God's special elect: "I am a Father to Israel, and Ephraim is my first born" (Jer 31:9).

Finally, the idea of God's "individual" Fatherhood in Judaism, where God is addressed as "my Father," or approached as a "person" by the Jews, begins in gradual stages to unfold in the *Old Testament*.[10] Two verses in *Sirach* reveal this insight: "O, Lord, Father and Master of my life, permit me not to fall by them" (Sir 23:1), and "Lord, Father and God of my life, abandon me not to their control." (Sir 23:4).

This emergence of God as a "personal Father," the words of the prophet Jeremiah indicates, is what God seeks from His chosen people when he says: "I thought you...would call me, 'My Father'" (Jer 3:19).

Indeed, the Old Testament reveals the Jews had many names for God, but none of them, individually or together, meant the name He longed most to hear – *Father!*[11]

"In Paradise the Son is residing within the *Heart of the Father*, conversing with the Father in the Garden over Adam."
—St. Hippolytus

Chapter Three

ONE WITH THE FATHER

"Let what you heard from the beginning remain in you. If what you heard from the beginning remains in you, then you will remain in the Son and in the Father. And this is the promise that he made us: eternal life" (1 Jn 2:24-25).

The New Testament illuminates the significance of human fatherhood and brings the complete revelation of God's divine Fatherhood. It is a revelation that the Gospels place at the heart of Christ's mission, for Jesus came to reveal a father's love for his children is not just human but rooted in the divine.

Organized into three groups of fourteen ancestors, St. Matthew's genealogy of Christ unfolds a procession of "fathers" that begins with Abraham through the coming of Christ. St. Luke's genealogy traces the descendants of Jesus beyond Abraham back to Adam, and beyond that back to "God the Father" (Lk 3:38), in order to stress Jesus' divine Sonship.

Almost immediately, two significant *fathers* are introduced in the opening pages of the New Testament. Zechariah, who is to be the father of John the Baptist, is tested in his faith by an angel and comes up wanting. But like Abraham, God grants him the *gift of fatherhood* in his old age. Likewise, the Gospels introduce St. Joseph, Jesus' earthly father, who *exemplifies* human fatherhood while reflecting the light of Christ's heavenly Father.

Throughout the New Testament, wherever key figures are introduced, often their *fathers* are recalled. Phanuel is the father of Anna, the prophetess (Lk 2:36). Zebedee is the father of James the Greater and John (Mt 4:21). Alphaeus is the father of James the Lessor (Mt 10:13). The father of Levi, known as Matthew, is also named Alphaeus (Mk 2:14). Judas' father is James Iscariot, as is the first name of the father of the other Apostle named Judas (Acts 1:13), and the father of Andrew and Peter is Jonah (Mt 16:17).

Significantly, Peter's declaration of Christ being the Messiah is met by Jesus' response, "Blessed are you, Simon, *son of Jonah!*" (Mt 16:17), followed by, "No mere man has revealed this to you but my heavenly Father" (Mt 16:17). This passage of Scripture, in a special way, illustrates God's intent to have man understand human fatherhood is related to divine fatherhood in an inseparable way – by paternal love.

Over and over, human and divine *fatherhood* is accentuated throughout the pages of the New Testament. St. Joseph is called by the angel, "Joseph, son of David" (Mt 1:20). Jesus is revered as the "Son of David" too and the "Son of God," while the Jews are identified as "the sons of Abraham."

Through these passages and others, the importance of *fatherhood* is kept at the forefront of Scripture's message.

FOREKNOWLEDGE OF THE FATHER

The mission of Christ is to fully reveal the divine "Personhood" of the Father within the revelation of the Trinity. But *a degree of awareness* of this mystery existed around the time of His birth, many years before his public ministry. According to New Testament scholars, this is discernable in the words and events of some of the prominent figures in the opening pages of the Gospels.

When examined, the words of Zechariah (cf. Lk 1:76) and Elizabeth (cf. Lk 1:42-45) reflect a *certain reality* of the Father, Son and Holy Spirit, as do Mary's from the *Annunciation* (cf. Lk 1:26-28) through the *Visitation* (cf. Lk 1:39-45). As we read in Mary's response to the angel Gabriel, Mary understands that the Holy Spirit will come upon her and that the *child* she is to carry is the "Son of the Most High" (cf. Lk 1:32). And, she acknowledges in her *fiat* that the power of *the Most High*, God the Father, will "overshadow" her (cf. Lk 1:35).

The words and experiences of St. Joseph and St. John the Baptist reflect this reality too. St. Joseph is told by an angel of the Lord in a dream that Mary had "conceived a child by the Holy Spirit" (cf. Mt 1:20). Moreover, he is instructed that this Child "would save his people" – in essence, He is to be a *divine* Messiah. This revelation, Scripture recalls for us, fulfills Isaiah's prophecy of the coming of Emmanuel, which means "God is *with* us." The account of John the Baptist's role reveals a similar concept of the Triune God. John foretells "'One' to come who is more powerful than him and will baptize *in the Holy Spirit*" (cf. Mt 3:11). He later sees "the Spirit of God," or rather the *Spirit of the Father* (cf. Mt 3:16) and *experiences* the voice of God the Father, "This is my beloved Son. My favor rests on him" (cf. Mt 3:17).

There are more passages in the early chapters of the Gospels that support an unfolding foreknowledge of a Triune God, and by discernment the emerging reality of not just the coming of Christ, but also the reality of His Father. The account of Simeon's discovery of the *Presentation of Jesus* in the Temple reveals he was inspired by the "Holy Spirit" (cf. Lk 2:25) with the promise of seeing the "Anointed" or the "Messiah of the Lord"(cf. Lk 2:26). This is fulfilled, after which, Simeon is then said to "praise God" (*the Father*) (cf. Lk 2:28-32) while holding the "Glory of Israel" (*Jesus*) in his arms (cf. Lk 2:29).

Even Jesus at the age of twelve, long before His public ministry, speaks of the Temple in Jerusalem as His "Father's House" (Lk 2:49). It is a revealing statement not only because of its revelation of the divine *Personhood* of the Father, but also of Christ's awareness of His own divine Sonship. While seemingly addressed only to Mary and Joseph, His words reveal the times at hand, the foretold times the Jewish people are coming to better understand and sense are upon them. Moreover, Jesus' response to Mary and Joseph holds profound insight into His mission. This is because they are His very *first* words in Scripture and are directed towards His Father and His Father's plan for mankind's redemption. Through Christ's Incarnation, it is a plan now visible in the world and in the hearts of man. And through Christ's words in the Temple, it is a plan beginning to shed its secrecy.

By the time Christ *is* to begin His ministry, an even more trinitarian awareness of God, and His Fatherhood, appears prevalent. Indeed, the Jews, the Gospel of John states, tell Christ, "We are no illegitimate breed! We have but one *Father* and that is God himself" (Jn 8:41). God, the Jewish religious leaders now openly declare, is their "Father."

Likewise, the Apostles already sense at the onset of Christ's ministry, prior to His teaching them, that Jesus is the "Son of God" (Jn 1:49). The words of Andrew (Jn 1:41) Phillip (Jn 1:45) and Nathaniel (Jn 1:49) imply such and are in agreement in meaning with each other. The Gospels seem also to reflect an expectation among many that the prophesied Savior – also called the *Anointed One, God's Chosen One* or the *Messiah* – is of a divine nature. Again, this expectation is best confirmed in Nathaniel's unhesitating response that Jesus is the "Son of God" (Jn 1:49). All of these statements appear rooted in a progressive belief arising over time through the discernment of the Hebrew Scriptures that the Messiah is to be the *divine Son* of a *divine Father.*

Indeed, Jesus Himself tells His listeners to "search the Scriptures" (Jn 5:39, cf. 5:46) to find the truth about Him, and, in essence, the truth about the "One" who sent Him, His heavenly Father.

ONE WITH THE FATHER

But it is through the teachings of Christ, the Son of God made man, who is the Father's one, perfect and unsurpassable *Word,* that God is revealed to be a divine Person – a heavenly Father. This is because Christ, the new Adam, is the very revelation of the mystery of the Father and His love, and forever asserts in His words that God is His Father and our Father too: "I am ascending to my Father and your Father, my God and your God!" (Jn 20:17).

Throughout the Gospels, Christ reveals the grandeur of the heavenly Father's great love and mercy for His adopted children. He is a "perfect" Father, Christ tells us, a Father to put *faith and trust* in and to *pray* to for all of one's needs. Most significantly, He is a Father we need to come to see, know and understand through Christ. This is because Jesus is "one with the Father" (cf. Jn 10:30) and "the very stamp of his nature" (Heb. 1:3). Therefore, whoever sees Jesus has "seen the Father" (cf. Jn 14:9).

Moreover, Christ's words not only reveal the truth of our heavenly Father but emphasize the consequences of man living outside of the Father's will. With the fall in Eden, man separated himself from the love and peace found in its Father, preferring *the world* and its enticements. Power, materialism, and pleasure became the desires of his "restless" heart. These inclinations spurred man to want to possess, control and accumulate. As Scripture reveals, the results have been anxiety and fear, suffering, misery and death for every generation since our first parents departed the Garden.

The words of *Sirach* reflect this reality of man's journey through time separated from its heavenly Father:

> "A great anxiety has God allotted,
> and a heavy yoke, to the sons of men;
> from the day one leaves his mother's womb
> to the day he returns to the mother of all living,
> his thoughts, the fear in his heart, and his troubled
> forebodings till the day he dies –
> Whether he sits on a lofty throne
> or grovels in dust and ashes,
> Whether he bears a splendid crown
> or is wrapped in the coarsest of cloaks –
> Are of wrath and envy, trouble and dread,
> terror of death, fury and strife.
> Even when he lies on his bed to rest,
> his cares at night disturb his sleep.
> So short is his rest it seems like none,
> till in his dreams he struggles as he did by day,
> terrified by what his mind's eye sees,
> like a fugitive being pursued;
> As he reaches safety, he wakes up
> astonished that there was nothing to fear.
> So it is with all flesh, with man and with beast,
> but for sinners seven times more" (Sir 40:1-8).

Christ's words offer light to dispel the shadows that hover over man's way of thinking; man must *trust* God in order to live without fear, to live in peace and happiness; man must surrender his will to the "will of the heavenly Father" (cf. Mt 12:50): "Do not to lay up for yourselves an earthly treasure" but instead "heavenly treasure" (Mt 6:19-21), "No man can serve two masters," "You cannot give yourself to God and money" (Mt. 6:24-25). "Look at the birds in the sky. They do not sow or reap, they gather nothing into barns; yet your heavenly Father feeds them. Are not you more important than they?" (Mt 6:26), "Stop worrying then, over questions like, 'What are we to eat, or what are we to drink, or what are we to wear?' Your heavenly Father knows all that you need" (Mt 6:32).

Throughout the Gospels and the Epistles, the New Testament makes it clear that the world and its ways contradict the Father and His ways. St. John's first letter offers no illusions: "Have no love for the world, nor the things that the world affords. If anyone loves the world, the Father's love has no place in him, for nothing that the world affords comes from the Father (1 Jn 2:15-17).

St. Paul's words are in agreement. They call us to a *new life* as adopted sons of the Father (Rm 6:4). It is a life that is free of our fear of the Father, free of our bondage to the ways of the world: "All who were led by the Spirit of God are sons of God. You did not receive a spirit of slavery leading you back into fear, but a spirit of adoption through which we cry out "ABBA," that is "Father" (Rm 8:15).

While learning to live according to the Father's will is the heart of His teachings, Christ explains that God the Father desires to be truly known, loved and honored by His children.

In the *Gospel of John*, Christ teaches that the Father is "spirit and truth" and wants His children to seek to worship Him in spirit and truth (Jn 4:23). He wants them to become His "sons of light"

(Jn 12:36) in order to share in the divine life with God forever (Jn 5:24-26). Consequently, Jesus says our heavenly Father is ready to *"come"* to a soul and to *"dwell* in him" (Jn 14:23), to be a *personal* Father (Jn 20:17). Through such love, Christ tells us our Father hopes to welcome His children back home to Him. As St. John Paul II writes, "Infinite and inexhaustible is the Father's readiness to receive his prodigal children home."[1]

A FATHER AT WORK

Clearly, Christ's Gospel presents the path the world is invited to take after His redemptive mission. Through the victory of the Cross, man is invited to turn away from sin and follow in Jesus' footsteps. Man is invited to do the will of the Father and to seek His Kingdom "within" in order to build His Kingdom "on earth as it is in heaven."

Thus, the New Testament completes the doctrine introduced in the Old; through God's *everlasting* and *steadfast* love, through His *Word* and His *Spirit*, our Father remains committed to His children and is "at work" (Jn 5:17) fulfilling His plan to help the sons and daughters of Adam overcome through faith their *separation* from Him – to counter the darkness first brought upon man through Original Sin – by intensifying the light of His *rays of Fatherhood* upon the path back to Him.

This time, though, the *Light* of the Father's rays is His only begotten Son, Jesus Christ (Jn 8:12), who fully reveals His Father's plan to man.[53] It is a simple plan; Christ "is the Way, the Truth, and the Life" (Jn 14:6) of the Father's doctrine of faith and love (Jn 7:17). He is the portal back to restoration and communion in the divine life with the Father.

Indeed, Jesus' words are straight forward : "No one comes to the Father but through me" (Jn 14:6).

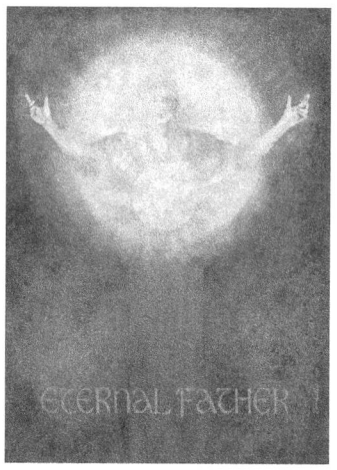

> "The great mystical tradition of the Church of both East and West has much to say in this regard. It shows how prayer can progress, as a genuine dialogue of love, to the point rendering the person wholly possessed by the divine Beloved, vibrating at the Spirit's touch, resting filially within the *Father's Heart*."
> —St. John Paul II

★ *Eternal Father by Gerry Simboli*

Chapter Four

THE THRESHOLD OF THE FATHER

*"Do not live in fear, little flock. It has pleased your
Father to give you the kingdom" (Lk 12:32).*

The importance of coming to know God as a Father is reinforced in our minds and hearts through the Church today, the visible plan of the Father's love for humanity. This is especially found in the Sacred Liturgy – which is offered to the Father – and in the Eucharist, the sum and summary of our faith.[1]

At every Mass, the faithful also pray the *Our Father*, asking for God's "will to be done on earth as it is in heaven." Unlike our first parents, who rebelled against the will of the Father, believers are called through the words of the *Our Father* to be like Christ: "Not my will, but yours be done" (Lk 22:42, cf. Jn 4:34, 5:30; 6:38). Likewise, in the first words of the *Apostles Creed*, faith in the Father's providence is enscribed: "I believe in God the Father Almighty."

Liturgical prayers and devotions focus attention on the Father too, such as the Fourth Eucharistic Prayer (Canon IV), which addresses man's *original separation* from its heavenly Father. "*Father*, we proclaim your greatness! All your actions show your wisdom and love. You formed man in your own likeness and set him over the whole world to serve you, his Creator, and to rule over all creatures. Even in disobedience he *rejected your friendship* but you *did not abandon* him to the power of death…"

BAPTISM: FAITH IN OUR FATHER

Many Church traditions appear to cast light on divine Fatherhood in various ways too. Priests are called "Father," the Pope is the "Holy Father," Patrology is the study of "the Fathers of the Church" and every new life in Christ is presented at *Baptism* by a "Godfather."

Following Christ's example (cf. Jn 3:22, 4:2) and mandate (cf. Mt 28:19), Baptism in Christ is the principal assault on Original Sin, a Sacramental mystery designed to help bridge through Sanctifying Grace a soul's separation from God and to begin reunification with Him through Jesus and the Holy Spirit.

Baptism, in fact, initiates the process of "professing faith" in the Father's divine will for a soul.[2] According to the *Catechism of the Council of Trent*, the prescribed words that accompany the solemn ceremony of Baptism are intended to do just that – to begin a soul's *life of faith* in God.[3] The ceremony's words require the renunciation of Satan and the public declaration of belief in "God the Father Almighty" by the Godparents and those in attendance.

Centuries ago, St. Augustine wrote that Baptism was called "the Sacrament of Faith."[4] Others termed it, "the Illumination," because by *faith* we profess in Baptism that "the heart is illumined."[5] St. Denis called Baptism "the beginning of the most Holy Commandments," as a soul begins its walk in the truth of the Creator and His will for that soul.[6] Most of all, Baptism gives us new life in the Father. St. Irenaus writes,

"Baptism gives us the grace of new birth in God the Father, through his Son, in the Holy Spirit. For those who bear God's Spirit are led to the Word, that is, to the Son, and the Son presents them to the Father, and the Father confers incorruptibility on them. And it is impossible to see God's Son without the Spirit, and no one can approach the Father without the Son for the knowledge of the Father is the Son, and the knowledge of God's Son is obtained through the Holy Spirit."[7]

There is one more important note regarding Baptism and God the Father. The Baptism of Jesus by John the Baptist in the Jordan – who was baptized not because He needed to be cleansed of Original Sin, but in order to show Baptism was to remain essential and to be instituted by His Church – was accompanied by a "voice from heaven," the *voice of the Father*: "You are my beloved Son. On you my favor rests." It was an event in the life of Christ so pivotal that it is recorded in all four Gospels (Mt 3:17, Mk 1:11, Lk 3:22, cf. Jn 1:34). Accordingly, theologians believe this holds great significance to the role of the Sacrament and its relationship to placing our faith in God the Father.[8]

CROSSING THE THRESHOLD OF THE FATHER

Today, in a world filled with uncertainty, confusion and mounting danger, the time has come for mankind to turn towards its heavenly Father, to mend our *separation* from Him in a greater and more visible way.

In *Crossing the Threshold of Hope*, editor Vittorio Messori asks St. John Paul II if he thought God's children were ready to surrender their *fear of the Father* and cross the threshold of hope, in order to rediscover their heavenly Father.[9] The Pope replied that through wisdom and prayer the world can find its heavenly Father is *truly present* and *ever ready* through His merciful love to free man from his fear of God.[10]

As Christians, baptized in Christ, we are free of *Original Sin*. We are free to take hold of our divine inheritance, free to become incarnations of the filial love of Christ for His Father – free to be sons and daughters of our Father for all eternity. In faith, the gifts of our Father, of His paternal love, are given to us to discover and search, to embrace and cherish.

Unlike the fallen angels – *who denied the Fatherhood of God, who rebelled against His paternal will* and *rejected His love, and from the beginning have tried to keep man from knowing the love of the Father* – we are made in God's image, created in Him, and redeemed by His Son. We are His children called to be "one" in Him, as the Father, Son and the Holy Spirit are "one" in each other.

Thus, through Christ, with Christ, and in Christ, mankind needs to return to its Father, to his Heart, for the love of our Father calls His children to see Him in our hearts so we may come to fully know, love and honor Him, so we, like the angels, may unceasingly resound the Church's praise "Glory to God in the highest!"

THE MYSTERY OF THE FATHER'S HEART

Now in our time, dwelling in unapproachable light, the Father's face becomes more radiant and visible to man, His presence more discernable, His love incarnate in the eyes of our souls. As St. John Paul II stated, the Father wants to make Himself more known in order to reveal more of His undying love so we can better see His *rays of Fatherhood*, so we can help bring His Kingdom more fully on earth.

With Mary our Mother leading the way, the Holy Spirit points to the Father, to His love for all mankind. Confronted by this great calling, the first words of St. John Paul II's papacy are clear: We must "be not afraid!" We must trust the truth about ourselves and "not fear the Father,"[11] not fear His love.

This is the *mystery of the Father's love*, the mystery of His merciful Heart that we are called to embrace,[12] in order to set contemporary man free from fear of himself, of the world, of its loving Father. It is the *mystery* we are called to embrace in order to replace this fear with an authentic concern that God's *will* is done on earth, the *will* which is the *good* found in the love of the Father – *the threshold of hope*[13] – that we are called to cross over in order to come to know and love our Father, in order to realize we are called to return to Him for all eternity.

Do we now draw near to our *Father of Lights*?

Do we seek Him out and return to His loving arms and embrace?

Mired in a *crisis of civilization*,[14] the state of the world reveals that the time is right to give Him our love, to surrender and unite our hearts to His Fatherly Heart[15] – the great wellspring of His divine paternal love for us and the *Abyss* of His unfathomable *mystery*.

Yes, in the Father's Divine Paternal Heart are all of the answers mankind is searching to find. In His Heart is the mystery of His love in Christ for mankind. For St. John tells us, "It is only the Son, who is nearest to the Father's Heart, who has made him known" (Jn 1:18).

Part II

NEAREST TO THE FATHER'S HEART

"... No one has ever seen God; It is the only Son, who is nearest to the *Father's Heart*, who has made him known." (Jn 1:18)

Chapter Five

NEAREST TO THE FATHER'S HEART

*"Now glorify me, Father, with you, with the glory that
I had with you before the world began" (Jn 17:5).*

"In the beginning was the Word:
the Word was with God
and the Word was God.
He was with God in the beginning.
Through him all things came to be,
not one thing had its being but through him.
All that came to be had life in him
and that life was the light of men,
a light that shines in the dark,
a light that darkness could not overpower.
A man came, sent by God.
His name was John.
He came as a witness,
as a witness to speak for the light,
so that everyone might believe through him.

He was not the light,

only a witness to speak for the light.

The Word was the true light

that enlightens all men;

and he was coming into the world.

He was in the world

that had its being through him,

and the world did not know him.

He came to his own domain

and his own people did not accept him.

But to all who did accept him

he gave power to become children of God,

to all who believe in the name of him

who was born not out of human stock

or urge of the flesh

or will of man

but of God himself.

The Word was made flesh,

he lived among us,

and we saw his glory,

the glory that is his as the only Son of the Father,

full of grace and truth.

John appears as his witness. He proclaims:

'This is the one of whom I said:

He who comes after me

ranks before me

because he existed before me'.

Indeed, from his fullness we have, all of us, received—

yes, grace in return for grace,

since, though the Law was given through Moses,

grace and truth have come through Jesus Christ.

No one has ever seen God;

It is the only Son, who is nearest to *the Father's Heart*,

Who has made him known."[1]

These words—the magnificent *Prologue* of St. John's Gospel—are among the most memorable in all of Scripture. They proclaim Jesus Christ as the incarnate *Word* of God the Father, His only beloved Son, begotten before all time, and the One who has *revealed the Father* to us.

The importance of this theological truth is paramount to our faith. Through Jesus, the Father makes it clear that *Divine Revelation* is complete and fulfilled. It is the Father, in all His richness, who has manifested Himself in a human life – a Father who wanted to conceal nothing from us, thus He revealed Himself totally to humankind.[2] It is a revelation, therefore, that stresses the "Word was with" and the "Word was God."[3] St. John means by this "that the Word possesses the divine nature, that He is simply not some attribute or extension of God, but that He is strictly and integrally God and from all eternity, Christ was oriented to the Father." [4]

But more explicitly, St. John's *Prologue* reveals the depth of this orientation and the extraordinary intimacy of the Father and Jesus—as St. John himself tells us that this Son is **"nearest to the Father's Heart."**[5]

This revelation, of Jesus being "nearest to the Father's Heart," has intrigued and challenged scholars for centuries. St. John recognizes that unlike any mortal, Jesus enjoys a perfect union with His Father not only in grace, but in *substance* and *nature*. However, many commentators say that his words imply more.

A renowned theologian in his own right, Pope Benedict XVI writes, "The saying at the end of the *Prologue* is the decisive *key* to the image of Jesus in John's Gospel: 'No one has ever seen God; it is the only Son, who is *nearest to the Father's Heart*, who has made him known' (Jn 1:18). Only the one who is God sees God—Jesus. He truly speaks from his vision of the Father, from unceasing dialogue with the Father, a dialogue that is his life."[6]

St. John Paul II concurs that the end of St. John's *Prologue* is the key to understanding that the Son is the complete reflection of the Father, "The *Prologue* of John is certainly the *key* text that gives full expression to the truth about the divine sonship of Christ. He who "became flesh" in time, is the Word himself from all eternity. He is the only-begotten Son–God "who is in the Bosom of the Father." He is the Son 'of the same substance of the Father,' he is 'God from God.' He receives the fullness of the glory from the Father."[7]

This decisive *key* in St. John's *Prologue*, the divine dialogue of love and life in the Heart of the Father, is a profound mystery of the faith. In numerous writings, the Fathers of the Church expressed their understandings of this divine inner life and all of its workings. They envisioned the boundless, inexpressible abyss of the Son's love for the Father and the Father's love for the Son—a love that existed "before the foundation of the world" (Jn 17:24) – the indefinable love that led to the Cross (cf. Jn 3:16).

Many of the Fathers describe this divine love as especially revealed and comprehended in the Father and the Son's completeness, along with their *Oneness of Being* in bringing the Paschal Mystery to fulfillment: "You, Father, are in me as I am in you"

(Jn 17:21), "[E]verything of mine is yours and yours is mine" (Jn 17:10), "Father, into your hands I commend my spirit" (Lk 23:46).

CLIMAX ON CALVARY

It is especially on Calvary—in the final, climactic scene of Jesus' life—that we find the greatest testimony of the Father and Son's divine love, along with its greatest *visible sign*. For out of this frozen second in time, we come to understand the pierced Heart of the Savior at the moment of His death on the Cross is completely embraced and subsumed into the arms and Bosom of His Father. It is a fusion of divine love, of divine Hearts, expressed in both the visible and the invisible – the Son's *blood* and the Father's *grace*. It is, Pope Benedict XVI states, the perfect communion in knowledge, unity and being of the Father and the Son.[8]

Indeed, in the waning seconds of the Crucifixion, we are given a visual theophany for the eyes of our souls. Christ's death becomes the ultimate expression of the Father and the Son's love for one another and the perfect closing denouement of a divine and human diorama of love that begins in Bethlehem, takes us to the Temple, follows the Jordan to the heights of Tabor, and then winds through the Garden of Gethsemane on the way to the bloody summit at Golgotha.

Consequently, the decisive moments on Calvary forever illuminate the rich meaning of St. John's words. In surveying the full landscape of Scripture, the conclusion of the *Prologue* amounts to a declaration of a supreme affirmation—one that precisely pinpoints the innermost truth of this mystery, the all consuming love of the Father for the Son and the Son for the Father. St. John Paul II writes, "Only the Son was capable of introducing us to this mystery. Since "no one has seen God" no one knew the mystery of his inner life. The Son alone knew it. It is only the Son, *who is nearest to the Father's Heart, who has made him known"*[9], who is "in the Father as the Father is in him, even on the Cross,"[10] who "embraced death as an entrance into the immutable peace of the Father's Bosom...whose soul entered into the beatific vision in the Bosom of the Trinity."[11]

BACK TO THE GARDEN

There is more to unfold in this endless epiphany. The mystical side of the moment transcends time both backwards and forward as Christ's crucifixion becomes the *visible sign* of the Father's everlasting love – not only for His Son, but for humanity too. Behind the horror of Jesus' death, we find paradox: God is inviting His prodigal children back home to Him through it all. Henceforth, both the Passion and Resurrection of Jesus Christ reveal nothing less than the turn of the ages; salvation has finally arrived for the children of Adam. Out of His perfect obedience (cf. Heb 5:8,9), the only begotten Son is nailed to the *Tree* by the Father's love for mankind, raining down the blood that opened heaven to the disobedient man and, like the rising sun erases all darkness, the bright day of forgiveness dawned upon an eclipsed world.

But there was even a greater mystical fulfillment to God's triumph of mercy. In the world of the *invisible*, the summit of Calvary is understood to perforate the heavens in the fullness of time and blossom in Paradise. The Cross becomes not only the key to mankind's redemption but also to our return to the *Garden* – the Father's *garden of life*. In essence, as Christ empties Himself in love on Calvary in returning to His Father's Heart, He also opens the door for mankind to return in love to the Father's Heart – His *Heart of Life*. Thus, man is once more invited to share in the fruits of the divine (cf. Rv 22:19) that were lost when Adam and Eve were barred from the *Tree of Life* (cf. Gn 3:22) and banished from the Garden of Eden (cf. Gn 3:23). The Apostles and early disciples had understood the significance of this mystical drama in time. Subsequently, Christ's salvific act leads to the birth of the Church, the Sacraments, and the coming of the Holy Spirit.

As can be seen, the *Prologue* of St. John's Gospel leads us to contemplate the profound mysteries of the faith. However, from this enlightened wisdom, one more enigmatic mystery stands before us — one that now demands a closer look and a better understanding — for it lies at the core of all the other mysteries.

It is the unfathomable mystery of *God the Father's Heart* — the *Divine Paternal Bosom* of all life that St. John writes "the only Son is nearest to" — that allows Christ "to make his Father known." Fr. Enrique Llamas Martinez, O.C.D., a Professor Emeritus of the Pontifical University of Salamanca, writes, "The mystery is contained in the Heart of the Father: God will reign from a tree (*Regnabit a ligno Deus*). The triumph of the Cross explains the *Life* of the Church to be established on the *Law of Love*."[12]

"'No one has ever seen God: it is the only Son, who is nearest to the *Father's Heart*, who has made him known' (Jn 1:18). Just as Jesus, the Son, knows about the mystery of the Father from resting in his *Heart*, so too the Evangelist has gained his intimate knowledge from his inward repose in *Jesus' Heart*."
—Pope Benedict XVI

Chapter Six

THE MYSTERY OF THE FATHER'S HEART

> *"O' Lord, for thy servants sake, according to thy own Heart, thou has shewn all this magnificence, and wouldst have all the great things to be known" (1 Chr 17:19).*

From the beginning, we have all seen this love – this mystery of the Father's Heart – who allowed us to see His love in Christ. St. John Paul II writes in his encyclical letter, *Dives in Misericordia,* that it is a mystery to be revealed by the Church simply because it is "[t]he reason for her existence."[1]

To study the mystery of the Father's love, therefore, is to bring this mystery down to us. It is the mystery of a Father who *is* Love, who dwells in unapproachable light in His invisible nature, yet becomes visible through Christ. He dwells there to make His love for man known, and to make His mystery present in our world—a world where each of His children is made in His image and formed in His likeness out of His love.[2]

The Father's love speaks to the world by means of the whole universe and all of visible creation. However, He does not remain *closely* linked with the world as the Creator or as its source of existence, but by the very essence of a bond that is more intimate than that of creation.[3] He is "Our Father," who grants us life and participation in *His* very life. It is the life of His Paternal Heart, which is overflowing with the harmonious passion of His divine truth: His divine paternal love. Indeed, He who loves desires to give of himself – to give *all* of Himself, to give *all of His Heart*!

And we have all experienced this love of our Father, this emptying of Himself. The quintessential manifestation of God the Father's love and the establishment of the New Covenant occurs in the ultimate giving of the Father's love: the *Passion* and *Crucifixion* of His only begotten Son, Jesus Christ: "God so loved the world that he sent his only Son, so that everyone who believes in him may not perish but have eternal life" (Jn 3:16).[4]

In his encyclical letter, *Redemptor Hominis,* St. John Paul II unfolds this great mystery of the Father's love and how it may be best understood: "He it was, and he alone, who satisfied the Father's eternal love, that fatherhood that from the beginning found expression in creating the world, giving man all the riches of creation and making him 'little less than God,' in that he was created 'in the image and after the likeness of God.' He and he alone also satisfied the Fatherhood of God and that love which man in a way rejected by breaking the first covenant and the later covenants that God 'again and again offered to man.' The redemption of the world – this tremendous mystery of love in which creation is renewed – is, at its deepest root the fullness of justice in a human heart – *the Heart of the first-born Son*."[5]

It is in the pierced Heart of Jesus Christ, therefore, where the Father's love springs forth the great mysteries of our faith within our hearts. This love, the mystery of the Father's divine paternal love and His salvific gifts, is undeniably seen in the symbol par excellence of the Heart of the Savior.[6] This truth was recognized to a degree from the beginning. Contemplating the Heart of the One whom they have pierced, the founders of the Church saw the birth of the Church in this scene, along with the gift of the

Sacraments and the pouring forth of the divine grace and effusion of the Holy Spirit upon the world.[7]

Thus, from Christ's Heart flowed the Father's *visible love* upon mankind in a most radiant way, spreading to the four corners of the world.

THE LOVE OF THE FATHER

But there is more to the greatest story ever told that needs to be understood, that beckons to be more closely examined in the light of divine truth to better grasp *the mystery of the Father – the mystery of His loving Heart*.

Throughout his papacy, the writings of St. John Paul II illuminated God the Father's great love for mankind in the minds of the faithful. From *Redemptor Hominis* to the prophetic *Tertio Millennio Adveniente* and beyond, St. John Paul II's insights helped to better reveal the progressive unfolding of the Father's visible love in creation, the *Incarnation*, and in the *Paschal Mystery*. He especially taught us to see how the Father's love slowly brought about the Paschal Mystery to fulfillment, giving God's children through His great plan for them the *Heavenly Food* that will allow them to live forever.

St. John Paul II tells us in *Dives in Misericordia* that the profound mystery of the Father's love is one that the Church must unfold and develop if we are to come to better know, love, and honor our heavenly Father—and to see the depth of His love for us.

Not surprisingly then, it is a mystery of love that can be better understood in the way our faith has previously come to see and comprehend God's infinite love—*in and through the symbol of the heart* – the universal symbol of love.

THE HEART OF THE FATHER

Over the centuries, the Church began to recognize that the love of Jesus and Mary would be more clearly understood if their Hearts, the undeniable emblems of their great love for humanity, were contemplated. These movements took hold, and by the early middle ages, the Church had begun to encourage the spread of devotion and consecration to the Immaculate Heart of Mary and the Sacred Heart of Jesus.

Now, following in this tradition, it is the *Divine Paternal Heart of God the Father* that we are called to see and understand; the mystical womb of the Creator, where all mankind is formed in the image of God. And like the Hearts of Jesus and Mary, the Heart of the Father holds for us in a special way what humanity is being called to better understand – our heavenly Father's great love for His children, His Church and all creation. It is a love perfectly captured in coming to know His Heart – the symbolic source of His divine paternal love.

The truth of this emerging reality can be seen in the work of the Holy Spirit as the Father's Heart has been cited more and more in the writings of theologians and popes. On December 7, 1988, St. John Paul II spoke of the *Heart of the Father* being present in the mystery of the Cross:

> "Jesus realized in the depths of his being the loving and immediate presence of the Father, since Jesus is in the Father as the Father is in him" (cf. Jn 10:38; 14:10), even on the Cross. By his death Jesus reveals that at the end of life man is not doomed to immersion in obscurity, in the existential void, in the abyss of nothingness. But man is invited to *meet the Father* toward whom he moved in the journey of faith and love during life, and into whose arms he threw himself with holy abandonment at the hour of death. It is an abandonment which, like that of Jesus, implies a total gift of self on the part of a soul which ac-

cepts to be despoiled of the body and of earthly life, but in the knowledge that it will find **in the arms and Heart of the Father** the new life, a participation in the very life of God in the Trinitarian mystery."[8]

In these words, St. John Paul II explains that the mystery of creation, the mystery of man, and the mystery of the Redemption are like gifts springing from love – and these great mysteries bear witness not only to the love of Christ but also to the love of the Father. This is because the Father is He who establishes the world in existence, and subsequently man in the world; He who gave His only begotten Son to redeem mankind, He who is "Love" (1 Jn 4:8),[9] "an authentically paternal love."[10] In essence, the Holy Father shows us that we are led to glimpse in love the divine motive of creation and the Redemption, and the source from which they spring—which is the love of the Father, the love of His Paternal Heart for us, for only love gives a beginning to good and delights in good (cf. 1 Cor 13).

In *Tertio Millennio Adveniente*, St. John Paul II wrote again of the Father's paternal love as seen in His Paternal Heart – a divine Heart he tells us we are being called through our faith and religion to know: "The religion which originates in the mystery of the Redemptive Incarnation is the *religion of dwelling in the Heart of God*, of sharing in God's very life. St. Paul speaks of this in the passage already quoted: 'God has sent the Spirit of his Son into our hearts, crying, 'Abba! Father!'" (Gal 4:6).[11]

IN CHRIST WE SEE THE FATHER

Perhaps in no better way, St. John's *Prologue* illuminates the importance of this understanding of the Father's love as seen in His Paternal Heart.[12] This is because, the Apostle tells us, Christ was one in Heart (cf. Jn 1:18) with the Father before all time,[13] and therefore it is in the Heart of the Son that we can best come to understand the Paternal Heart of the Father – the great source of the love for the Son and for man.[14] He writes, "This image of the man, in the image of the Creator, became flesh and dwelt among us and was filled with enduring love, the love coming from the Father"(cf. Jn 1:14).

From St. John's words, we are called to know that this is the same *paternal love* of the Father for us in which He bore the Son "before the foundation of the world" (Jn 17:24), the same paternal love whose "Heart was grieved" by our "actions" (cf. Gn 6:6), the same paternal love for Christ that led to the Cross (cf. Jn 3:16).

It is in the Incarnate Christ, therefore, that we come to see, know, and understand the Father's great paternal love for man, and to understand His Fatherly Heart is the source of this love. This is because the Father and the Son "are one" (Jn 10:30) and, as Christ said to Philip, "Whoever has seen me has seen the Father" (Jn 14:9). Christ can say this, Pope Benedict XVI writes, because only He from all eternity was in the Father's Heart, living before the face of the Father: "'[I]t is only the Son, who is *nearest to the Father's Heart*, who has made him known' (Jn 1:18). ...He lives before the face of God, not just as a friend, but as a Son; he lives in the most intimate unity with the Father."[15]

Moreover, Pope Pius XII tells us that it is in this very truth that we are brought to realize that to see the Heart of the Son is to see the Heart of the Father, because the way to the Heart of the Father is found through the Heart of the Son.[16] Henceforth, it is in this perspective, St. John Paul II explains, that we are invited to not only "see" the Father (cf. Jn 14:9), but to "know" the Father (cf. Jn 10:14-15), to know His great paternal love for man (cf. Jn 16:27) and, as Christ did on the Cross, to "return" to the Father (cf. Lk 23:46). For to return to the source of His great love – to return our heart, like Christ did, to our Father's Paternal Heart (cf. Jn 1:18) – is God's desire for man.

In essence, our love for our Father is to be like Christ's love for His Father (cf. Jn 15:9-11). It is a love of the *Heart* – our heart for the Father's Heart – a love greatly needed in our times, and a love we are called to seek because it seeks us.

THE PLAN OF THE FATHER

In *Tertio Millennio Adveniente*, St. John Paul II writes that God's search for man begins in His "Fatherly Heart" and continues endlessly as He calls His children to Him through the Church and the Sacraments. He writes: *"In Jesus Christ* God not only speaks to man but also *seeks him out.* The Incarnation of the Son of God attests that God goes in search of man. Jesus speaks of this search as the finding of a lost sheep (cf. Lk 15:1-7). It is a search which *begins in the Heart of God* and culminates in the Incarnation of the Word. God goes in search of man, created in his own image and likeness, he does so because he loves him eternally in the Word, and wishes to raise him in Christ to the dignity of an adoptive son. God therefore goes in search of man who *is his special possession* in a way unlike any other creature. Man is God's possession by virtue of a choice made in love: God seeks man out, *moved by his Fatherly Heart."*[17]

Seeking man's return to Him has always been God's plan – a plan that the Church tells us originated in His Paternal Heart. Reflecting the words of the psalm, "the plan of the Lord stands forever, the designs of his Heart" (Ps 33:11), the *Catechism of the Catholic Church* tells us that God's search for man is **"the mysterious design of his wisdom and goodness,**[18]**...[a] plan born in the Father's Heart."**[19]

Thus, it is this divine plan "born in the Father's Heart," unfolded and made visible in the Incarnation and the Redemption, and fully revealed in the mystery of the Eucharist – that Christ calls the world to His Father, to the Father's love, for conversion to

God is always the fruit of the rediscovery of this Father, who is rich in mercy.[20]

This call of God for His children to return to Him has been the call of the ages, but now in our time, it has taken on a new urgency. This is because a *crisis of civilization* has erupted, fueled and driven by a *culture of death*.

The signs of the times need no heralding. One cannot escape the obvious. The world is moving forward in unchartered waters, and as St. John Paul II, Pope Benedict XVI and Pope Frances have cautioned, it is trying to do so without its Creator—its one, true God, who wishes only to build it up in His love and truth, the radiance of His Divine Paternal Heart.

"Behold, the Lord God shall come with strength, and his arm shall rule: Behold his reward is with him and his work is before him. He shall feed his flock like a shepherd: he shall gather together the lambs with his arm, and shall take them up in his *Bosom*, and he himself shall carry them that are with young" (Is 40:10-11).

Chapter Seven

A CRISIS OF CIVILIZATION

"I called out: Lord, you are my Father, my champion, my savior! Do not abandon me in time of trouble, in the midst of storms and dangers" (Sir 51:10).

Pope Pius XI defined the pressing dangers of his times in the encyclical letter *Caritate Christi Compulsi* (1932); he reached out to the mercy of the Sacred Heart of Christ, pouring out the sorrows of mankind and of the human heart. In a world suffering from the aftermath of World War I – a world mired deep in economic depression and on the brink of World War II – Pope Pius XI prayerfully called for public worship so that "we may obtain mercy and find grace in seasonable aid" (Heb 4:16). [1]

Almost fifty years later, St. John Paul II recognized in *Redemptoris Hominis* that the world, the Church, and present-day humanity were all living through a solemn moment: the height of the Cold War, along with emerging modern-world perils brought about by science, materialism, and continued violations of human dignity. As he commenced his pontificate in 1978, he cited the "atomic stockpiles" and the unpredictable scenario of "a world in which man has become the means and instrument for unimaginable self-destruction." Trusting in the Father's merciful design and faithful promise, the Holy Father emphasized that it is a "world 'groaning in travail.'"[2]

His successors, Pope Benedict XVI and Pope Francis, have found no reprieve from the urgency of our times. Wars, poverty and social injustice still grip much of the world, while immorality, humanism, and practical atheism have spread to every nation, every people. Moreover, over the past several decades, secular thought has become institutionalized in many nations, burgeoning the popular view that Christian morality is archaic and regressive.

According to studies, a growing plurality today embrace a permissive outlook regarding all the major social issues of the past half century. In addition, sociologists conclude that the roles of the foundational cornerstones of civilization – marriage and the family – are approaching a transitional point of influence, no longer seen as unquestionable pillars of truth.

During the *Year of the Family* (1994), St. John Paul II observed that the sanctity of marriage and the human family, as God intended them to be, was in serious danger. Over the years, both stalwart institutions of civilization have been continuously marginalized, discredited and redefined. St. John Paul II emphasized in his *Letter to Families* that it was vital for the Church to not only promote the dignity of marriage and the family, but to bring this teaching into every home. "The mystery of the Incarnation and the very history of humanity is seen in the family," said St. John Paul, "was it not through a family, the family of Nazareth, that the Son of God chose to enter into human history?"[3]

A FRAGILE WORLD

Then there is the question of international peace: the fragile atmosphere of coexistence on a planet containing over seven billion inhabitants. Somehow, human beings must continue to find a way to live with each other—and to do so without triggering a cataclysmic confrontation, one that can carom out of control and unleash the apocalyptical scenarios that numerous authors and filmmakers have imagined in their works.

Since the detonation of the two atomic bombs over the Japanese cities of Hiroshima and Nagasaki in 1945, the world has stumbled forward through a "Cold War,"[4] all the while clinging to a nuclear deterrence plan based upon the concept that threatening a holocaust to prevent one is the best way to stymie calibrated dangers of annihilation.[5] Over the last fifty years, whether through good fortune or the mercy of God, mankind has survived repeated close calls with the potential use of weapons of mass destruction.[6] Pope John Paul II confronted the ongoing strain of this protracted nightmare in many of his writings.[7]

However, humanity's worst fears are not relics of the past. The Cold War atmosphere of the twenty-first century – while viewed by most as significantly thawed because of the collapse of the Soviet Union – is in fact very much alive and even intensifying in risk.[8] According to experts, the bipolar system of deterrence between the East and the West is still in play, filled with the flaws and terrifying assumptions that guide it.[9]

And to broaden this threat, the continued rise of nuclear capabilities among many more nations is presenting countless emerging scenarios that many now believe could see a regional crisis explode into a worldwide conflagration.[10] For many nuclear proliferation specialists, such a reality is seen as almost inevitable. This is because there appears to be no sure way of containing the spread or preventing the use of weapons of mass destruction.[11] There is also the growing understanding that the nuclear deterrence strategies of the past will not impede fanatic movements or rogue nations who intend to use such weapons; some of whom, it is believed, are contemplating a first-strike approach despite certain nuclear retaliation.[12]

A CRISIS OF CIVILIZATION

But the most worrisome threats to the future of civilization are the attacks on *life* itself.

In his encyclical letter, *Evangelium Vitae*, St. John Paul II sought to illuminate the growing threat against life, describing a "culture of death" as being at the heart of the *crisis of civilization*.[13] Human society, he wrote, was being poisoned by gravely misguided and disordered moral precepts. Confronting the rational behind a woman's choice to have an abortion along with the justification for euthanasia, St. John Paul II called such thinking "a disturbing 'perversion' of mercy"[14] and a "conspiracy against life."[15] "True compassion does not kill," he added, "abortion and euthanasia," therefore, "take the form of murder, regardless of the views of doctors, scientists, legislators, or those in power, those who hold authority to decide life and death."[16] There can be no true peace, he concluded, "unless life is defended and promoted, for 'every crime against life is an attack on peace,'"[17] and a "supreme dishonour to the Creator" that "attributes to human freedom a perverse and evil significance."[18]

St. John Paul II acknowledged these escalating perils to life on not only human and political levels, but spiritual levels as well. He wrote of the presence of evil and warned of the "wages of sin" and of "Satan."

A CRISIS OF LIFE

Whether it is the politics of economic and social injustice, abortion and population control, or terrorism and nuclear proliferation, the question at hand is one of *life* itself. Our *crisis of civilization* is a *crisis of life*; man denying and abusing the principle, the preciousness, and the sacredness of human life – all life – the life of the unborn and the life of the living.

During his papacy, Pope Benedict XVI affirmed his concerns regarding the dangers of the growing threat to all life on earth: "Openness to life is at the center of true development. When a society moves towards the denial and suppression of life, it ends up no longer finding the necessary motivation and energy to strive for man's good." We must cultivate, he urged, "the fundamental right to life of every people and every individual."[19]

Pope Francis has spoken of his concerns, too, and sees sin as the culprit, as the cause of the *crisis of life*: "Death, destruction, enormous economic and environmental damage[20] ...Turn to us, O Lord, and have mercy on us because we are sad, we are distressed. See our misery and our pain and forgive all sins, because behind every war there always are sins: the sin of idolatry, the sin of exploiting others on the altar of power, sacrificing them."[21]

Across the religious spectrum, spiritual leaders concur that it is sin that has led to the *crisis of civilization* now upon us. Decades ago, the poignant words of Pope Pius XII weighed the profound gravity of the "domination of sin" (Rom 3:9) in the world: "the sin of the century is the loss of the sense of sin" (cf. *Discorsi e Radiomessaggi*, VII, 1946, 285).

In recalling Pius XII's observation, St. John Paul II, in his general audience on November 12, 1986, called attention to the fact that *a total disintegration of all morality* was looming if the world no longer recognized sin and its consequences, "Evil is not complete or at least not without a remedy, as long as man is aware of it. But when even this is lacking, the *complete collapse of moral values* is practically inevitable and there looms over man as a terrifying reality the risk of definitive perdition. For this reason the grave words of Pius XII (which have become almost proverbial) should always be remembered and meditated on with great attention."[22]

THE MERCIFUL LOVE OF THE FATHER

Pushing aside fear, while calling for the Father's mercy and "a season of a New Advent, a season of expectation,"[23] St. John Paul II turned to Christ, who is united in heart with each modern man and leads all in today's dangerous and perilous world to the mercy of the Father: "Jesus Christ is the chief way for the Church. He himself is our way to the 'Father's house'... Christ communicates to us the Spirit who places within us the sentiments of the Son and directs towards the Father", towards the 'vision of the Father' in the holiness of his mercy."[24]

In 1994, as St. John Paul II prepared the Church for the *Jubilee Year 2000*, he emphasized in *Tertio Millennio Adveniente* the need to counter the emerging magnitude of the crisis he foresaw—a *crisis of civilization*—by bringing about Pope Paul VI's repeated call for a *civilization of love* through the mercy and love of the Father for all His children.[25] Again, as in *Dives in Misericordia*, St. John Paul II turned to the *Parable of the Prodigal Son*.

The Pope pointed to our Father's merciful love, which calls all souls through a conversion of heart to return to their Father, to share in the *divine life*. Most significantly, he emphasized "[t]he whole of the Christian life is like a great *pilgrimage to the house of the Father*, whose unconditional love for every human creature, and in particular for the 'Prodigal Son' (Lk 15:11-32), we discover anew each day."[26]

Indeed, our Father's unconditional love for His creation, including all of His children in the world, guides our destiny in times so threatened by the unique evils of our world. Hearts of stone, as Scripture says, need to be transformed into "hearts of flesh"[27] (cf. Ez. 36:26), rendering life on earth divine and more worthy of humanity.

Thus, as Pope Pius XI turned in 1932 to the Sacred Heart of Jesus in the uniqueness of his times, we are invited to turn to the Paternal Heart of God our Father, who has never abandoned a single child of His and who is ready to receive His prodigal children, as St. John Paul II stated, into His arms and Fatherly Heart[28] in the uniqueness of this moment in history.

THE HOLY SPIRIT POINTS TOWARDS THE FATHER

Our return to the Father is ordained by Him as a process. It is a process of His divine paternal love that begins with our Mother Mary, who lovingly guides all His children to her Son. Jesus then mercifully lifts us upon His Cross to our Father. While comforting us on this journey home, the Holy Spirit purifies and refines us so that God the Father can come and dwell in us as living temples; we, in turn, can dwell in Him. This was reflected in St. John Paul II's preparation for the *Jubilee 2000*—1997, the Year of Jesus; 1998, the Year of the Holy Spirit; and 1999, the Year of God the Father. The Church teaches that our spiritual journey, then, is intended to move always in the direction of the Father.[29]

In moving towards the Father, in answering His invitation to turn away from a *crisis of civilization* towards a *civilization of life*, the Holy Spirit shows us the surest means to approach Him in order to hasten our journey back to Him: it is through the furnace of His merciful love, the Father's Divine Paternal Heart.

This revelation of the Father's merciful love, this work of the Holy Spirit, is manifested in the Church today. St. John Paul II writes in his encyclical letter *Dominum et Vivificantem*: "The supreme and complete self-revelation of God, accomplished in Christ and witnessed to by the preaching of the Apostles, continues to be manifested in the Church through the mission of the invisible Counselor, the Spirit of Truth. How intimately this mission is linked with the mission of Christ, how fully it draws from this mission of Christ, consolidating and developing in history its salvific results, is expressed by the verb 'take': 'He will take what is mine and declare it to you' (Jn 16:14). As if to explain the words 'he will take' by clearly expressing the divine and Trinitarian unity of the source, Jesus adds: 'All that the Father has is mine; therefore I said that he will take what is mine and declare it to you' (Jn 16:15). By the very fact of taking what is 'mine,' he will draw from 'what is the Father's.'"[30]

REVEALING THE FATHER'S HEART

In this light – like all mysteries of the faith—the Holy Spirit now reveals that the Father's Paternal Heart is the Heart that we need to come to know, to see, and to love. This is because it is the Heart that, out of love, bore such love for Christ before the world began (cf. Jn 17:24). It is the Heart that, out of love, brought forth the universe and all its wonders (cf. Jn 1:10), and it is the Heart that lovingly brought forth mankind, each and every soul (cf. 1 Jn 3:1). It is, in essence, the Heart of a Father who lives, loves, and speaks in every line of Scripture in the Old and New Testaments, calling mankind to Himself (cf. Lk 24:44-48).

Most of all, it is the merciful Heart of a Father who has been waiting to be better known in order to be loved, in order to pour out His greatest sign of love and mercy upon mankind. It is to be an outpouring of His paternal love that St. John Paul II says will stir people hearts by renewing their hope in the *"coming of the Kingdom of God."*[31]

Pope Benedict XVI's words in *Deus Caritas Est* reflect this mystery and truth of our Father: "True, no one has ever seen God as he is. And yet God is not totally invisible to us; he does not remain completely inaccessible. God loved us first, says the *Letter of John*... (cf. Jn 4:10) and this love of God has appeared in our midst. He has become visible in as much as he 'has sent his only Son into the world, so that we might live through him' (1 Jn 4:9). ...in Jesus we are able to *see the Father* (1 Jn 14:9)."[32]

To *see the Father*, therefore, is to *first* reveal His great paternal love for His children as recognized and understood in the Old Testament, a love story that cannot help but begin to unfold the sublime *mystery of the Father's Paternal Heart*.

Part III

THE HEART OF GOD IN SCRIPTURE AND THE CHURCH

86 *The Mystery of the Divine Paternal Heart of God Our Father*

"God is wise in his *Heart* and mighty of strength" (Jb 9:4).

Chapter Eight

A FATHERLY GOD

"...but it is your providence, O Father, that steers its course, because you have given it a path in the sea, and a safe way through the waves" (Wis 14:3).

"Christ reveals the Father within the framework of the same perspective and in ground already prepared, as many pages of the Old Testament writings demonstrate," St. John Paul II writes in *Dives in Misericordia*.

Moreover, the Holy Father writes that the Old Testament framework is the "foundational basis" of Christ's words to St. Philip in the New Testament: "Have I been with you so long, and yet you do not know me...? He who has seen me has seen the Father." (Jn 14:8)[1]

From the beginning, the Church recognized God's love for His children as recorded in the words of the early authors of Scripture. This divine paternal love of the Father is first seen in *Genesis* (cf. Gn 1:31) and unfolds throughout the Old Testament as ancient Israel came to understand God's great love for His chosen people. We read of this love in *Hosea*:

"I will heal their defection,
I will love them freely;
for my wrath is turned away from them.
I will be like the dew for Israel:
he shall blossom like the lily;
He shall strike root like the Lebanon
cedar, and put forth his shoots.
His splendor shall be like the olive tree
and his fragrance like the Lebanon cedar,
Again they shall dwell in his shade and raise grain;
They shall blossom like the vine,
and his fame shall be like the wine of
Lebanon" (Hos 14:5-9).

ANTHROPOMORPHISM

God's love for His people is presented often through the anthropomorphic language of the Old Testament. This is part of God's revelation intended to reveal His will and closeness to His people through *human characteristics* attributed to Him.

In his apostolic letter, *Mulieris Dignitatem*, St. John Paul II writes that the Bible—especially in the early chapters of the Old Testament – is abundantly anthropomorphic, which is God's pedagogy in the early stages of unfolding revelation: "Speaking about himself, whether through the prophets, or through the Son (cf. Heb 1:1,2) who became man, *God speaks in human language*, using human concepts and images. If this manner of expressing himself is characterized by a certain anthropomorphism, the reason is that man is 'like' God: created in his image and likeness. But then, *God too* is in some measure 'like man,' and precisely because of the likeness, he can be humanly known. At the same time, the language of the Bible is sufficiently precise to indicate the limits of the 'likeness,' the limits of the 'analogy.' For Biblical Revelation says that, while man's 'likeness' to God is true, the '*non-likeness*' which separates the whole of creation from the Creator is *still more essentially true*. Although man is created in God's likeness, God does not cease to be for him the One 'who dwells in unapproachable light' (1 Tim 6:16): He is the 'Different One,' by essence the 'totally Other.'"[2]

It is through this anthropomorphic language, therefore, that the God of the Old Testament is described to us. It is said that He "has eyes (Am 9:3, Sir 11:12), ears (Dn 9:18), hands (Is 5:25), [and] feet (Gn 3:8), as seen in one of the most beautiful uses, 'they heard the sound of the Lord walking in the garden in the cool of the day...'"[3] In the *Psalms*, the Lord is said to have a face. "The Lord is just, he loves just deeds; the upright will see his face" (Ps 11:7).

In many passages of the Old Testament, God appears and takes action, as He closed the door in Noah's Ark (cf. Gn 7:16) and walked with Enoch (cf. Gn 5:24). He appeared to Abraham at Mamre, and is described as standing, resting, eating, walking and speaking to him (cf. Gn 18:22, 18:33). In *Isaiah*, we read that the Lord even "whistles" (cf. Is 7:18). In addition to Abraham, God appeared to Jacob (cf. Gn 35:9) and Solomon (cf. 1 Kgs 11:9), spoke to Moses (cf. Ex 3:4), and called to Samuel (cf. 1 Sm 3:4). In *Exodus*, God is said to witness, hear, and know: "I have *witnessed* [italics added] the afflictions of my people in Egypt and *heard* [italics added] against their taskmasters, so I *know* [italics added] well what they are suffering" (Ex 3:7).

Throughout the Old Testament, God is represented as subject to certain emotions: He "rejoices" (Ps 104:31), is "regretful" (Jer 42:10), "revengeful" (Dt 32:35) and "kind" (Jl 2:18). He gets "angry" (1Chron 13:10), but "does not persist in anger forever" (Mi 7:18). He is "loathe to punish" (Jn 4:12), "though when he punishes, he takes pity" (Lam 3:22). He also is described as being "disgusted" (Lev 20:23), "jealous" (Ex 20:15, Jos 24:19, Na 1:2,

Dt 5:9) and even possesses a sense of humor: "The one enthroned in heaven laughs" (Ps 2:4).

Most importantly, the Old Testament speaks of God's love for His people (cf. Hos 11:8-9), especially in relation to Him as a Father (cf. Sir 51:10). He is a Father, the prophets reveal, that has a merciful Heart (cf. Jer 31:20) – a Heart He calls His people to see, to recognize, and to understand that is the source of His *everlasting love* (cf. Jer 31:3) – His *steadfast love* for Israel (cf. Is 54:10).

A GOD WHO IS A FATHER

In their writings, the Fathers of the Church explain that the God of the Old Testament is a God who desires His children to know and understand Him as a Father because of His great paternal love for them seen so uniquely in His providence and mercy:

> "But it is your providence, O *Father* [italics added], that steers the boat's course, because you have given it a path in the sea, and a safe way through the waves" (Wis 14: 3).

> "I will be a *Father* [italics added] to him, and he shall be a son to me" (2 Sm 7:14).

> "I called out: Lord, you are my *Father* [italics added], my champion, my savior!

> Do not abandon me in time of trouble,
> in the midst of storms and dangers" (Sir 51:10).

> "Have we not one *Father* [italics added]?
> Has not the one God created us?" (Mal 2:10)?

As with His love for His Son, Scripture reveals that God's Fatherly communion with mankind exists by virtue of His *will* to be a universal Father before creation. It was God's paternal intention, manifested through His paternal love, that formed human beings outside of Himself as well as the created universe for our dwelling. The *Catechism of the Council of Trent* summarized this truth declaring that "[b]y a special superintending care and providence over our interest God displays a paternal love for us."[4]

The *Catechism of the Catholic Church* states that the mystery of this Fatherhood in the Old Testament[5] has its root in the divine revelation of the Old Covenant.[6] While the Trinity has yet to be revealed, God's love for Israel is compared to a father's love for his son.[7] In Israel, God is called Father in as much as He is Creator of the world.[8] Even more, God is Father because of the Covenant and gift of the law to Israel, "His chosen."[9] God is also called the Father of Israel.[10] Most significantly, "He is 'the Father of the poor,' of the orphaned and the widowed, who are under His loving protection."[11] By calling God "Father," the language of the Jewish faith indicates two main things: God's Fatherhood is the first origin of everything and transcendent authority; and He is at the same time the source of goodness and loving care for all His children.

The *Catechism* notes that "God's parental love and tenderness can also be expressed by the image of motherhood,"[12] but God "transcends human fatherhood and motherhood."[13] "No one is father as God is Father.[14] Thus, the divine works and Trinitarian mission in creation – before the New Testament revelation – unfolds in this divine paternal love of God, as the Jews came to understand nothing is forever but God and His love for them: "Such is the 'plan of His loving kindness,' conceived by the Father before the foundation of the world, in His beloved Son."[15]

"Is Ephraim not my favorite son, the child in whom I delight? Even though I threaten him, I must still remember him! My *Heart* stirs for him, I must show him compassion! (Jer 31:20).

Chapter Nine

THE HEART OF GOD IN THE OLD TESTAMENT

"But the plan of the Lord stands forever; the design of his Heart, through all generations" (Ps 33:11).

Beginning in *Genesis*, we find passages referring to God's love emanating from His Heart that are intended to better reveal the divine paternal love of a Father:

> "When the Lord saw how great the wickedness of human beings was on earth, and how every desire that his heart conceived was ever anything but evil, the Lord regretted making human beings on the earth, and his *Heart* [italics added] was grieved" (Gn 6:5-6).

In *Judith*, we read how God's chosen ones are to be near His Fatherly Heart:

> "[L]et us rather give thanks to the Lord Our God who, as he tested our ancestors, is now testing us. Remember how he treated Abraham, all the ordeals of Isaac, and all that happened to Jacob…For as these ordeals were intended by him to search their hearts, so now this is not vengeance that God is exacting on us, but a warning inflicted by the Lord on those who are near his *Heart* [italics added]"(Jdt 8:25-27).

In the *Prophetic Books*, the God of the Old Testament submits Himself to complete disclosure of His love for His children; therefore, it is His intent to compare the hearts of His creatures to His own Heart. In *Jeremiah*, we read that God's decisions and actions are stirred from the depth of His Heart, the source of His Fatherly love and concern for His chosen people:

> "The anger of the Lord will not abate until he has done and fulfilled what he has determined in his Heart" (Jer 30:24).
>
> "Is Ephraim not my favorite son, the child in whom I delight?
> Even though I threaten him, I must still remember him! my *Heart* [italics added] stirs for him, I must show him compassion!, says the Lord" (Jer 31:20).
>
> "The Lord said to me: Even if Moses and Samuel stood before me, my *Heart* [italics added] would not turn toward this people" (Jer 15:1).
>
> "I will appoint over you shepherds after my own *Heart* [italics added], who will shepherd you wisely and prudently" (Jer 3:15).
>
> "The anger of the Lord will not abate until he has done and carried out completely the decision of his *Heart* [italics added]. In days to come you will fully understand it" (Jer 30:24).
>
> In *Hosea*, we read how God's Heart invokes His mercy:
> "When Israel was child, I loved him,
> out of Egypt I called my son...
> Yet it was I who taught Ephraim to walk,
> who took them in my arms...
> I drew them with human cords

With bands of love;
I foster them like one
Who rouses an infant to his cheeks;
I bent down to feed them...
They have refused to repent.
My *Heart* [italics added] is overwhelmed,
My pity is stirred.
I will not give vent to my blazing anger,
I will not destroy Ephraim again;
For I am God and not a man,
the Holy One present among you.
I will not come in wrath" (Hos 11:8-9).

The passage in *Hosea* is especially significant, writes Pope Benedict XVI, because it reveals God's love, His mercy – "His Heart" – transforms His justice. Pope Benedict writes, "Because God is God, the Holy One, he acts as no man could act. God has a Heart, and this Heart turns, so to speak, against God himself: Here in Hosea, as in the Gospel, we encounter once again the word *compassion*, which is expressed by means of the image of the maternal womb. *God's Heart* transforms wrath and turns punishment into forgiveness."[1]

In *Isaiah*, God's Heart is revealed to temper His anger. Theologians explain that God speaks to His people through His servant Isaiah's experience and words:

"The wine press I have trodden alone,
and from the people no one was
with me.
I trod them in my anger,
and trampled them down in my wrath;
Their blood spurted on my garments;
all my apparel I stained.
For the day of vengeance was in my *heart* [italics added],

> My year for redeeming was at hand.
> I looked about, but there was no one to help,
> I was appalled that there was no one
> to lend support;
> So my own arm brought about the victory,
> And my own wrath lent me its support" (Is 63:3-5).

Depending on the Scriptural translation and interpretation, there are considerable references to God's Heart in the Old Testament. According to Biblical historians, researchers, and scholars, perhaps as many as thirty or more references to the Heart of God were in the original texts. Over time, some of the passages reveal the word *heart* was replaced with the word *mind*. Nevertheless, the context of the Old Testament writings reveals a God who connects His own Fatherly love, joy, providence, sorrow, and mercy to a Paternal Heart of His own – implying emotions and decisions related to the experiences of the human heart, and implying a God who wishes His people to abide in His Heart, as He abides in theirs.

DIVINE PATERNAL LOVE

The Old Testament passages which refer to the Heart of God can best be described as containing language intended to be associated with the *paternal love* of God, the love of a heavenly Father for His children – for nothing could better convey such love than a father's heart.

In his encyclical letter *Haurietis Aquas*, Pope Pius XII traces this divine love in the Old Testament "*Psalms*, writings of the prophets, and the *Canticle of Canticles*" and called it "an expression of human, intimate, and paternal love …which God continued to sustain the human race."[2] St. John Paul II writes that it is the love of a Father, who is "pure paternity."[3]

Although the God of the Old Testament possesses Fatherhood attributes that are undeniably paternal and presented as such in the language of the Old Testament books, the Fatherhood in the Old Testament is for the most part a collective Fatherhood. God not only presents Himself as Father, but as Son and Spirit, who acts within the richness of His Trinitarian Being, but without revealing this Being as such. Significantly, there is never reference to God as a direct ancestor, as "one who begets."

Hence, Christians often believe that God's presence in Old Testament's writings is the same presence of the divine Person of 'God the Father' as later revealed in the New Testament; however, the God of Judaism is a theology of one God, *exempt of Trinitarian Personhood*, and therefore a different doctrine. This means that Old Testament references to the individual Persons of the Trinity are to be seen as not as a divine Person—instead, they are to be seen as a power or a personification of the divine power proceeding from God, which gives life, bestows strength, illuminates and propels toward good. Perhaps the words of *Job* summarize this understanding the best: "God is wise in his Heart and mighty of strength" (Jb 9:4).

Nevertheless, for the record, there are four moments in the Old Testament when the *plural* for God is raised in biblical language, arousing suspicion of a Trinitarian presence. At one time, these passages were taken as at least hints of the Trinity speaking, although most modern scholars generally agree they do not necessarily support such a conclusion about the Holy Trinity: "Then God said, 'let *us* make man in our image, after *our*[italics added] likeness'" (Gn 1:26); "Then the Lord God said, 'behold, the man has become like one of *us* [italics added], knowing good and evil'" (Gn 3:22); "Come, let *us* [italics added] go down, and there confuse their language that they may not understand one another's speech" (Gn 11:7); "And I heard the voice of the Lord saying, 'Whom shall I send and who will go for *us* [italics added]?'" (Is 6:8)"[4] "It is not because you are the largest of all nations that the Lord set his Heart on you and chose you, for you are really the smallest of all nations. It was because the Lord loved you and because of his fidelity to the oath he had sworn to your fathers…" (Dt 7:7-8).

"It is not because you are the largest of all nations that the Lord set his *Heart* on you and chose you, for you are really the smallest of all nations. It was because the Lord loved you and because of his fidelity to the oath he had sworn to your fathers…" (Dt 7:7-8).

Chapter Ten

THE PROPRIETY OF THE FATHER

> *"See what love the Father has bestowed on us that we may be called the children of God. Yet so we are. The reason the world does not know us is that it did not know him" (1 Jn 3:1).*

Jesus Christ revealed the triune God; with this, the doctrine of the Holy Trinity had its beginning in the economy of salvation. This means that the existence and relationship of the Father and the Holy Spirit is defined by Jesus Himself, as well as His relationship with the Father and the Holy Spirit.[1]

In the two great ecumenical councils of Nicaea (325) and Constantinople (381), the unity and trinity of God was unequivocally defined. The Magisterium of these councils bore fruit in the *Nicene–Constantinopolitan Creed* and the *Athanasian Creed* of the fifth century, establishing the Church's faith in the triune God—Father, Son and Holy Spirit. The Creeds, in examining the presence of God the Father in the Old Testament, profess in faith "that God the Father almighty is 'Creator of heaven and earth' (*Apostles Creed*), 'of all that is, seen and unseen' (*Nicene Creed*)."[2] Creation, then, is revealed as the first step toward God's covenant with His people, the Father's paternal love made visible, "a universal witness to God's all powerful love."[3]

Seen in this light, "[t]he Old Testament suggests and the New Covenant reveals the creative actions of the Son and the Spirit, inseparably one with that of the Father."[4] We also discover that "[t]his creative cooperation is clearly affirmed in the Church's rule of faith: 'There exists but one God…he is Father, God, Creator, the author, the giver of order. He made all things *by himself*, that is by his Word and by his Wisdom', 'by the Son and the Spirit' who, so to speak, are 'his hands.'"[5] However, as none of the Persons of the Holy Trinity are revealed prior to Christ, we should not interpret the language of the Old Testament as speaking of the Personhood of the members of the Trinity.

In affirmations defined in the creeds on the Father, Son, and Holy Spirit, the Church further addressed this understanding of the Holy Trinity. By 1215, at the ecumenical Fourth Latern Council, a more complete doctrine emerged: "[T]he true God is one alone, eternal, immense, and unchangeable, incomprehensible, omnipotent and ineffable, Father and Son and Holy Spirit: indeed three Persons but one essence, substance, or nature entirely simple. The Father from no one, the Son from the Father only, and the Holy Spirit equally from both: without beginning, always, and without end; the Father generating, the Son being born, and the Holy Spirit proceeding: consubstantial and coequal and omnipotent and coeternal; one beginning of all, creator of all visible and invisible things, of the spiritual and of the corporal; who by his own omnipotent power at once from the beginning of time created each creature from nothing, spiritual and corporal, namely, angelic, and mundane and finally the human, constituted as it were alike of spirit and the body."[6]

THE DOCTRINE OF APPROPRIATION

Convened by Pope Pius IX, the First Vatican Council (1869-1870) was content in its teaching of creation to repeat the Latern Council's words in its explanation of the trinitarian presence of God in the Old Testament. However, the Second Vatican Council (1962-1965) related creation to the Trinity while emphasizing God the Father, working the *Principle of Appropriation*: "The Eternal Father, in accordance with the utterly gratuitous and mysterious design of his wisdom and goodness, created the whole universe, and chose to raise up men to the divine life."[7]

Similarly, the *Catechism of the Catholic Church* attributes creation to the Trinity, emphasizing again the *Appropriation of the Father*: "Though the work of creation is attributed to the Father in particular, it is equally a truth of the faith that the Father, Son, and Holy Spirit together are the one, indivisible principle of creation."[8]

According to St. Thomas Aquinas, the *Doctrine of Appropriation* is to apply what is common to that which is proper. This means what is common to the whole Trinity cannot be applied to the propriety of any Person because it agrees with One more than the other; this would offend their equality of Persons, *but only because what is common has a greater resemblance to the propriety of one Person than to that of another.*

St. Thomas warned, however, that when we appropriate essential attributes to individual Persons we do not *exclude* the others, nor do we set up a *scale of participation*. As an example, St. Thomas illustrated the process of appropriation in God the Father: "Power implies beginning; it is therefore, *appropriate to the Father* who is the beginning without beginning…Thus it is the resemblance of the attribute which is appropriated to the propriety of the Person, which is the objective basis of the appropriation."[9] Theologians note that this is seen in the creeds, which recognize the Father's and the Holy Spirit's action in the unfolding of the Old Testament.

In the light of the New Testament, the *Fatherly* presence of God the Father in the Old Testament is one God, whose trinitarian presence is seen by St. Augustine and others as having its starting point in the unity of God – a divine mystery discernable in the Old Testament through an overwhelming sense of God. He is the One who reveals Himself, who takes the initiative of self-disclosure. He manifests Himself to the Jews by His paternal love, as expressed in His care, His compassion, His demands, and His power. Simply stated, the Prophets told the Jews what God desired of them, but they did not open up to speculation of the Godhead's inexhaustible treasures – specifically the divine Persons.

THE PROPRIETY OF THE FATHER

With this rule in mind, the actions of God the Father in the Old Testament clearly demonstrate, as with all of the Father's creative actions, His *great paternal love* for His children—a love best understood in the anthropomorphic language of revealing Himself as possessing a *Heart*.

In *De Trinitate*, St. Augustine considered the theophanies and anthropomorphic language of the Old Testament and asserts these manifestations are "of the whole Trinity." He did, however, not want so much thought of the divinity of the Trinity in the Old Testament as to make it *so* separate as to appear almost a "fourth Person" or again so dominate that it absorbs the other "three Persons." He suggests that "this would be a new kind of Seballianism.[10] St. Augustine believed and was upheld by St. Bonaventure and St. Thomas that the monotheistic revelation of the God of the Old Testament remains identical to the God of the New Testament. However, His full trinitarian constitution, which acts with the infinite richness of His trinitarian Being, is as of yet unrevealed; it will be revealed only when Christ distinguishes Himself manifestly from the other two Persons through the Incarnation.

Nevertheless, when God manifests Himself in the language and theophanies of the Old Testament, endowed with various attributes which will *later appear* belonging more to those of God the Father as revealed by Christ in the New Testament doctrine, we are in St. Augustine's reasoning, recognizing the Father's attributes and characteristics and are to see within the God of the Old Covenant the "workings" of the Person of the Father.

Indeed, the *Catechism of the Council of Trent* specifically recognizes the presence of the Father in the Old Testament when it states that it is "God the Father" speaking in *Isaiah*. In defining the *Creed*, the catechism of Trent reads: "But that Christ the Lord was also delivered over to death by the Father and by himself, the Scripture bears witness. For in *Isaiah*, God the Father says; "For the wickedness of my people have I struck him."[11]

Seen in this light and context, the passages in the Old Testament that refer to God's paternal love, and to God having a *Heart*, are best understood to be associated with God the Father's paternal love and presence in the Old Testament as later revealed in the New Testament[12], because they have a greater resemblance to the *propriety of the Father.*

St. Gregory Nazianzen especially viewed the Old Testament as being deliberately revealing of God the Father in relation to the mystery of the Trinity. "In effect," said the great Father of the Church, "the Old Testament expressly told us about the Father, and less clearly about the Son; the New Testament manifested the Son and suggested the divinity of the Holy Spirit" (Orat. XXXI, Theol. V, 26: pg. 36, 165). Likewise, the *Catechism of the Catholic*

Church states, "The Old Testament proclaimed the Father clearly."[13]

In his general audience of October 16, 1985, St. John Paul II addressed the *hidden Trinity* of the Old Testament, especially God the Father: "The mystery of the divine paternity with the Trinity was not yet explicitly revealed in the Old Testament. However, the whole context of the Old Testament was rich with allusions to God's Fatherhood in a moral and analogical sense. Thus, God is revealed as "'Father' of his people."[14]

THE PATERNAL HEART OF GOD THE FATHER

It must be emphasized that divine attributes of the God in the Old Testament that appear to be of a particular divine Person—in this case the paternal love and mercy of the Father, as represented in passages that speak of God's Heart—are not, as St. Thomas writes, necessary to be understood as *proof* of an argument for that particular divine Person. Rather, as St. Augustine suggests, such manifestations or theophanies can be permissibly understood as "deliberately present on purpose" to manifest in a special way 'one' of the Persons."

In fact, it is not only understandable and theologically permissible to associate, as in this case, the paternal love of God the Father as represented in His Heart in specific passages of the Old Testament; it is actually somewhat encouraged in order to help better prepare for the more *full disclosure* of such attributes or qualities of that divine Person as later revealed in the New Testament.

As we read in the Gospels of Luke and John, Jesus Himself tells us we are to *look* for such evidence of manifestations of the divine Persons of the Trinity in the Old Testament: "[S]earch the Scriptures...they testify on my behalf" (Jn 5:39, cf. Jn 5:46); "[I]f you had believed Moses, you would have believed me, because he wrote about me" (Jn 5:46); "'[E]verything written about me in the law of Moses and the prophets and psalms must be fulfilled.' Then he opened their minds to understand the scriptures" (Lk 24:44-45).

In this regard, we find that the authors of the New Testament had no reservation in citing what they understood to be the actions of the individual, divine Persons of the Trinity in the Old Testament. St. Luke writes in Acts: "[T]he Holy Spirit spoke beforehand through the mouth of David" (Acts 1:16), and he writes, "then Paul made one final statement. 'Well did the Holy Spirit speak to your ancestors through the prophet Isaiah'" (Acts 28:25).

Likewise, and significant for our purposes, St. Paul's words in his *Letter to the Hebrews* clearly speak of the Father as the source of revelation to the prophets of the Old Testament: "In times past, God spoke in partial and various ways to our ancestors through the prophets; in these last days, he spoke to us through the Son" (Heb 1:1-2).

In following the progression of Sacred Scripture, the anthropomorphic language and images of God as possessing a *Heart* in the Old Testament can be understood through reason and faith to reveal divine pedagogy: the wise arranging of "the New Testament being hidden in the Old Testament and the Old Testament being made manifest in the New Testament." As in the creeds—where we affirm that the Father is *Creator* of heaven and earth and the Holy Spirit *spoke* through the prophets—the multiple verses in the Old Testament that speak of God's Heart are not to be taken simply metaphorical. Rather, they are intended to convey to us the truth of the individual Persons of the trinitarian God not yet fully revealed, and the truth of their individual attributes or qualities not fully revealed.

In this understanding, the *Heart of the paternal God in the Old Testament is best understood as being the Paternal Heart of God the Father*, for nothing could convey better His great paternal love for His people—a love that desired to *shine* in their hearts. St. Paul does exactly this in his recognition of the Heart of the Father when speaking of God choosing David as a "man after his own Heart" (cf. Acts 13:22).

MOSES: "THE LORD HAS SET HIS HEART ON YOU"

In revealing God's "plan of loving goodness," we believe in faith that the Old Testament prophets conveyed God's true words, words intended to establish His desire for His children to *know* His "love" for His chosen people. It is a love that is completely fulfilled for Israel in the coming of Christ, who tells us that it was He who Moses spoke of: "Moses wrote about me" (Jn 5:46), Jesus says to His adversaries.

Likewise, St. Phillip's words concern this truth: "We have found the one about whom Moses wrote of in the Law, and also the prophets" (Jn 1:45). According to Pope Benedict XVI, this fulfillment in Christ of God's love for His chosen people is a fulfillment that is true because of God's Fatherly Heart, for His Paternal Heart is understood by Israel to possess the fullness of His love: "'No one has ever seen God; it is the only Son, *who is nearest to the Father's Heart* [italics added], who has made him known' (Jn 1:16-18). We began this book with Moses' prophecy: 'The Lord your God will raise up for you a prophet like me from among you, from your brethren – him you shall heed' (Dt 18:15). We saw that *Deuteronomy*, which contains this prophecy, ends with the observation: 'and there has not arisen a prophet since in Israel like Moses, whom the Lord knew face to face' (Dt 34:10). Until that hour, the great promise had remained unfulfilled. Now he is here, the one who is truly close to the *Father's Heart*, the only one who has seen him, who sees him and who speaks out of this seeing—the One of whom it is therefore fittingly said: 'him you shall heed' (Mk 9:7; Dt 18:15). The promise to Moses is fulfilled superabundantly, in the overflowingly lavish way in which God is accustomed to bestow his gifts."[15]

Indeed, we read in *Deuteronomy* – a Scriptural passage often used today as the first reading on the *Feast of the Sacred Heart*—how Moses speaks to his people about the gifts of God, who has His Paternal Heart set on His chosen people: "For you are a people sacred to the Lord, your God; he has chosen you from all nations on the face of the earth to be a people peculiarly his own. It is not because you are the largest of all nations that the Lord set his *Heart* [italics added] on you and chose you, for you are really the smallest of all nations. It was because the Lord loved you and because of his fidelity to the oath he had sworn to your fathers, that he brought you out with his strong hand from the place of slavery, and ransomed you from the hand of Pharaoh, King of Egypt. Understand, then, that the Lord, your God, is God indeed, the faithful God who keeps his merciful covenant down to the thousandth generation toward those who love him and keep his commandments" (Dt 7:6-11).

DAVID: "THE PLAN OF THE LORD STANDS FOREVER, THE DESIGNS OF HIS HEART"

But perhaps it is in the *Psalms*, so filled with praise of the glory of God, where we find Scripture's most powerful call to recognize and understand God's loving presence and plan for His people in the Old Testament, stemmed from His Fatherly Heart.

It is a call from His servant, David, who the Lord God chose to be King because he was "a man after His own *Heart* [italics added]" (1 Sm 13:14). In his *Psalm*, David speaks of the Heart of His Fatherly God in a special way: "Let all the earth fear the Lord; let all who dwell in the world show him reverence. For he spoke, and it came to be, commanded, and it stood in place. The Lord foils the plan of nations, frustrates the designs of peoples. But the plan of the Lord stands forever, the designs of his *Heart* [italics added] through all generations. Blessed is the nation whose God is the Lord, the people chosen as his inheritance" (Ps 33:8-12).

While some may argue that biblical use of anthropomorphic language is imaginative, theologians argue that there is a higher form which seeks human terms to provide an explanation of divine reality beyond physical traits or activities. Consequently, God's transcendence from what is intelligible as well as what is sensible must be heeded.[16]

The Old Testament unlocks the secrets of the Father's paternal love as symbolized and expressed in the many passages that speak of God possessing a Heart. But this mystery, which is somewhat unveiled in the Old Testament, becomes apparent in the New Testament; where the Father's divine paternal love, like His divine Personhood, is revealed to us through a deeper understanding of the life and the words of Christ Himself.

And as Christ's passion and death were forewarned in the Old Testament, the revelations of the Heart of God in the Old Testament can be seen as glimpses of the light of the truth of the Father's Paternal Heart that cannot be contained.

Part IV

THE DIVINE PATERNAL HEART OF GOD THE FATHER

"Learn the *Heart of God* in the words of God, that you may long more ardently for things eternal."
—St. Gregory

Capter Eleven

THE THEOLOGY OF GOD THE FATHER

> *"This is how you are to pray: Our Father in heaven, hallowed be your name, your kingdom come, your will be done, on earth as in heaven. Give us today our daily bread; and forgive us our debts, as we forgive our debtors; and do not subject us to the final test, but deliver us from the evil one."(Mt 6:9-13)*

Before we examine the New Testament and the Paternal Heart of God the Father, it is important that we first take a brief look at the theology of God the Father and its relevance to the mystery of the Father's love.

Although the Church has recognized the three divine Persons of the Holy Trinity since her founding, it has not given to each of the Persons the same theological emphasis. According to theologians, the theology of God the Father is significantly less developed than the theologies of Christ and of the Holy Spirit.[1] Most significantly, no specific term is used to identify the study of God the Father; this is further complicated by the usage of the term *Patrology*, or *Patristics*, to describe the field of study of the Fathers of the Church.[2]

Our faith formation, from a theological perspective, concentrates on the Person of Jesus Christ, since the mystery of the Incarnation is at its center. While the Father willed to send His Son, who is the perfect image of the Father, He did not send Himself. This has always kept the focus of the faith on Christ, rather than the Father or Holy Spirit.[3]

As is not surprising, reflections on the teachings of the Gospels have especially centered on Jesus Christ, although the revelation of His Father is at the center of His orientation as a divine Person.[4] Even Christ's teaching of "seeing the Father in him" (Jn 14:9) has not led, for the most part, to a more deeper discovery over the centuries of the mysterious features of the Father,[5] especially the deeper mysteries of His paternal love.

Recent development of a broader understanding of the Holy Spirit in relation to Christ has included a maturation of our own personal understanding of the Holy Trinity.[6] But, the specific theology of the Father has still remained less developed in comparison to that of Christ and the Holy Spirit.[7] The more recent writings of St. John Paul II and Pope Benedict XVI have significantly forwarded theologically the invitation to "see the Father in Christ" and the more profound implications of this truth.

THE "FATHER" GOD OF THE OLD TESTAMENT

Two primary factors appear to be at the core of this situation, factors that have historically existed from the beginning of the Church and are seen to have contributed to our unfamiliarity with God the Father in a theological sense.

The first is the long held belief of the need to separate the theology of God's Revelation in the writings of the Old Testament and the Gospel's Revelation of the Father by Christ. Too many writers over time have held the opinion that the "Fatherly" God of Judaism is an identical doctrine to the God the Father doctrine revealed in the New Testament.[8] This has led simply to identifying the God of the Old Testament as being the first Person of the Trinity, God the Father, and seeing only the revelation of the Son and the Holy Spirit as being truly unique to the New Testament. Doctrinal reflection on these two divine Persons has consequently been greater at the expense of a true development of the theology of God the Father, a development in which many believe has already been made in examining the God of the Old Testament.[9]

The second factor that has historically existed in hindering development of a profound theology of the Father—and also somewhat contributes to the first factor—is the use of theological language that has caused, by consequence, a certain confusion and misunderstanding in our communication of this entire doctrinal issue.

The Old Testament is manifest in the usage of the word "God" to designate Judaism's single true and revealed "God," who is at times also referenced in certain passages as "Father."[10] For the record, the word "Father" is found fourteen times in the Old Testament. In the context of the Old Testament, neither of these words are intended to be understood as the divine Person of God the Father that is revealed by Christ in the New Testament.

In the New Testament, the words "God" and "Father" are also used, but now primarily refer to God the Father, the First Person of the Holy Trinity. However, the use of the words "God" and "Father" in the New Testament often become understood for many as *synonyms* that refer to Israel's monotheistic God, which is in truth, not the correct doctrine of God the Father as revealed in the New Testament.[11]

GOD OUR FATHER

In the Gospels, Christ presents Himself as Son of the "Father" and also uses the title "Son of Man."[12] He did not refer to Himself as the Son of God. But, He did not dispute those who called Him "Son of God," as Peter said to Him, "You are the Son of the living God" (Mt 16:6), and He did not dispute those who said or asked if He claimed to be the Son of God: "Are you then the Son of God" (Lk 22:70)?[13]

To further complicate the matter, God the Father is often referred to simply as "God" in many passages of the Epistles, once again creating interpretative issues because of the Old Testament's use of the word "God." There is no evidence that theologians have ever struggled to interpret the writings of Sts. John and Paul in regards to their usage of the word "God" when speaking of God the "Father." But, it is obvious that the dual meaning of the terminology can cause some to be uncertain whether the word "God" is referring to God the Father of the New Testament or to the God of the Old Testament. For example, St. John writes at the beginning of his Gospel: "In the beginning was the Word, and the Word was with God, and the Word was God. He was in the beginning with God" (Jn 1:1-2). In this passage, St. John uses the word "God" three times, two of which are used in speaking of the Person of God the Father. In St. John's Letters, the usage of the word "God" when speaking of the "Father" is found again: "In this way the love of God was revealed to us: God sent his only Son into the world so that we might have life through him" (1 Jn 4:9).

Similarly, St. Paul often uses the word "God" in his Letters when he is referring to God the Father: "God is faithful, and by him you were called into fellowship with his Son, Jesus Christ" (1 Cor 1:9). Likewise, for the record, the Epistles of Sts. Peter, James, and Jude also use the word "God" when referring to God the Father.

In essence, all of this is seen to have somewhat affected the development of the theology of God the Father.

Father Jean Galot explains that this difficulty with the language surrounding the God of the Old Testament and God the Father has spanned the centuries and has influenced the theology of God the Father. Fr. Galot writes:

> "From the very beginning, the language of the Christian faith, in affirming that Jesus is the Son of God, maintained a certain identification between "God" and the "Father." This manner of speaking has been transmitted over the centuries and encouraged the equivalent use of the words "God" and "Father."
>
> It is important, nevertheless, to remember that this terminology which was still subsidiary in the Old Testament was accompanied by another terminology that counterbalanced it and stemmed from the Gospel revelation. The term "God" was applied to Jesus in the Profession of Faith in the council of Nicea: "God (born) from God." In the title "Mother of God" given to Mary, God designates solely the person of the Word incarnate. In fact, the two modes of expression have subsisted side by side, balancing or complementing one another. The one would seem to reserve the name of God for the Father, and to the other confers it is on the Person of Jesus. Since the more ancient language has been preserved, we should not be surprised that it provided support for those who use the words "God" and "Father" interchangeably.
>
> We can add that the liturgy has often favored the assimilation of the notion of Father with notion of God. Many prayers name the One to whom they are addressed "God," "Almighty and Eternal God." Now, they are really addressing God the Father, because at the end of the prayer recourse to the mediation of Christ is expressed: "Through Jesus Christ, your Son, our Lord." The Father is simply being invoked by the name "God," as if "God" and "Father" were equivalent. Or else he is called

"Lord" after the manner of the Old Testament which applied this title to God. This liturgical language therefore suggests that the Father is identical with the one God revealed in the Old Covenant.

We are so accustomed to this language that the identification of the *Doctrine of the Father* with the *Doctrine of God* might seem quite normal, and we might therefore think any effort to develop theological reflection more appropriate to the Father superfluous. If we allowed ourselves to take this view, yielding to the path of least effort, we would fail to grasp the value of a theology of the Father."[14]

THE FULL REVELATION OF THE FATHER

In retrospect, the authors of the Epistles cannot be questioned for their approach, for it was their intent at that time in the early Church to emphasize the fact that Jesus Christ was "God" and that His Father was "God," and that these separate truths of the divinity of the individual Persons of the Trinity needed to be visible and paramount in their writings. In reading Scripture, we can see that there were many divergent influences on them as even Christ in some of His words on the Cross did not use the word Father, but exclaimed, "My God, my God, why have you forsaken me?" (Mt 27:46, Mk 15:34).

For our purposes, however, it is necessary to illuminate this important matter so that the unfolding of these mysteries – mysteries of the divine Person of God the Father and His paternal love as understood in His Paternal Heart – are seen in the fullest light and meaning of both the Old and New Testaments. In this way, we will be able to better grasp the full revelation of God the Father as intended in the teachings of Jesus Christ, and to also better grasp those passages in both the Old and the New Testaments that help us to see and understand the Father's Paternal Heart.

In the remaining chapters of this book, whenever it is important that a clear distinction is needed to emphasize that the word "God" is being used in reference to "God the Father," it will sometimes be followed by the words "the Father" in *italics* and in *brackets*. For example, we read in the *Epistle of St. James*, "James the servant of God [*the Father*], and of our Lord Jesus Christ, to the twelve tribes which are scattered abroad, greetings" (Jas 1:1).

> "But the Son possesses a position of singularity above others in having by nature what He receives, as Basil also declares; hence He is called only begotten; the only begotten who is in the Bosom of the Father, He hath declared unto us.
> —St. Thomas Aquinas

Chapter Twelve

CHRIST REVEALS THE FATHER

*"I ascend to my Father and your Father, to
my God and your God" (Jn 20:17).*

Who is this God that all Christians and even other religions call "Father?" The history of theology reveals that this question is one for the ages. As we have noted, the Fatherhood of God in the Old Testament is a Fatherhood as it pertains to God's people as a whole and as a community. Although at times, individuals are seen as sons and daughters of a God they call "Father," the God of the Old Testament is a collective Father, as He presents Himself to His chosen people.

In the New Testament, the revelation of God the Father by Jesus – although to a degree the continuation of the revelation of this *Fatherly* God of the Old Testament – is one of a personal Father, who through His Son, Jesus Christ, affirms to us a new perspective: God the Father is totally and solely our Father, too. He is a Father who wishes us to know and love Him as our heavenly Father,[1] and who wishes us to *trust* and *rest* in His tender paternal love and mercy.

THE FATHER'S DIVINE ATTRIBUTES

Over the centuries, many of the Church's greatest theologians report a sense of weakness and inadequacy in their efforts to truly know and explain this mystery of the First Person of the Holy Trinity. For the most part, in our Christian understanding of the Father, we also are aware of our limitations in comprehending Him; He who preexisted before all existed, He who is the source of all existence and all life, He who is wise, powerful, just, and merciful, He who is wisdom, beauty, knowledge, and love, He who is all of these, and so much more.

All of this teaches us about the limitations of language in attempting to adequately define and explain God. However, there are four basic attributes that constitute God's divine nature:

Our Father is *eternal*. There never was a time He did not exist. He always was and always will be. He is our "Eternal" Father.[2]

Our Father is *infinite*. He is without limitation, unconstrained in any sense. Our Father is everywhere, endless in all directions, not just spatially but in every dimension. He is fullness, without occupying space, in His Being. His divine nature is whole and original, ultimately infinite in finite explanation.[3]

Our Father is *perfect*. He lacks nothing, which defines His divine nature. He is fully realized within Himself, as all His perfections are something He has, not something He lacks. All His perfections are of the highest order, as He is infinitely perfect.[4]

Our Father is *immutable*. He never undergoes any change, in any way, whatsoever. This unchangeable reality means He never matures or grows into completeness. There are no transitions in our Father, for He is and was and will be always all that He can be, which is part of the perfection of God's eternal, divine nature.[5] We read in *Psalms*:

Long ago you laid the foundation of
the earth, and the heavens are the
work of your hands.
They will perish, but you endure;
they will all wear out like a garment.
You change them like clothing, and
they pass away;
but you are the same, and your
years have no end.
The children of your servants shall
live secure,
their offspring shall be established
in your presence" (Ps 102:25-28).

"THE FATHER OF LIGHTS"

As we read in the *Epistle of St. James*, God our Father is "the Father of lights, with whom there is no alteration or shadow caused by change" (Jas 1:17). In his general audience of July 24, 1985, Pope John Paul II provided in the fullness of our faith a progressive revelation that succinctly reveals this mystery of "the Father of lights:"

> "The God of our faith, whom we profess in the Creed, is the God of Abraham, our father in faith (cf. Rom 4:12-16), he is "the God of Isaac and of Jacob," that is, of Israel (Mk 12:26 and parallel passages), the God of Moses – and finally and above all he is God, "the Father of Jesus Christ" (cf. Rom 15:6) . We affirm this when we say "I believe in God the Father..." He is the one and identical God of whom the *Letter to the Hebrews* tells us that having already "spoken in many and various ways of old to our fathers by the prophets, finally in these last days he has

spoken to us by the Son…" (Heb 1:1-2). He who is the source of the word which describes his progressive self-revelation in history, is fully revealed in the Incarnate Word, the eternal Son of the Father. In this Son – Jesus Christ – the God of our faith is definitively confirmed as Father. As such he is recognized and glorified by Jesus who prayed: "I thank you, Father, Lord of heaven and earth…" (Mt 11:25), clearly teaching us also to discover in this God, Lord of heaven and earth, *Our Father* (Mt 6:9). "Thus the God of revelation, "God, Father of Our Lord Jesus Christ" (Rom 15:6), is placed before our faith as a personal God, as an inscrutable divine "I" before our human "I," before each and all. He is indeed an inscrutable "I', in his profound mystery, but he has "opened" himself to us in revelation so that we can turn to him as the most holy divine "You." Each one of us is in a position to do so, because our "God, who embraces in himself and surpasses and transcends in an infinite way everything that exists, is very close to all, and indeed intimate to our innermost being – "*interior intimo meo.*" as St. Augustine wrote (*Confessions*, bk. III, c. VI, 11; PL: 32, 687).[6]

In the light of this understanding of God the Father, we see that He is not only "the Father of Israel, the Father of all mankind, but "Our Father," our perfect Father (cf. Mt 5:48). The Father, Pope John Paul II summarizes in his teaching, "is pure paternity."[7]

Two passages of the New Testament make this truth about our heavenly Father and His relationship to us abundantly clear. Christ reveals in the *Gospel of St. John*: "I am ascending to my Father and to *your* [italics added] Father, to my God and *your* [italics added] God" (Jn 20:17) and Jesus states, "Whoever loves me will keep my word, and my Father will love him, and we will come to him and make our dwelling with him" (Jn 14:23). Through both passages, believers are invited to know that Christ's Father is *truly* our Father and that we can best come to know, understand, and love Him through the Incarnate Christ, who is "in the Father" (cf. Jn 14:11), who has "seen the Father" (Jn 6:46), and who is our way to the Father (cf. Jn 14:5), the same Father who loved and chose us in Christ "before the foundation of the world" (Eph 1:3-6).

THE ANTHROPOMORPHISM OF GOD THE FATHER IN THE NEW TESTAMENT

The monotheistic God of the Old Testament presented Himself through anthropomorphic features that had their own *Biblical motivation*.[8] But the New Testament profoundly reveals the immense love God the Father has for His children: St. John Paul II writes, "Seeing that man is created in the image and likeness of God, there is reason for speaking of God in the image and likeness of man. Nevertheless, this anthropomorphism does not obscure God's transcendence. It does not reduce God to human dimensions. This marvelous preparation carried out by God in the history of the Old Covenant, especially by means of the prophets, awaits its definitive fulfillment. This fulfillment is as we know, in Christ, the Word made flesh, *"who is the perfect reflection of the Father."* And following the pedagogic progression in the New Testament, the proprieties of his Being, usually called his *attributes*, reveal to us the Father, the God who is "love", in all the glory and magnificence of his Personhood."[9]

Like the Old Testament, the New Testament reveals the Father and His attributes in definitive, anthropomorphic terms. The Father has a ""side" (cf. Jn 1:17) a "right hand" (Lk 22:69), "hands" (Lk 23:46), a "face" (Mt 18:10) and a "voice" (cf. Jn 1:17). He "speaks" (Jn 8:26), "works" (cf. Jn 5:17), "teaches" (cf. Jn 8:27), "shows" (Jn 5:20), "assigns" (cf. Jn 5:22), and "gives testimony" (cf. Jn 5:37). He "reigns" (cf. Jn 3:3), expresses "wrath" (Jn 3:36) and is "pleased" (cf. Jn 8:29). He "gives" (Jn 6:37), "grants" (cf. Jn. 6:65), "testifies" (Jn 8:18) and He "prunes" (cf. Jn 15:2). He possesses a "seal" (Jn 6:27) and "raises the dead" (Jn 5:21). He has a "presence" (Jn 8:38) and a "will" (Jn 5:30). And, our Father "hears us" – "always hears us" (cf. Jn 11:42).

Moreover, the New Testament reveals the grandeur of the *divine* Personhood of God the Father, His properties or attributes in their entire splendor. In Christ's powerful words, the Eternal Father is unfolded as our *awesome* God. Christ reveals that the Father *is* "life" (Jn 5:26) and "gives life" (Jn 6:33). He *is* "love" (cf. Jn 3:35) and "loves" (cf. Jn 15:10). He *is* "truth" (Jn 4:23) and *is* "truthful" (cf. Jn 8:26). He *is* "power" (cf. Mk 14:36) and "gives power" (cf. Jn 5:27). Most significantly, Christ emphasizes the Father *is* "divine" (cf. Jn 17:3) and "holy" (cf. Jn 17:11).

Scripture states we are to have "faith" in the Father (cf. Jn 5:24) and He is to be "honored" (cf. Jn 5:23) and "glorified" (Jn 14:13), for He is a "good" (Mk 10:17-18) and "perfect" Father (Mt 5:48), "infinitely perfect" (Vat I DS 3001). Confirming God's most powerful sign of His divine paternal love in the Old Testament, Jesus attests that our Father is "merciful" (Lk 6:36), a "Father who judges impartially according to each one's works" (1 Pt 1:17). And our Father is a "living God," as St. Peter proclaimed: "You are the Messiah, the Son of the living God" (Mt 16:16, cf. Jn 5:26). He is the Son who dwelled before creation in the "Heart" of the Father (cf. Jn 1:18), or in some translations, in His Father's "Bosom."

THE "BOSOM" OF THE FATHER

As with the many references to the "Heart of God," the term "Bosom" is synonymously used in the Old Testament to convey a symbolic reality of the source of God's passionate love for His people: "Behold, the Lord God shall come with strength, and his arm shall rule: Behold his reward is with him and his work is before him. He shall feed his flock like a shepherd: he shall gather together the lambs with his arm, and shall take them up in his *Bo-*

som [italics added], and he himself shall carry them that are with young" (Is 40:10-11).

In the New Testament, the word "Bosom" is used in some translations when quoting St. John's *Prologue* (cf. Jn 1:18). For the most part, theologians define God's Bosom as the intimate domain of the Father's divine Heart – the quintessential seat of the unity shared between the divine Persons as understood in the *Prologue* (cf. Jn 1:18).[18]

Based on Scripture, some writers emphasize that it is the "inner sanctuary" of the love of the Father's divine Being, and therefore the fountainhead of His divine paternal love for His Son: "[F]or the Father loves his Son" (Jn 5:20). St. John Damascene writes: "For the Son is in the Father and the Spirit…without ever leaving the Father's Bosom."[10] St. Basil (*the Great*) writes, "A Father's Bosom is a fit and becoming seat for a Son."[11] St. Athanasius writes, "They are united with each other without mediation or distance, and they exist inseparable: all the Father *embosoming* the Son, and all the Son hanging from and adhering to the Father, and alone resting on the Father's *Breast* continually."[12]

St. Clement understood the Father's Bosom to be the "*Abyss, the invisible and inexpressible*," which Moses had encountered in the shadow.[13] In the *Vulgate* translation of the *Canticle of Zechariah*, the Lord's words are "*per viscera misericordiae Dei Nostri.*" This means the "Abyss of the mercy of our God." As with the word "Bosom," the term *Abyss* is also used in reference to the Father's divine Heart. For the record, the Greek and Hebrew translations of this part of the *Canticle* read "the loving-kindness of the Heart of our God" (*Jerusalem Bible*, 1966).[14] In examining this question of terminlogy, we find that most Scriptural scholars infer that the word "Bosom" is synonymous with "Abyss," and that both of these terms mean the Heart of God the Father.

ST. JOHN PAUL II AND POPE BENEDICT XVI

According to St. John Paul II, in the tradition of the Fathers of the Church and the Liturgy, the words *Side* and *Breast* are also understood as meaning the Father's *Heart*. However, John Paul II himself often spoke or wrote specifically of the "Heart of the Father." For example, in his general audience of August 19, 1987, he continued this traditional teaching of the unity of the Father and the Son as revealed in St. John's Gospel in the clearest and starkest of terms: "It is only the Son, who is nearest the *"Father's Heart,"* who has made him known" (Jn 1:18).[15]

For the most part, Pope Benedict XVI prefers in his writings the same terminology. In his book, *Jesus of Nazareth*, he quotes the *Prologue* of the *Gospel of John*, specifically John 1:18, at least eight times. In each reference, he uses the words the *"Father's Heart"* rather than *Father's Bosom* or *Abyss*.

In one reference, Pope Benedict distinguishes that Christ's *Breast* is to be understood in the same context as when speaking of the Father's Heart, and that St. John's intimate relationship with Christ is to a degree parallel with Christ's relationship to His Father because of their "nearness" to the divine "Heart." The Pope writes, "These statements concerning the external origin of the Gospel take on deeper dimension in the story of the washing of the feet, which points to its inward source. Here it is said that this disciple reclined at Jesus' side during the meal and that, when he asked who the betrayer was, he 'leaned back on Jesus' Breast' (Jn 13:25). These words are intended to parallel the end of the Prologue of John's Gospel, where it is said apropos of Jesus: 'No one has ever seen God; it is the only Son, who is nearest to the Father's Heart, who has made him known' (Jn 1:18). Just as Jesus, the Son, knows about the mystery of the Father from resting in his Heart, so too the Evangelist has gained his intimate knowledge from his inward repose in Jesus' Heart."[16]

" Alone begotten of God, in a way peculiar to Himself, from the *Womb of his own Heart* – even as the Father Himself testifies, "My *Heart*, says He, has emitted My most excellent Word."
—Tertullian

Chapter Thirteen

THE HEART OF THE FATHER IN THE NEW TESTAMENT

> *"No one has even seen God; it is only the Son, who is nearest to the Father's Heart, who has made him known" (Jn 1:18).*

The *"Propriety of the Father,"* according to the Doctors of the Church, permits us to recognize those passages of the Old Testament that speak of the Heart of God as being most appropriately in reference to the Heart of God the Father.

In this regard, St. Paul's words in the *Acts of the Apostles* reveal that he held this view too, "Then God removed him (*King Saul*) and raised up David as their King; on his behalf God testified, 'I have found David son of Jesse to be a man after my own Heart who will fulfill every wish.' According to his promise, God has brought forth from this man's descendants Jesus, a savior for Israel" (Acts 13:23).

Perhaps more than any of the New Testament authors, the doctrines of Sts. John and Paul unfold and develop the divine paternal love of the Father for the Son – His absolute gratuitous love shared so intimately in His divine Fatherly Heart – in which He "chose to raise men up to divine sonship through the 'richness of His grace.'" It is a grace abundantly emanating from His divine paternal love for His only begotten Son: "He [*the Father*] who did not spare his own Son but handed him over for us all, how will he not also give us everything else along with him?" (Rom 8:32) St. Paul affirms, "nothing in all creation will ever be able to separate us from the love of God [*the Father*] that is revealed in Christ Jesus our Lord" (Rom 8:39).

St. Paul also envisions, above all, the fulfillment of the plan by which the Father has *predestined* man to reproduce the image of His Son (Rom 8:29); the perfect divine image of the Father in the Son that is self-evident and born out of the Father's love for the Son and His adopted children.[1] Because man is created in the image of God and He had not assumed the form of man until the Incarnation, Christ – who is "the image of the invisible God" (Col 1:15) and first born of all creation – reveals this divine image. Christ, writes St. Paul, is "the image of God" (2 Cor 4:4) or the *image of the Father.*

St. John also reflects this truth abundantly in his Gospel, especially in his *Prologue*. He writes, "No one has even seen God. The only begotten Son, who is in the *Heart* of the Father, he has revealed him" (Jn 1:18).[2] St. Paul, again in *Colossians*, writes that the image of the Son is that of the Father: "Stop lying to one another, since you have taken off the old self with its practices, and have put on the new self, which is being renewed, for knowledge, in the image of its creator" (Col 3:9-10).

ST. JOHN'S PROLOGUE

In Jesus, the Father makes it clear that Divine Revelation is complete from two points of view: It is the Father Himself, in all His inmost richness, who has manifested Himself in a human life; a

God who wanted to hide nothing about Himself, thus He manifested Himself in a way that revealed Him totally to humankind. It is a revelation, therefore, that St. John in his Prologue stresses "the Word was with God" and "the Word was God " (Jn 1:1).[3]

In saying this, St. John "means that the Word possesses the divine nature, that He is not simply an attribute or extension of God, but that He is strictly and integrally God."[4] That explains why the manifestation of the Word-made flesh is the full manifestation of the Father. Nonetheless, the truth does not prevent us from acknowledging "the Word was with God," meaning that from all eternity Christ was oriented to His Father.[5]

In *Abba, We Long to See your Face*, Fr. Jean Galot writes: "More explicitly, at the end of St. John's *Prologue* there is the question of "God the only Son who is at the Father's Side", or still more precisely, who penetrates, who is immersed "in the Bosom of the Father" (Jn 1:18), who is 'nearest to the Father's Heart.'" The purpose of St. John's revelation is to delve us into the Heart of the Father and into his intimacy. This is because full communion with the Father, with his Paternal Heart, is the most essential goal of the Christian life. St. John writes that this is what makes "our joy complete" (1 Jn 1:4), for Jesus says that this is what makes his joy complete, remaining united with the Father in his love" (Jn 15:10).[6] In his general audience of June 19, 1991, Pope John Paul II echoed this teaching: "Every true joy has the Father as its final goal."[7]

In many of his writings, St. John Paul II repeatedly spoke of the divine communion of the Trinity and of the Father's paternal love for the Son, which he writes emanates from "His Fatherly Heart," and can be especially seen in the *union* of the Heart of the Son in the Heart of the Father as found in St. John's *Prologue*: "The truth concerning Jesus Christ, Son of God, constitutes the self-revelation of God, the keynote of the doctrine which unveils the inexpressible mystery of one God in the Blessed Trinity. According to the *Letter to the Hebrews*, God 'in our time…has spoken to us though his Son' (Heb 1:2), revealing the reality of his personal life – that life wherein he remains in absolute unity in the divinity, while at the same time it is the Trinity, the divine communion of the three Persons. The Son, 'who came from the Father and entered the world (cf. Jn 16:28) testified directly to this communion. The Son alone testified, none other. The Old Testament, when God 'spoke through the prophets' (Heb 1:1), knew nothing of this personal mystery of God. Undoubtedly, certain elements of the Old Testament revelation constituted a preparation for what we have in the Gospels. Nevertheless, only the Son was capable of introducing us to this mystery. Since 'no one has seen God' no one knew the mystery of his inner life, the Son alone knew it. It is only the Son, who is *nearest to the Father's Heart*, who has made him known" (Jn 1:18)."[8]

THE SUPREME LOVE OF THE FATHER

According to theologians, the Father's Paternal Heart proves this to be true when He allows His own divine Heart to be mystically opened in sending His beloved Son to the Cross.[9] Fr. Galot writes that in giving His only begotten Son, the Father *sacrificed* Himself: "The first sacrifice took place in the Father's Paternal Heart. Saint John has included this idea in his definition of supreme love: 'This is what love is: not that we loved God but that he *(the Father)* loved us and sent his Son as the expiation of our sins' (1 Jn 4:10)."[10]

Moreover, it is an act considered to be the summit of His paternal love, emanating from His Paternal Heart.[11] Fr. Galot explains, "The Father's suffering then, is a suffering of compassion, a suffering of *Hearts*, because of the completeness of his Oneness with his Son, a completeness best understood in their Hearts being together as one: "Father....everything of mine is yours and yours is mine" (Jn 17:1,10).[12] Likewise, the Redemptive Passion, while it belongs to the Son as His personal experience, also belongs to the Father by virtue of this compassion – a compassion best understood because of His paternal love, which emanates from His Paternal Heart: "The Father is in me and I am in him" (Jn 10:38), a divine paternal love that existed before the creation for His only begotten Son: "Because of the love you bore me before the world began" (Jn 17:24).[13] Fr. Galot concludes: "Admittedly, as God, in his divine nature, he remains immutable and impassible. Yet in the relations he has freely entered into with humankind through his paternal love, he experiences suffering or joy according to the attitudes and actions of each individual human being. Even though the Father bears no responsibility for men's sins, he has involved himself fully, with the plenitude of this Fatherly love, in the drama of the sins committed by men. He suffers from each offense and he is filled with compassion for the wretched state of every sinner. He reaches out in reconciliation and is eager to grant his forgiveness. An absolute paternal love governs all the Father's actions."[14]

THE MYSTERY OF THE FATHER AND THE CROSS

According to St. Hippolytus of Rome, Pope Callistus (217-222) attested to this belief of the Father sharing in the passion experience of the Son through their unity of divine nature, their unity of Hearts. St. Hippolytus writes, "For the Father who rested in the Son himself, having taken unto himself our flesh, raised it to the nature of Deity in uniting it to himself and made it one with himself, so that the names of Father and Son apply to one and the same God, and that his Person being one, cannot be two; thus *the Father suffered with the Son*, for we must not say that the Father suffered" (*Philos.* 9, 12, 16-19).[15]

This is, indeed, the mystery of the Cross, inescapably tied to the mystery of the Paternal Heart of the Father. Fr. Enrique Llamas Martinez, O.C.D., a Professor Emeritus of the Pontifical University of Salamanca, writes, "The mystery is contained in the *Heart of the Father*: God will reign from a tree (*Regnabit a ligno Deus*). The Triumph of the Cross explains the life of the Church to be established on the law of love."[16] It is a divine paternal love that St. John Paul II writes only the Son knows because "It is only the Son, who is nearest to the Father's Heart,"[17] …who is "in the Father as the Father is in him, even on the Cross!"[18]

In his first encyclical letter, *Lumen Fidei*, Pope Francis referred to this truth and explains how we too are to abandon ourselves, our sufferings, our crosses into the arms of the Father and unite with Him as Christ did on the Cross, "Christians know that suffering cannot be eliminated, yet it can have meaning and become an act of love and entrustment into the hands of God who does not abandon us; in this way it can serve as a moment of growth in faith and love. By contemplating Christ's union with the Father even at the height of his sufferings on the Cross (Cf. Mk 15:34), Christians learn to share in the same gaze of Jesus. Even death is illumined and can be experienced as the ultimate call to faith, the ultimate "Go forth from your land: (Gn 12:1), the ultimate "Come!" spoken by the Father, to whom we abandon ourselves in the confidence that he will keep us steadfast even in our final passage."[19]

Because of His unity in Heart with the Father, Jesus tells us that God our Father is the source of *all* His teaching, the truth of it, and why we are to believe and trust His words. Indeed, Christ asserts that He came only to accomplish the Father's works, especially the institution of the Eucharist, the real "Manna from heaven" that His "Father gives" to the world out of His infinite paternal love for all of His children.

It is through this Sacramental gift, therefore, that we also come to better understand that the life of Jesus is in the Father and the life of the Father is in the Son. It is a dialogue of life in the Father's Heart, writes Pope Benedict XVI.[20]

And like the Cross, it is a *life* they share together in Heart that, Christ explains, is the divine essence of the great truth revealed in St. John's *Discourse on the Bread of Life*.

"Return to that most loving *Heart of your Father*, which is full of love and mercy for you, which will receive you home, heaping upon you blessings. Return, you transgressors, to the *Heart*, 'which means to My *Heart* that is all yours, since I have given it entirely to you."
—St. John Eudes

Chapter Fourteen

THE PATERNAL HEART AND THE BREAD OF LIFE

"Amen, amen, I say to you, it was not Moses who gave the bread from heaven; my Father gives you the true bread from heaven. For the bread of God is that which comes down from heaven and gives life to the world." (Jn 6:32-33).

"The Father is in me and I am in the Father" (Jn 10:38). In these words, Christ leads us to understand how the mystery of the divine paternal love of the Father, the love of the Father's Paternal Heart, also involves the mystery of the Eucharist. This is because Christ's words help us realize that the *life* contained in the Eucharist due to God's unity of divine nature is also, in essence, a *life in our Father's Heart* – a life in which we are invited to share through His great love for us in the Sacrament.

The Church teaches that it is our path to perfection, the perfection Christ invited us to seek in our "perfect" Father (Mt 5:48), for, as St. Irenaeus writes, "a creature receives its 'perfection' in the Sacraments."

UNFOLDING THE PASCHAL MYSTERY

Jesus tells us that the truth of the Eucharistic food is found in the truth of this life He possesses in the Father; therefore, this truth is to be possessed by those who eat this food: "Just as the living Father sent me and I have life because of the Father, so also the one who feeds on me will have life because of me" (Jn 6:57). This life, this eternal life found in the Eucharist, comes from the source of all life: the providential paternal love of the Father, the *Heart* of all life, where all life was and will forever be conceived, sustained, and inevitably returned to have "eternal life" (Jn 6:40), to "live forever" (Jn 6:58).

After confirming through miracles, deeds and words, the divinity of Christ – miracles that St. John Paul II states "have their source in God's loving and merciful 'Heart' which lives and beats in the human heart"[1] – the Paschal Mystery continues to unfold. The Father leads Peter to confess his profession of faith near Caesarea Phillipi: "You are the Christ, the Son of the living God" (Mt 16:6). Jesus replies this was not a human revelation, but a revelation of "[His] Father in heaven" (Mt 16:17). Essentially, this profession confirms the truth of Christ's divine Sonship, the One who comes from the Father—only the Father "knows the Son" (Mt 11:27), only the Father knows "who the Son is" (Lk 10:22) and only the Father can convey the truth to Peter: "No mere man has revealed this to you, but my heavenly Father" (Mt 16:17).[2]

This inward reality is then *confirmed externally* on Mt. Tabor during the Transfiguration where the Father speaks:[3] "This is my beloved Son" (Mk 9:7). On Tabor, Christ reveals this *living Father* to His Apostles; they *hear* the Father's voice; they *see* Elijah, who was *fed* by God and kept *alive* in the desert; they *see* Moses, who was also *fed* by God and kept *alive* in the desert—thus, the Paschal Mystery continues to shape and unfold. Christ then tells the three Apostles to not reveal the vision until after "the Son of Man had risen from the dead" (Mk 9:9). The theophany of the Transfiguration of the Lord is thus undeniably connected to what is to happen in Jerusalem. Pope John Paul II writes, "If the Father now confirms the interior revelation about Christ's divine sonship: "This is my beloved Son. Listen to him" (Mk 9:7). It seems that he wishes to prepare those who had already believed in him for the events of the Passover which is drawing near, for his humiliating death on the Cross. It is significant that "as they were coming down the mountain" Jesus commanded them, "tell no one about the vision until after the Son of has been raised from the dead" (Mt 17:9, cf. Mk 9:9 and Lk 9:21). The theophany on the mountain of the Transfiguration of the Lord is thus situated in relationship with Christ's Paschal Mystery."[4]

In the *Gospel of St. John*, the Apostle writes in his *Discourse on the Bread of Life*: "Do not work for food that perishes but for the food that endures for eternal life, which the Son of Man will give you. For him the Father, God, has set his seal" (Jn 6:27). The Jews reply, expecting a miracle as before with the multiplication of the loaves at Passover, that their ancestors too were fed with manna to eat from the heavens. But then Jesus says to them: "Amen, amen, I say to you, it was not Moses who gave the bread from heaven; *my Father gives you the true bread from heaven* [italics added]. For the bread of God is that which comes down from heaven and gives life to the world" (Jn 6:32-33). Jesus tells them, "I am the bread of life" (Jn 6:35) and that "[e]verything the Father gives me will come to me...this is the will of the one who sent me [*the Father*]" (Jn 6:37-38).

Through these words, Christ reveals that His flesh and blood are the food and drink – the *real* food and drink that will provide *life eternal*. This is because the Father who has *life* sent Him, and He has life "because of the Father." So, as Christ says, "whoever feeds on Me" will have this same life. It is a *taste* of the divine life the Trinity shares, St. Gregory tells us.

This mystery of the Father and Christ as One – this paternal mystery of the divine life and love that comes from the Father and existed between the Father and the Son before the world began – is also a mystery of *the Father's giving of His divine life and love to humanity* before the world began, and is intended to be seen, understood, and continued in the "Bread of Life" that *"comes from the Father."* In essence, the Father, who is life, permits His own divine Person to also be "the giving of Himself" in the Sacrament. This is because He is consubstantial with the Son in the great mystery of the Holy Trinity. Thus, the unity of the Father's Paternal Heart with the Son's Heart on the Cross, together with the Holy Spirit, brings the Paschal Mystery to fulfillment for mankind, who are called to "feed on God" and "live forever" – who are called to share in the divine life "coming from the Father."

THE FATHERS OF THE CHURCH

For the most part, this understanding is not new. St. Athanasius writes, "Christ was 'God' not by nature, but by participation, he could never have formed the likeness of God, through the Sacrament, in anyone. For he that possesses nothing, but that which he has borrowed from another, cannot hand down anything to others...By partaking of him (*Christ*), we "partake" of the Father; because that the *Word* is the Father's own. Whence, if he was himself too from participation, and not from the Father his essential Godhead and Image, he would not deify being deified himself. For it is not possible that he, who merely possesses from participation, should impart of that partaking to others, since what he has is not his own, but the Giver's; and what he has received, is barely the grace sufficient for himself" (*De syn.* 51 LNPF, EP 787).

St. Hilary of Poitiers, Doctor of the Church, also writes of the Father's sharing of His divine life through the Son in the Sacrament: "For so are we all one, because the Father is in Christ and Christ in us. Whoever then shall deny that the Father is in Christ naturally, or Christ in him, because the Father in Christ and Christ in us make us one in them... And thus there might be taught a perfect unity through a Mediator, whilst we abiding in him, he abode in the Father, and as abiding in the Father abode also in us; and so we might arrive at unity with the Father..."[5]

In *Dives in Misericordia*, St. John Paul II writes, "And yet the divine dimension of the Paschal Mystery goes still deeper. The cross on Calvary, the cross upon which Christ conducts his final dialogue with the Father, emerges from the very heart of the love that man, created in the image and likeness of God, has been given as a gift, according to God's eternal plan...It is love which not only creates the good but also grants participation in the very life of God: Father, Son and Holy Spirit. For he who loves desires to *give himself*."[6]

In his general audience of July 13, 1988, St. John Paul II expanded on this truth: "The Eucharist as a sign of the fraternal meal is closely connected with the promulgation of the *Commandment of Mutual Love* (cf. Jn 13:34; 15:12). According to Pauline teaching, this love intimately unites all members of the ecclesial community: "Because there is one bread, we who are many are one body" (1 Cor 10:17). This union, the fruit of fraternal love, in some way reflects the trinitarian unity formed by the Son with the Father as is evident from Jesus' prayer : "That they all may be one, as you, Father, are in me and I in you" (Jn 17:21). It is the Eucharist that makes us partakers in the unity of God's (*the Father's*) life according to the words of Jesus himself: "As the living Father sent me, and I live because of the Father, so he who eats me will live because of me" (Jn 6:57).[7]

The Eucharist in a Trinitarian setting permits us to see the analogy of Christ's unity with us, and also to share in the natural bond between the Father and the Son. However, St. Hilary adds that the distinction must be preserved between *unity in the Godhead* and *unity between the communicant and Christ.*

THE HEART OF THE FATHER IN ALL CHRIST'S MIRACLES

With that noted, the truth of this reality does not end with the Eucharist. St. John Paul II tells us that it is not only in the miracle of the Eucharist, but in *all* of Christ's miracles that we find the full immersion of the Paternal Heart of God our Father at work; because of His unity of nature with His Son, He continually reveals His love of and for humanity by giving and sharing His *life*, the *life* emanating from His Paternal Heart.

In his general audience of December 9, 1987, Pope John Paul II spoke of the truth of the presence of the Father's Paternal Heart in the Savior's many miracles: "Christ's miracles recorded in the Gospels are signs of the divine omnipotence and salvific power of the Son of Man. They also reveal God (*the Father's*) love for humanity – particularly those who suffer, who are in need, who implore healing, pardon and compassion. They are therefore signs of his (*the Father's*) merciful love proclaimed in the Old and New Testaments. Especially the reading of the Gospel makes us understand and almost feel that Jesus' miracles have their source in God's (*the Father's*) loving and merciful *Heart* which lives and beats in his human heart…all that he does, even in working miracles, is done in close union with the Father!"[8]

Pope John Paul II's words, which surround the mystery of the Father, the Eucharist, and Christ's miracles, reveal the truth of the Father who is *love*, who is *life*; a divine paternal *love* and *life* emanating from His Divine Paternal Heart so infinite that "all paternity in heaven and earth is named" (Eph 3:15), for truly there is "one God and Father of all, who is above all and through all and in all" (Eph 4:6).

"For this is the religion of Jesus which is centered on the Mediator who is man and God, and in such a way that *we* cannot reach the *Heart of God (the Father)* save through the *Heart of Christ*, as He Himself says: 'I am the way, the truth and the life. No one cometh to the Father save by Me.'"
—Pope Pius XII

Chapter Fifteen

THE SACRED HEART OF JESUS

*"For in him all the fullness of God was
pleased to dwell" (Col 1:19).*

The theological framework of God the Father's Divine Paternal Heart as revealed in the Old and New Testaments is evident and reflects a deliberate and progressive unfolding of a sublime mystery and truth of God. However, it is in the history and theology of Jesus' Sacred Heart and its devotion, where we find the undeniable truth of the Father's Paternal Heart perfectly positioned to await its complete discovery, understanding, and inescapable reality.

Through the writings of the great men and women that have led the Church over the centuries, we understand the truth of the paternal love of God the Father is symbolized in the Sacred Heart of His Son, whose Heart is, the Church teaches, *human and divine.*[1]

In light of this proclaimed truth of the Sacred Heart of Jesus, is it not altogether proper to ask if the Father's love, whose *love* is in union with Christ (cf. Jn 15:9), who He is One with (cf. Jn 10:30) and who are in each other (cf. Jn 14:10), should not come to be better known and understood through the official recognition of a Heart of His own?

From a theological perspective, many great voices of the Church have already established the reality of the Father's Divine Paternal Heart in their writings. These writings suggest the understanding that if the Son possesses a divine Heart, the Father must also possess a divine Heart. This is because of their unity of divine nature and because all divine traits and characteristics of God must first be possessed in the Father. We clearly see this in the Gospels and the Epistles. Jesus said of His Father during the *Last Supper*, "everything of mine is yours and everything of yours is mine" (Jn 17:10). St. Paul writes that the Son is "the very stamp of his [*the Father's*] nature" (Heb 1:3).

In these passages of Scripture, we find that the groundwork for a developed theology of the Divine Paternal Heart is present and has been applied in the writings of theologians. But despite Scripture's use of anthropomorphic language and the many writings that speak of the Father's Heart, perhaps some will argue the Father was never incarnate and, therefore, the Church cannot theologically say the Father truly possesses a Heart.

The answer to this theological question, this great mystery, lies in the Church's recognition of Christ's Sacred Heart. For in this action, the Church opened the way for the recognition of the Paternal Heart of God our Father, an unfolding mystery of the Father and His love that Scripture tells us, like all divine mysteries, that God wants us to understand: "O Lord, for Your servant sake, and according to Your own *Heart* [italics added], You have wrought all this greatness, to make known all these great things" (1 Chr 17:19).

All *divine truths* are to be known to man, St. Peter writes, for man is called by God to "share in the divine nature" (2 Pt 1:4) because He "made him in the image of his own nature" (Wis 2:23). Thus, in the Sacred Heart of Jesus, we find the undeniable divine truth of the Father's Divine Heart.

THE HEART OF JESUS IN SCRIPTURE

Devotion to the Sacred Heart of Jesus consists of attention to the inexhaustible source of mercy and love poured out by God the Father through the pierced Heart of Jesus. Christ's Heart, unlike anything else, came to symbolize God's love for man in a way that was humanly understood.

Three passages in the New Testament that speak of Christ's Heart, however, are also seen to help us understand God's love for man as found in Jesus' Sacred Heart:

> -"At the sight of the crowds, his *Heart* [italics added] was moved with pity for them because they were troubled and abandoned, like sheep without a shepherd" (Mt 9:36).
>
> - "Come to me, all you who labor and are burdened and I will give you rest. Take my yoke upon you and learn from me, for I am meek and humble of *Heart* [italics added]; and you will find rest for yourselves. For my yoke is easy and my burden light" (Mt 11:28-30).
>
> - "My *Heart* [italics added] is moved with pity for the crowd, for they have been with me now for three days and having nothing to eat" (Mt 15:32).

After the New Testament, the earliest references to the Heart of Christ are found in the writings of St. Justin (100-163). He writes, "We Christians are the true Israel which springs from Christ, for we are drawn out of his Heart as out of a rock."[2] Less than a hundred years later, St. Irenaeus wrote, "The Church is the fountain of living water that flows to us from the Heart of Christ."[3] Two centuries after, St. Augustine cited in his writings how St. John, in laying his head on the breast of Christ, "drew loftier mysteries from his inmost Heart."[4]

DEVOTION TO THE SACRED HEART

History reveals that the central features of the devotion to Jesus' Sacred Heart have been present since the earliest days of the Catholic Church. But many notable Church figures, such as St. Bonaventure, St. Mechtilde of Magdeburg, Julian of Norwich, and St. Catherine of Siena, propagated attention to the Sacred Heart through their experiences and writings, as did St. Francis de Sales and St. John Eudes.

The apparitions to Saint Margaret Mary between 1673 and 1675, later approved by the Catholic Church, led to more widespread devotion. St. Margaret received a set of twelve promises that exerted strong influence on popular piety and devotion to the Sacred Heart.[5] In the early eighteenth century, Fr. Joseph Francois Galliffet presented petitions to the *Congregation for the Rites* in promoting the devotion to the Sacred Heart, defending the physical heart as the seat of emotion and love. In 1765, a petition was presented by the Polish bishops and the feast was established in Poland by Pope Clement XIII and the Roman Arch Confraternity.[6]

Pope Pius VI published in his bull of 1794, *Auctorem Fidei*, the doctrinal basis for adoration of the Sacred Heart. It held that *in* such adoration of the Sacred Heart, the human heart of Christ, is the *Hypostatic Union*. Thus, the humanity of Christ belongs to the divine Person of the Word and it is therefore right to give it adoration or *latria* (the worship due to God alone).[7] In 1856, Pope Pius IX established the Feast of the Sacred Heart in the universal Church. Essentially, this truth is expressed by the mysteries of God's love held in the image of the Sacred Heart of Christ.[8]

THE HEART AS A SYMBOL

For the record, the use of images, symbols, and representations of the spirit life was controversial in the early Church. During the iconoclast controversy of the eight century, the Church's Magisterium justified the use of icons and images. The foundation for this acceptance is the mystery of the Incarnation itself. God had forbidden representation of Himself in the Old Testament. However, the invisible became visible in the Incarnation, permitting depictions of Himself in word and image. Also, we are composed of body and soul. For this reason, it is impossible for us to enter the spiritual without the corporeal.

Icons and other representations are images of a reality which man cannot see. Since this reality is the ontological foundation of the images themselves, the cult and veneration given is not directed at the images for what they are in themselves, but for what they represent. Images are not to be understood as doubles of what they represent; rather, they only lead to what they represent. This means to contemplate the Sacred Heart is to lead us to Christ.[9]

THE POPES AND THE SACRED HEART

Pope Leo XIII consecrated the world to the Sacred Heart in 1899. In *Annum Sacrum*, he justified the action. Pope Benedict XV recommended consecrating families to the Sacred Heart. Pope Pius XI established the Liturgical Feast of Christ the King through his encyclical letter, *Quas Primas*, in 1925, referring to Christ's kingship in connection to the Sacred Heart and calling on the faithful to renew their consecration to the Sacred Heart on the Feast of the Kingship of Christ.[10]

In 1928, Pope Pius XI published his encyclical letter on reparation to the Sacred Heart, *Miserentissimus Redemptor*.[11] Pope Pius XII, likewise in his first encyclical letter, *Summi Pontificatus*, speaks of the influence of his own consecration to the Sacred Heart and in the encyclical letter, *Mediator Dei*, emphasizes that adoration of the Blessed Sacrament is closely associated with devotion to the Sacred Heart.

Pope Pius XII continued to develop devotion to the Sacred Heart. The *Heart*, he wrote, is the symbol of the love of Christ for His Father, the Father of all mankind. As a divine Person, Christ shares the divine love with the Father and the Holy Spirit, but only He manifests it in a human body.[12]

At the beginning of *Haurietis Aquas*, Pope Pius XII writes that worship offered to the Heart of Christ is a most excellent act of religion; it involves giving and consecrating ourselves to the divine Redeemer's love, to which His Heart is a "living pointer and symbol." He further explains we are called to make "a return of love to the divine love."[13]

Citing his predecessor, Pius IX, Pius XII added, "You shall draw waters of joy out of the Sacred Fountain" (Eph 2:7). He wrote to enumerate the heavenly gifts which devotion to the Sacred Heart poured out on the souls of the faithful to help endure the trials and difficulties of the past two centuries, emphasizing again the devotion to the Sacred Heart is based on love. In his apostolic letter of 1952, *Sacro Vergenti*, which consecrated Russia in response to Our Lady's requests at Fatima in 1917, Pope Pius XII grounded the consecration to the Sacred Heart on the Kingship of Christ by *nature* and acquired right.[14]

In 1959, Pope John XXIII announced the intention of calling a General Council of the Church, which began in 1962. The *Second Vatican Council* commended devotion to the Sacred Heart, and in the Pastoral Constitution, *Gaudium et Spes*, uses the symbolism of the human heart as the center of man's interior personality and moved conscience. *Gaudium et Spes* teaches that "it is only in the mystery of the Word made flesh that the mystery of man truly becomes clear." This is a theme frequently used by St. John Paul II in reference to the mystery of man and God's paternal love for man,[15] as represented in His Paternal Heart.

Pope Paul VI, in his 1965 apostolic letter, *Investigabiles Divitias Christi*, recommends devotion to the Sacred Heart, citing such devotion has "ability to affect a true change of Heart." In his encyclical letter, *Diserti Interpretes*, he emphasizes that Christ's wounded Heart is a symbol of the Incarnate Word's eternal love.[16]

POPE JOHN PAUL II AND POPE BENEDICT XVI

St. John Paul II expanded our understanding of the Heart of Jesus in almost all of his teachings and writings. In his encyclicals, apostolic letters, homilies, angelicus addresses, general audiences, and various pronouncements, he delved further into the mystery and spirituality of God's Heart.[17] In *Redemptor Hominus* (1979) and *Dives in Misericordia* (1980), he made references to the Heart of Christ. And in *Dominum & Vivificantem* (1986), the encyclical letter on the Holy Spirit, and his apostolic letter, *Dominicae Cenae* (1980), he continued this teaching. In essence, the Pope reminded us that man's heart is, like the rest of him, made in the image and likeness of Jesus' divine Heart, thus holding the key to happiness and peace in this life.

During his 1986 Papal visit to France, St. John Paul II gave a homily at Paray-le-Monial, where he emphasized the words of the prophet Ezekiel concerning mans' heart: "I will give you a new heart" (Ez 36:26). The Pope said that all the history of Christian spirituality bears witness that the life of the person who believes in God, looking towards the future of hope, is enlightened by the marvelous truth of the Heart of Christ, who offers Himself to the world. He spoke of divine providence, which revealed this message of Christ's Heart at such a crucial time in the history of the Church.[18]

"Man's heart," said St. John Paul II, "is created to be the center of love but too often becomes the center of rejection of God. It is the central core of the conversion which God desires on the part of man and for man so as to enter into his intimacy, his love. Man is to be given a heart capable of letting itself be moved by the Holy Spirit. The ultimate testimony of love of God for man will be the pierced Side, the pierced Heart, of Christ on the Cross. Through the Heart of his Son, pierced on the Cross, the Father has freely given us everything."[19]

The Pope also said that the Heart of Jesus has a fundamental role in the construction of the *civilization of love*.[20] In many ways, it is essential in the definitive coming of the Father's Kingdom on earth, in which he wrote of in *Tertio Millennio Adveniente*.[21]

In his Angelus Address on June 1, 2008, Pope Benedict XVI said, "I invite everyone to renew his devotion to the Sacred Heart of Christ in the month of June, making use of the traditional prayer of the offering of the day and keeping in mind the intentions that I have proposed to the whole Church."

THE SACRED HEART OF JESUS: HUMAN AND DIVINE

The devotion to the Sacred Heart, a worship that is rightly paid to the Heart of flesh and the symbol of a human heart, brought forth questions between the material, the metaphysical, and symbolic sense of the word "heart." It was understood that the devotion to Christ's Heart represented His love, but not just His love for men; it could not exclude His love for the Father, which included His love for men. The Church concluded that Christ's Heart encompasses all His manifestations of love—both His human and His divine love—for Jesus loves us as man and He loves us as God. *The Heart of Jesus, therefore, like all else within Him, has two natures that cannot be separated.* Although devotion is directed to the material Heart of Jesus, it does not stop there: it also includes love, which is its principal object, but which it reaches only in and through the Heart of flesh—the sign and symbol of this love. This love is devoted to His divine body and *His divine Heart*; these two elements constitute the whole, which is as much the cause of the devotion and its reason for existence.[22]

The Sacred Heart of Jesus, like all else belonging to Him, is worthy of adoration. However, it would not be so if it was considered to be isolated from His divine Person, having no connection with it. In his bull *Auctorem Fides* in 1794, Pope Pius VI authoritatively vindicated this type of devotion against the calumnies of the Jansenists. The devotion is to the Person of Jesus, paid to the Heart of Jesus, as a living and expressive symbol, *inseparable from His divinity.*

Over the years, the Popes have not failed to emphasize in their writings the truth and understanding of Christ's Sacred Heart being a human and a divine Heart.[23]

In *Annum Sacrum* (1899), Pope Leo XIII wrote: "[S]eeing that whatever honor, veneration, and love is given to this '*divine Heart*' [italics added] is really and truly given to Christ himself."[24] In *Miserentissimus Redemptor* (1928), Pope Pius XI wrote of "a marvelous increase that has been made in the number of faithful of both sexes who with eager mind endeavor to make satisfaction for the many injuries offered to the divine Heart."[25] And again in *Caritate Christi Compulsi* (1932), Pius XI wrote of "all the offenses that wound that divine Heart."[26] Pope Pius XII, in *Haurietis Aquas* (1956), wrote too of "those beatings of the divine Heart."[27] The Holy Father also recalled the words of Pope Gregory the Great who advised the faithful to "[l]earn the *Heart of God* [italics added] in the words of God."[28]

> "They are united with each other without mediation or distance, and they exist inseparable: all the Father *embosoming* the Son, and all the Son hanging from and adhering to the Father, and alone resting on the Father's *Breast* continually."
> —St. Athanasius

Chapter Sixteen

DIVINE HEARTS

"*The Father is in me and I am in the Father*" (Jn 10:38).

Faced with the truth that the Father sent His Son into the world to expiate the sin of His children's misuse of free will, the drama of Calvary reveals that the efficacy of the Father's gift is only accomplished through His willingness to be the first to endure the consequences: "God so loved the world that he gave his only Son" (Jn 3:16). And in giving what He held most precious—His Son—our Father is the first to remedy the harm in which we human beings inflict upon ourselves.[1]

Indeed, the Father's paternal love, in creating, sustaining, and redeeming His creation, challenges us to the truth of its source: a Divine Paternal Heart of His own – a rich, full Heart, the *Cradle of Infinite Love*, where all reality—visible and invisible—found its first loving conception.

This Divine Paternal Heart, though not an Incarnate Heart as Christ's Heart, is the source of the Father's divine properties, including His act of generation. The Fathers of the Church, particularly the Greek Fathers, thought of God the Father as the source of the other divine Persons. Divine Fatherhood is, they wrote, His propriety; His Fatherhood is primordial, original, and eternal. In Him, Fatherhood is subsistent, independent, and absolute; it is the model and source of every lesser paternity in heaven and on earth.[2]

DIVINE NATURE

The Church teaches that if we are to understand and accept this truth, we must then accept that for the Son to have a divine Heart, He must have a divine nature whose divine attributes and qualities *draw* from the Father; even though His human heart is a distinctive characteristic of His human nature. The Fathers of the Church held that all such divine attributes, qualities, traits, and characteristics must first be possessed in the divinity of the Father, who derives nothing from outside Himself. In *Colossians* we read, "For in him all the fullness of God was pleased to dwell" (Col 1:19), and, "For in him dwells the whole fullness of the deity bodily (Col 2:9). In his general audience of March 8, 1989, St. John Paul II referenced St. Paul's words, "The Resurrection reveals the fact that 'in Christ the whole fullness of the deity dwells bodily' (Col 1:19). Thus, the Resurrection completes the manifestation of the content of the Incarnation."[3]

Since the earliest centuries of the Church, theologians have written of God's divine nature, explaining and clarifying the doctrine. The writings of Tertullian, St. Hilary of Poitiers, St. Clement, St. Basil the Great, St. Gregory of Nazianzus, St. Anselm of Canterbury, and others explored the life of the Trinity. The following are some of the more referenced and quoted writings on the subject of God's divine nature – including its unity, consubstantiality, and the relations of the Persons and their divine properties.

ST. AUGUSTINE

In *De Trinitate*, St. Augustine emphasizes the unity of the divine nature, the consubstantiality of the Three Persons, and that everything the Son is *must come* from the Father. He attributes these to the role of the *principle of existence*, and if *latria* is forthcoming, as Pope Pius VI commended in defending the divine Heart of Christ, it is for the Trinity itself, one only God: Father, Son and Holy Spirit. St. Augustine writes, "The Father communicates to the Son all that he is except that he is Father. Therefore, *everything that the Son has comes from the Father* [italics added]."[4]

ST. ATHANASIUS

Known as the great defender of the faith during the Arian crisis, St. Athanasius believed that what is said of the Son must be said of the Father; for the Son, he writes, is in the "Heart" of the Father: "God, being without parts, is Father of the Son without partition or passion; for there is neither effluence of the immaterial, or influx from without, as among men; and being uncompounded in nature he is Father of one only Son. This is why he is only-begotten, and alone in the Father's *Bosom* [italics added], and alone is acknowledged by the Father to be from him, saying, 'This is my beloved Son, in whom I am well-pleased' (Mt 3:17). And he too is the Father's Word, from which may be understood the *impassible* [italics added] and *impartitive* [italics added] nature of the Father, in that not even a human word is begotten with passion or partition, much less the Word of God."[5]

ST. JOHN DAMASCENE

In his writings, St. John Damascene emphasized the truth of the Trinity's divine nature and the full meaning of the Father's act of generation regarding the Son and Holy Spirit: "The Father derives from himself his Being, nor does he derive a single quality from another. Rather, he is himself the beginning and cause of the existence of all things both as their nature and mode of being: and unless the Father is, neither the Son nor the Spirit is. *And unless the Father possesses a certain attribute, neither the Son nor the Spirit possesses it:* and through the Father, that is, because of the Father's existence, the Son and the Spirit exist."[6]

ST. THOMAS AQUINAS

St. Thomas Aquinas, in his writings in the *Summa Theologica* on the Hypostasis, the substance of God, and the paternity of the Father, sees Him as the *principle* from which the Son proceeds in likeness. He emphasizes the inseparability of their divine natures and attributes, especially the divine paternal love of the Father and His love *in union* with the Son's love. Quoting St. Ambrose and St. Hilary, St. Thomas asserted that "in the Father and the Son there is no discrepancy but one Godhead, and according to St. Hilary, in God there is nothing alien or separable." St. Thomas also notes that "the Father loves the Son and the Son loves the Father, an indivisible relationship in *all its necessary traits, possessions and attributes.* All that the Father has he has given to the Son in his generation with the exception of being Father."[7]

ST. JOHN PAUL II

In his general audience of Nov. 20, 1985, St. John Paul II spoke of the unity of the divinity among the Persons of the Trinity, especially the absolute unity of the Father and the Son: "Only the Word, the Son, "proceeds" from the Father by eternal generation. God (*the Father*), who eternally knows himself and everything in himself, begets the Word. In this eternal begetting, which takes place by way of intellect *(per modum intelligibilis actionis),* God, in the absolute unity of his nature, that is, of his divinity, is Father and Son. "He is" and not "he becomes," "he is" so eternally. "He is" from the beginning and without beginning. With this aspect, the word "procession" must be understood correctly; there is no connotation proper to a temporal "becoming." The same is true of the "procession" of the Holy Spirit.[8] "Therefore, by means of generation, in the absolute unity of the divinity, God is eternally Father and Son. The Father who begets loves the Son who is begotten. The Son loves the Father with a love which is identical with that of the Father. In the *unity of the divinity*, love is on one side paternal and on the other, filial. At the same time the Father and the Son are not only united by that mutual love as two Persons infinitely perfect, but their mutual gratification, their reciprocal love, proceeds in them and from them as a Person."[9]

A week later, the Holy Father expanded on this unity of divine nature in his general audience of November 27, 1985: "When we speak of "human nature," we indicate what makes a human being a human being, with his essential components and properties. Applying this distinction to God, we recognize the unity of nature, the unity of the divinity, which belongs in an absolute and exclusive way to him who exists as God."[10]

INSEPARABLE DIVINE HEARTS

In applying this understanding of God's inseparability of divine nature and that the Father communicates all that He is to the Son, we see that the reality of the Father's Divine Paternal Heart has been recognized by many of Catholicism's most influential writers, from the early Church to the present.

The inseparable divine Hearts of the Father and the Son were the object of St. Theophilus of Antioch's writings; he was the sixth Bishop of Antioch in Syria, and is also credited with being the first to use the word *Trinitas* for the union in nature of the three divine Persons in God. In Paradise, St. Theophilus writes, the Word resided in the *Heart of the Father*; before anything came into being, the Father, in His Heart, had His Son as Counselor, being His own mind and thought. He writes, "This Logos spoke to Adam in Paradise: The God and Father of all, indeed, cannot be contained and is not found in a place, for there is no place of his rest: but his Word, through whom he made all things, being his power and wisdom, assuming the Person of the Father and Lord of all, went to the Garden in the Person of God, and conversed with Adam. For the divine writing itself teaches us that Adam said that he had heard the voice. But what else is this voice, but the Word of God, who is also his son? Not as the poets and writers of myths talk of the sons of gods from intercourse, but as truth expounds, the Word, that always exists, residing within the Heart of God [*the Father*]. For before anything came into being he had him [the *Son*] as counselor, being his own mind and thought."[11]

The words of St. Ambrose, one of the *great Fathers* of the Church, provide another excellent summation of this truth – the unity of God's divine nature, and that all attributes must first be possessed in the Father, especially as it applies to the Divine Paternal Heart of God the Father: "The Son lives by the Father, because he is the Word given forth from the Heart of the Father, because he comes forth from the Father, because he is begotten of the bowels of the Father, because the Father is the fountain and the root of the Son's Being."[12]

POPE PIUS XII AND POPE BENEDICT XVI

In more recent times, both Pope Pius XII and Pope Benedict XVI have written of the Father's Divine Paternal Heart. In their writings, Pope Pius XII and Pope Benedict XVI explore the unity and inseparability of the divine nature as evidenced in the Father's Heart.

In *Haurietis Aquas*, Pope Pius XII acknowledges the divine nature and inseparability of the Persons of the Trinity regarding the divine Hearts of Jesus and the Father. He declares that the Sacred Heart of Christ by the essential truth of the Hypostatic Union gives us the only way to reach the Heart of the Father: "Once this essential truth has been established we understand that the Heart of Jesus is the Heart of a divine Person, the Word Incarnate, and by it is represented and, as it were, placed before our gaze all the love with which he has embraced and even now embraces us. Consequently, the honor to be paid to the Sacred Heart is such as to raise it to the rank—so far as external practice is concern – of the highest expression of Christian piety. For this is the religion of Jesus which is centered on the Mediator who is man and God, and in such a way that *we* cannot reach the Heart of God *(the Father)* save through the Heart of Christ, as he himself says: 'I am the way, the truth and the life. No one cometh to the Father save by me.'"[13]

In *Jesus of Nazareth*, Pope Benedict XVI writes that the total "communion" of the Father and the Son is best understood in its depth through Christ being in the Heart of the Father: "'All things have been delivered to me by my Father; and no one knows the Son except the Father, and no one knows the Father except the Son and any one whom the Son wills to reveal him' (Mt 11:25-27; Lk 10:21-22). Let us begin with this last sentence, which is the key to the whole passage. Only the Son truly 'knows' the Father. Knowing always involves some sort of equality. ...Truly to know God presupposes communion with him, it presuppose oneness of being with him. In this sense, what the Lord himself now proclaims in prayer is identical with what we hear in the concluding words of the prologue of John's Gospel, which we have quoted frequently: 'No one has ever seen God; it is the only Son, who is nearest to the *Father's Heart* [italics added], who has made him known' (Jn 1:18). This fundamental saying – it now becomes plain – is an explanation of what comes to light in Jesus' prayer, in his filial dialogue. At the same time, it also becomes clear what "the Son" is and what this term means: perfect communion in knowledge, which is at the same time communion in Being. Unity in knowing is possible only because it is unity in being."[14]

It can be clearly seen, therefore, that the divine Hearts of the Father and the Son are inseparable from a theological standpoint. In recognizing the Sacred Heart of the Son, the Paternal Heart of the Father becomes an indisputable divine reality.

> "He is Father of one only Son. This is why He is only-begotten, and alone in the *Father's Bosom*, and alone is acknowledged by the Father to be from Him, saying, 'This is my beloved Son, in whom I am well-pleased.'"
> —St Athanasius

Chapter Seventeen

THE RIGHT HAND OF THE FATHER

"When he had accomplished purification from sins, he took his seat at the right hand of the Majesty on high" (Heb 1:3).

"The love of the Father," Pope Benedict XVI writes in *Deus Caritas Est*, "wishes to make humanity a single family in his Son."[1]

In these words, the Holy Father foresees a world that comes to know its Father's love through Christ – thus changing life on earth forever – and a world that unifies mankind in a way often foretold in the writings of the Old Testament prophets. This perfect, unifying love of the Father is a love that all humanity is called to know, to see is real, and to trust is eternal. And it is a love so great that it, like the love of Christ, deserves to be symbolized by a Heart of its own – a divine *Paternal Heart* that draws humanity to it like a guiding searchlight for wayward ships seeking the surest and safest way home.

However, because no one has seen the Father, and since He is spirit and does not possess an incarnate heart of His own, can we recognize and honor Him through a human symbol as we do with the Hearts of Jesus and Mary? From a theological standpoint, we have affirmatively answered this question. But what of its symbolic nature in relation to the history of understanding God the Father in the Church? Has the Church already established theological precedent by using corporeal images to express doctrine in relation to devotion to the Father?

THE CREEDS

The oldest authoritative doctrinal foundation of the Church's belief in the Trinity is the *Apostle's Creed*, which is rooted in the second century Trinitarian formula of Baptism. The *Nicene Creed* arose from the defensive struggle against Arianism, and it stresses the divinity of the Son and His consubstantiality with the Father. Both of the creeds in formula express that the Triune God is the Father of created things, and above all, creatures endowed with reason; they also express that there is a Fatherhood in God, a Fatherhood in the true and proper sense which belongs to the First Person only, and this is the model of God's Fatherhood of man, and of all "created paternity" (Eph 3:14).[2]

The Biblical teaching of the Trinity – of the divine Persons in God – can be reconciled with the basic Biblical doctrine of the unity of divine nature only if the three divine Persons subsist in one single divine nature. Thus, Christ declares the unity of His divine nature with that of the Father: "I and the Father are one" (Jn 10:30). This unity of the essence of God was sanctioned by the *Council of Nicea* (325).[3]

In the Ascension, both creeds are in agreement with what the Apostles confess: Christ ascended into heaven of His own power, as God in divine power, and as man in the power of His transfigured soul, which moves His transfigured body. In regard to the human nature of Christ, the Creeds assert that it was taken up into heaven as well. With His elevation into heaven, Christ now sits at the "right hand of God" (Mk 16:19).

THE RIGHT HAND OF THE FATHER

Often prefigured in the Old Testament, as in the psalm, "You will show me the path to life, abounding joy in your presence, the delights at your right hand forever" (Ps 16:11) and in *Isaiah* ,"my right hand spread out the heavens" (Is 48:13), the Scriptural reference to "the right hand of God" (*the Father*) is also found in the Epistles (cf. Rom 8:34, Eph 1:20, Heb 1:3, 8:1, 10:12, 12:2, 1 Pt 3:22). Therefore, Christ's Ascension is considered, from a soteriological angle, the crowning conclusion in the work of the Redemption, and from a Christological angle the final elevation of Christ's human nature into His condition of divine glory.[4] It also fulfilled the *Prophecy of the Lord* recorded in the *Psalms*, "A psalm of David. The Lord says to my lord: 'Sit at my right hand, while I make your enemies your footstool'" (Ps 110:1).

The Ascension of the Incarnate Christ in both natures is the completion and perfection of a mystery. The *Catechism of the Council of Trent* reads: "Nothing can be conceived more humble, nothing more lowly, than that the Son of God assumed our weak human nature and suffered and died for us. But nothing more magnificently, nothing more admirably, proclaims his sovereign glory and divine majesty than… [that] he rose from the dead, ascended into heaven, and sits at the right hand of God the Father."[5]

The glory of Christ in heaven, in His glorified body and in both natures – human and divine – is the focus of this mystery. But the words "Right Hand of the Father" deserve attention, for these words reveal that the early Church defined the presence and action of God the Father in language that, while not intended to be interpreted in a literal sense, validated the use of human features to accommodate a better understanding of the divine – a better understanding of God the Father.

CORPOREAL IMAGES AND DIVINE TRUTH

We have already noted the numerous references to the Father in the New Testament, which rely on anthropomorphic language to convey God the Father's divine Personhood, traits, actions, characteristics, and attributes. But in the creeds, rooted and written in the earliest days of the Church, the early Fathers followed and invoked Scripture, and thereby established precedent in the usage of corporeal images to convey and pronounce divine truths. Consequently, in transferring human ideas to celestial things in order to express doctrine, we find that the Fathers of the Church reasoned that there was no better way to convey the truth of God the Father, regardless of the fact that the Father is pure spirit.

The *Catechism of the Council of Trent* states: "The words, "He sits at the right hand of God (*the Father*)", observes a "figure of speech", other than the literal sense, as frequently happens in Scripture, to attribute human attributes and human members to God (*the Father*). God, who is spirit, admits of nothing corporeal. (Authors' note: most references to Christ have Him "sitting" at the right hand of the Father. However, St. Stephen reported he saw "the Son of Man *standing* at God's right hand (Acts 7:55)). This expression, "the 'right hand of the Father'" is meant to convey a meaning that the Father's "right hand is "an honorable" place.[6] Likewise, the *Catechism of the Catholic Church* reads that "the right hand of the Father [helps us] understand the glory and honor of divinity...of one being with the Father.[7]

THE LOVE OF THE FATHER

The Father possesses neither a hand nor a heart in a human context, but Scripture, doctrine, and precedent uphold that He possesses traits, characteristics, and attributes best understood in their intended meaning through the use of corporeal language and images. As the great Doctor of the Church, St. John Damascene writes: "All the statements made about God that imply *body* have some hidden meaning and teach us what is above us by means of something familiar to ourselves."[8]

Using the same reasoning, we see that the paternal love of God the Father can be best theologically apprehended, understood, and accepted through corporeal imagery. Although the Father is spirit and does not possess a corporeal heart, any understanding of Him is not limited by this reality. As the early councils of the Church recognized the honor, glory, and divinity that the *right hand of God the Father* symbolizes in the creeds, there is no better symbol of the Father's paternal providence, love, and mercy than His *Divine Paternal Heart*.

"Jesus' teaching is not the product of human learning, of whatever kind. It originates from immediate contact with the Father, from 'face-to-face' dialogue – from the vision of the one who rests close to the *Father's Heart*."
—Pope Benedict XVI

Chapter Eighteen

THE DIVINE PATERNAL HEART OF GOD OUR FATHER

"In my Father's House are many dwelling places. If it were not so, would I have told you that I am going to prepare a place for you?" (Jn 14:2)

If we look with the eyes of our soul, we will see that the world around us is a map of our Father's love, with all roads leading home to our *Father's House.*

In this time, God has shone a great light on these many roads, the light of our Mother, Mary, who is triumphantly bringing back her children to this *House.* From Guadalupe to Lourdes, from Fatima to Akita, from Kibeho to San Nicolas, the Church acknowledges that Mary is at work, always proving to be the perfect *Mother of all mankind.* St. John Paul II describes this to us: "*Mary Most Holy,* the highly favoured daughter of the Father, will *appear* [italics added] before the eyes of believers as the perfect model of love towards God and neighbor. ...The Father chose her for *a unique mission* in the history of salvation: that of being the Mother of the long-awaited Savior. ...Her motherhood, which began in Nazareth and was lived most intensely in Jerusalem at the foot of the Cross, will be felt...as a loving and urgent invitation addressed to all the children of God, so that they will return to the house of the Father."[1]

Like a gifted artist, Mary paints the picture, leaving no detail out of the undeniable truth of the Father's great love for all His children and of His great delight for each soul – marked for His glory – to come to know, love, and honor Him in a special way, *heart to Heart*. Through her pure and heartfelt "yes," Mary assembles in union the Father's family, divine, eternal, and complete to come to their Father.

Our Lord and Savior Jesus Christ began this work long ago and revealed His Father as *our* Father. He told us our Father loved us and called us to Him. But still God's children did not see Him nor hear His voice through His Son's. Obscured, hidden, forgotten, and buried, the truth of God our Father and His great love for His children has only been understood in glimpses by mankind, leaving us unsure of what to seek to make us complete and satisfy our desire for fulfillment.

Scripture reminds us that life is a treasure, a miracle to behold and appreciate. Now, the time has come for our human understanding of God our Father to be unlike ever before in order for the miracle of life to be better understood, for the story of salvation history to further unfold, and for the mystery of God our Father's love to come to be more seen.[2]

THE TIME HAS ARRIVED

Indeed, a unique and blessed moment has arrived in the Church and the world, for as God called out to Moses from the *Burning Bush*, telling him that "I am the God of your Fathers, the God of Abraham, the God of Isaac, the God of Jacob" and "I have come down to rescue My people," so God our Father is calling us, His children, from His *burning Paternal Heart*, telling us that "I am your Father, the Father of all mankind and I am coming down for all My children to be reunited with Me."

Now, through the power of the Holy Spirit permeating the world, Mary tells us in her visitations at Fatima and elsewhere that God wishes to pour out through her Immaculate Heart the fullness of His love, grace, and mercy on His children in order to lead them back to His loving Heart.[3] Moreover, as we read in the words of many of the popes over the past century, God is asking us to cast our eyes to the heavens and feel the sun of His Divine Heart rising in our souls as we approach a new epoch in time, an *Era of Peace* – a peace to be undaunted by sin and slavery to sin. This call of our Father – a gentle whisper to our hearts through His Spirit – asks us to choose Him over the world and its illusions, to turn to Him and the promise of our divine paternity and its inheritance, and to accept the truth of who we really are: children of the one, true, loving Father of all mankind.

In this light, as the doorway to the approaching *"Triumph of the Immaculate Heart"* is opened ever wider, the Shepherds of the Church echo Mary's words at Fatima. They tell us in their encyclicals, in their general audiences, and in their many words and ways that God our Father is deeply moved, hurrying to us like the father in the *Parable of the Prodigal Son*.[4] He hastens to us, they tell us, as the loving, caring father in the *Parable* does – as the most merciful and gentle Father to wipe away our tears and crush our fears in His mighty hands, in His forgiving embrace, and in His loving Heart.

Thus, as flowers before the sun – the Paternal Heart of God our Father – we are invited to turn towards Him and blossom in His arms, for He waits for us longingly to answer His invitation: to give Him our *fiat* and to come to His Heart!

RESPONDING TO OUR FATHER'S CALL

How are we to respond to this great call to our Father's Paternal Heart?

As Fr. Jean Galot writes, we are called to respond to the Father's invitation to intimacy *in* Him by inviting Him into our hearts, as He is now inviting us into His.[5] Thus, we need merely to say the words our Father has waited for all time to hear, for in these words is embodied the joining of hearts: "**Father, I love you and I give my heart totally to You, receive me into Your Heart.**"

In these words, we fulfill our heart's greatest desire by giving our heart to the Heart of our Father. In his book, *Introduction to the Devout Life*, St. Francis de Sales tells us that, the Father is *truly* in our hearts—as we are in His Heart—once we say *yes* to Him, like David did: "God's holy presence is in your heart and in the very spirit of your spirit. He enlivens it and animates it by his divine presence for he is there as the Heart of your heart and the Spirit of your spirit. For this reason David calls him "the God of his heart, and St. Paul says that "we live and move and are *in* God."[6]

And with our fiat to our Father, our joy is just beginning. According to the great Saints, once we are received into our Father's Heart, we will know no richer treasure, no holier splendor, and no greater happiness; we will have returned to where our divine resemblance was formed, where we were loved into existence, and where we were crafted by our loving Father in His image.[7] Like Jesus on the Cross, we will have returned to our *first* womb – the *Abyss* of our Father's love – where we can assimilate the rhythm and harmony of His holy will, and where we can imagine in our hearts the words our Father longs to say to us in reply, "I love you eternally – and I give you all *good* things – precious gifts – filling you with My immeasurable Spirit! Welcome into My Heart!"

THE HEART OF HEARTS

Once there, in our Father's Divine Paternal Heart, where divine *compassion*, divine *wisdom*, divine *beauty*, divine *yearning*, divine *fidelity*, divine *justice*, divine *mercy*, and divine *peace* infinitely exist, the great Saints who journeyed before us affirm that we will find the eternal awe and wonder of our Father's creative power and energy – forever at work infusing His divine graces into our souls while forming our immortality, assuring our destiny, and numbering us among His children forever. The words of St. Hilary help capture this unfathomable mystery: "It is the Father from whom everything that exists has been formed. He is in Christ and through Christ the source of all things…He transcends the realm of understanding. This is the true nature of the mystery of God, this name of the impenatrateable [*sic*] nature of the Father."

St. Hilary's words bring us deeper into the reality of the Father's Heart. In the *Heart of Hearts*, in the infinite *Bosom* of the Father, and where divine peace dwells and where it is safe and quiet, the perfection of our Father's divine paternity is found, constantly giving and transfusing *His paternal love* into His children; He covers them with it like the *morning dew*, formed from the essence of His divine Being. Here, we find our Father's providence showering upon us our every need in the humble sphere of our daily life. Like all His gifts and graces, our Father's Heart gives to us everything necessary, especially if we trust in faith, "So do not worry and say 'What will we eat' or 'What will we drink' or 'What will we wear?'…Your heavenly Father knows that you need them all." (Mt 6:31-32).

Scripture tells us that our Father gives us our daily bread, forgives our offenses, gives good things to us while knowing all before we ask, and most of all, lovingly pulls us away from temptation and evil. Most importantly, we see how He provides *all* of this for *all His children*, as His sun rises on the good and the bad; He is kind to even the unthankful. All are to simply *ask of their Father "in Jesus' Name."*

Perhaps *these* gifts of God's divine providence truly shows us the greatness of the love of His Paternal Heart, for He insures and provides the most mundane needs for His children, as seen in contrast to His *Sovereignty* over the earth, His *Lordship* over mankind's history, and His *Kingship* over His vast universe.

While modern doctrine objects to divine paternal providence as being incompatible to the functioning laws of nature, and while sin and suffering cannot be excluded in ceaselessly disturbing our Father's involvement with His children's lives, the Saints tell us that the Heart of our Father *provides in abundance*—even using our misguided moments and suffering on a loftier level of His divine plan, turning all into good!

"GOD MY FATHER"

Thus, arising from his Divine Paternal Heart, we find that our Father's divine perfection creates a Fatherhood that is totally paternal, *perfectly paternal*. This means God our Father is *infinitely* and *perfectly* an almighty omnipotent Father, exceeding anything we can understand, imagine, or hope for in a father.[8] It also means that God our Father is first and foremost a *Father*, and all the characteristics of His divinity first assume a paternal aspect, emanating from His Paternal Heart.[9]

But as the *Catechism* notes, in our Father's divinity is also a light casted on the importance of not just fatherhood but *motherhood*; our Father's Heart is the *first womb*, illuminating the truth of the great blessing that is motherhood, while divinely and humanly linking motherhood's *inseparability* with fatherhood. This is because in our Father, we discern the perfection of maternal love for us, which is found in the perfection of His paternal love.[10] *All of us were delivered from the womb of our Father's Heart.* It is an imagery that allows us to see our Father's Heart mystically transposed over every pregnant mother's profile, thereby further confirming the sacredness of life, the blessedness of motherhood, and the maternal love of the Father's Heart for each child.

According to St. Catherine of Siena, and many more of God's chosen ones, the paternal love of our ABBA reveals the *infinite grandeur* of a "perfect" Father, who though is thought of as being in eternity, is never more than just a prayer away from us; a whisper of love removed. And, once united in Heart with us through Christ, "the bridge on the world," our Father longs to hear our endless songs of love to Him, our cascading hymns of praise to His glory, our perpetual prayers for His assistance with our every need, our every fear, and our every dream, so that He can help unfold the unique design and plan He has for every one of His children. In essence, as He did with St. Catherine, He calls us into a *dialogue* with Him, a personal life of sharing our most intimate moments with our *concerned* and *committed* Father. Faced with this awesome truth, He is not only "God Our Father," but "God My Father!"

CHILDREN OF OUR FATHER'S HEART

While Jesus lived, our Father's Paternal Heart was forever in complete intimacy with His only begotten Son's Sacred Heart, whose human prayer – especially in the *Garden of Gethsemane* – was perfectly human. This allows us to discern that our hearts, though not in the same intimacy with the Father as Jesus, can offer such prayer that touches the Heart of our ABBA – prayer that moves His Heart to respond in paternal love for our every need too.

Appropriately, the words in *Jeremiah* are brought to life for all of us to better grasp the great love of the Paternal Heart of God Our Father,

> "Is Ephraim not my favored son, the child in whom I delight?
>
> Even though I threaten him, I still remember him!
>
> My *Heart* [italics added] stirs for him,
>
> I must show him compassion – oracle of the Lord" (Jer 31:20).

But our Father's Paternal Heart, St. Faustina Kowalska writes, longs for more than just our prayer and more than just our pleas for His mercy and favors. Rather, in our time, He wants us to now come to Him as a child taking its first steps, trusting the waiting, guiding, and protecting presence of a parent. According to St. Faustina, we are called to more deeply embrace "the will of the Heavenly Father" in our daily walk through life.[11]

Indeed, as a child falls into the outreaching arms of a parent, so are we to now grasp our Father's hand and fall into His comforting embrace. As Pope Benedict XVI writes in *Jesus of Nazareth*, we are invited to lean on our Father's Breast as St. John leaned on Christ's Breast[12] – *one heart in another* – and be amazed at the loving relationship between Father and child that must be fully explored for our lives and this world to come to fulfillment.

EACH CHILD IS PRECIOUS

As is clear in Scripture, there was and is only one purpose for man: the fulfillment of *God's Word*, which brings all God's children back into the *arms* and *Heart* of the Father where all were born and where all forever belong. This means, whether in peace or pain, the Father's love allows us to rest in His Heart, as He rests in ours.

But lest we forget, our Father's Heart is the greatest of hearts, the king of Hearts, because it is *perfect*, containing within it the truth of His singular and perfect love for *each* of us in a special, perfect way. Thus, in the sacred and paternal depths of God our Father's Heart, the Saints remind us that there lies His awareness of the *preciousness* of each and every child's *significance* in creation; regardless of their human shortcomings, failures, and sinful ways.

A good parent looks after the welfare of each child, and despite weaknesses, never doubts his or her individual worth or value. Even those who seem the most flawed draw a parent's heart even closer, for no better reason than need. This, *too*, is how our Father's Paternal Heart responds to each child's needs, and their needs for Him. *His infinite love is unique and infinite for each of us.* Moreover, those who are less perfect have greater need to which His Heart is strongly drawn. In every moment, our heavenly Father is with us in *every* need, for He created each one within His loving Heart—which resides in each, beating out a message of love. In this way and truth, we resemble our Father. As our hearts are bonded to our children's hearts and to their needs completely because of our unceasing, inseparable love for them, so is our Father's Paternal Heart bonded to ours even more. This is because the Father's infinite paternal love is truly a river of promises heard and kept for all His children's needs, hopes, and prayers. And that is why all can come to trust that every effort and every motion done in our Father's name will bear fruit when it is joined to His Paternal Heart, where He has written all our names.

THE FATHER'S HEART: OUR TRUE HOME

But Scripture teaches us that our Father's love for His children is so much more! In the fullness of this truth, God's sacred words tell us that our Father's Paternal Heart is a refuge, a fortress, and a sanctuary for us. It is an ocean of love and mercy, a sea of bliss, and a paradise for each and every child to return to when he or she is left alone in a world of emptiness and false illusion. Our Father's Heart is, as Christ showed us in Gethsemane, where we are to go when there is nowhere left to go and no one left to turn to. His Heart is, quite simply, our true *Home*, where we all are invited to return. This is the deeper mystery of the Father's Heart, a mystery we are all called to seek and to find.

Yes, our Father's Heart is our *Home*, where we are called to return. It is a true, loving home, a real home; for the Father's Heart is a house of comfort, solace, and rest. It is a house of protection – a place for the cold and the hungry and a place for the lost. We can go to the Father's Heart in the daytime of our life, when we are weary, when we need encouragement, and are tempted to give up. We can go to the Father's Heart in the night time of our life, when we are naked and scared, when we are alone and on our knees, and seek hope to prevent despair.

And so now, our Father summons us, one and all, back to Him – back into His arms, into His Heart. He summons the knowing, the confused, the floundering, and the proud. He summons the blind and the deaf. He summons the wicked. He summons the unwanted and separated. He summons those who are in despair and panicking, those who are frightened and devoured by evil, those who are misguided, and those who are *lost*.

Our Father *especially* seeks His little ones who are *lost*—lost to self, lost to power, lost to greed, lost to pride, lost to intellect, lost to disobedience, lost to willfulness, lost to apathy, lost to self abuse, lost to self indulgence, lost to hate, lost to lust, lost in their faith and no longer believe in a heavenly Father who loves them and has never forgotten them; a Father who has never left them and will *always* welcome them home to rest in His forgiving, loving Heart.

This is because no child is beyond the Father's Paternal Heart. Yes, it is truly a Heart, Pope Benedict XVI writes, that we are called to *rest* in, "just as Jesus, the Son, knows about the "mystery of the Father's Heart from *resting* in it."[13]

OUR DIVINE INHERITANCE

In this time, our Father is calling His children to His Paternal Heart. He asks us to make His Heart our pillow. He asks us to hear His Heart beat, a great bell tolling out the ancient vibration of love, beating in the rhythm and harmony of His will and calling all to become *one* with His music of mercy. He asks us to come and take root in His Heart as He takes root in ours – regardless of what our mind and senses tell us, regardless of the attractions and deceits of our lives and the world, and regardless of the many storms that cross our days.

Lovingly, our heavenly Father invites His children to enter and nestle into his Heart of warmth, tenderness, and reassurance, where He can cherish us, nurture us, renew us, rejoice in us, and where He can, as the prophet Isaiah writes, *delight in us*,[14] so that eventually we are made new, as Ezekiel tells us, in heart and spirit.[15]

The sustenance of the Father's love must draw us there in *repentance*, less we be chastised for our offenses. But the deprivation of this Heart should be more than enough to pull us away from our ingratitude and our selfishness, and pull us back home to our loving Father.

Yes, *we* are the prodigals, one and all, who need to set off for our Father's arms and Heart, longing for His kiss and for the celebration to begin. In this time, through intersecting hearts with our Creator, we are called by His love to bathe in His divinity; we are invited to become one divine *Family of God*,[16] prepared by Christ to return to our Father so we can not only embrace our divine inheritance and identity, but so we can live in God as God lives in us.

As Pope Benedict XVI writes in *Jesus of Nazareth*, "To pray for the Kingdom of God is to say to Jesus: Let us be yours, Lord! Pervade us, live in us; gather scattered humanity in your body, so that in you everything may be subordinated to God and you can then hand over the universe to the Father, in order that 'God may be *all* in *all*'" (1 Cor 15:28).[17]

Part V

TRIUMPH OF THE LIVING FATHER

"Only the Son was capable of introducing us to this mystery. Since "no one has seen God" no one knew the mystery of his inner life. The Son alone knew it. It is only the Son, *who is nearest to the Father's Heart*, who has made him known."
—St. John Paul II

Chapter Nineteen

THE PATERNAL HEART OF LIFE

"For this is the will of my Father, that everyone who sees the Son and believes in him may have eternal life" (Jn 6:40).

"Human life is sacred and inviolable at every moment of existence, including the initial phases which precede birth. All human beings, from their mother's womb, belong to God who searches them and knows them, who forms them and knits them together with his own hands, who gazes on them when they are tiny shapeless embryos and already sees in them the adults of tomorrow whose days are numbered and whose vocation is even now written in the 'Book of Life' (cf. Ps 139:1, 13-16). There too, when they are still in their mother's womb—as many passages of the Bible bear witness—they are personal objects of God's loving and Fatherly providence."

– Pope John Paul II, *Evangelium Vitae*[1]

From the *Tree of Life* to the *Book of Life*, God's Revelation from beginning to end is about life. Life – all human life – comes from God; it is His gift, the essence of His image, and His imprint. This is because our Father is, along with Jesus and the Holy Spirit, the *God of Life*, whose light, love, mercy, and peace flow to *all* His little ones, all His children. Consequently, Sacred Scripture warns that *man cannot* do with the gift of life as he pleases.

Throughout the Bible, the value of life is revealed as an indisputable treasure in the eyes of God, and His holy words take great care to convey this reality to His children. As God told Noah after the flood, "Indeed for your own lifeblood I will demand an accounting…from a human being, each one for the blood of another, I will demand an accounting for human life" (Gn 9:5). This is because the love and mercy which God has for His children is founded in the preciousness, sacredness, and holiness of life – the life of God Himself that He chooses to share with man: "Let us make human beings in our own image, after our likeness" (Gn 1:26).

It is a life that God did not *intend* to be marred by death, "[f]or God formed us to be imperishable; the image of his own nature he made us" (Wis 2:23) and "filled them with knowledge and understanding, and showed them good and evil" (Sir 17:7). But even after death entered the world, God remained a God of life: "God did not make death, nor does he rejoice in the destruction of the living. For he fashioned all things that they might have being" (Wis 1:13-14).

The many Scriptural texts are deliberate in content and extol the "greatness and inestimable nature of human life even in its temporal phase," writes St. John Paul II in his encyclical letter, *Evangelium Vitae*.[2] Moreover, the Pope tells us that the truth of the sacredness of life, both human and divine, is the *heart* of the New Testament, the heart of Jesus' message; for in every dimension, Christ's words are profound in meaning: "I came that they may have *life* [italics added], and have it abundantly" (Jn 10:10), "I am the way, the truth and the *life* [italics added]" (Jn 14:6), "No one has greater love than this, to lay down one's *life* [italics added] for one's friends" (Jn 15:13). "If you wish to enter *life* [italics added] keep the commandments" (Mt 19:17). As we can see, from the birth of Christ to the last moments of His life on the Cross, the New Testament's entire focus is on the priceless value and truth of having, giving, protecting, and possessing *life*, temporal and eternal.

THE WOMB: A SACRED SANCTUARY

And to those who challenge the belief that life begins at conception, the words of Scripture can be seen to clearly apply not only to the *visible* living. The unborn, undeveloped, and unseen child is no less precious in the eyes of God, no less *life*, and this truth is conveyed throughout the Bible in definitive passages: "[T]he Lord...made you...formed you in the womb" (Is 44:2), "for you formed my inmost being" (Ps 139:13), "Your hands have formed me and fashioned me...you fashioned me from clay!" (Jb 10:8-9), "Your eyes saw me unformed" (Ps 139:16).

Furthermore, as if to forewarn man from any thoughts of violating life in the womb, Scripture is abundant with passages that emphasize that the womb is a sacred sanctuary in the eyes of God: "I was cast upon thee from the womb. From my mother's womb thou art my God" (Ps 21:11), "the fruit of the womb is a reward" (Ps 127:3, cf. Ps 128:3-4), "The razor hath never come upon my head, for I am...consecrated to God from my mother's womb" (Jgs 16:17), "Before I formed you in the womb I knew you, and before you were born I consecrated you" (Jer 1:5), "Thus says the Lord who made you, who formed you in the womb and will help you: Do not fear, O Jacob my servant...whom I have chosen"(Is 44:2), "he will be filled with the Holy Spirit while yet in his mother's womb" (Lk 1:15), "the baby leaped in her womb" (Lk 1:41), "blessed is the fruit of thy womb" (Lk 1:42). Even the symbolic existence of whole nations are cited in Scripture as being "alive" in the womb: "Two nations are in your womb, and two peoples born of you shall be divided" (Gn 25:23).

To solidify the truth of this reality, life in the womb is often described in Scripture as *already* a child and a person in the eyes of God: "I have given birth to a man-child" (Gn 4:1), "a Virgin will be with child" (Is 7:14), "She was found to be with child" (Mt 1:18). Indeed, Christianity begins with the birth of a Child that is proclaimed as "joyful news," as should be the birth of every child.

In recent history, the Church has boldly called for all to respect, protect, proclaim, to love and serve human life. Pope John XXIII, in his encyclical letter, *Mater et Magistra* (1961), warned, "Human life is sacred—all men must recognize that fact." His successor, Pope Paul VI, echoed him in *Humanae Vitae* (1968): "God is the source of human life...there is no reason for the Church to abandon the duty entrusted to her of preaching the whole moral law firmly and humbly, both the natural law and the law of the Gospel." Similarly, St. John Paul II consistently confronted the attack on life. His profound words in his encyclical letter, *Evangelium Vitae,* cut to the heart of this issue in the clearest of ways, "How can anyone think that even a single moment of this marvelous [*sic*] process of the unfolding of life can be separated from the wise and loving work of the Creator, and left prey to human caprice?"[3]

The Creator, our loving *Father of Life*, holds the answer to today's perils that surround life itself. And it is in His Heart, *the Paternal Heart of Life*, that He calls us to find those answers.

"Let us rather give thanks to the Lord Our God who, as he tested our ancestors, is now testing us. Remember how he treated Abraham, all the ordeals of Isaac, and all that happened to Jacob…For as these ordeals were intended by him to search their hearts, so now this is not vengeance that God is exacting on us, but a warning inflicted by the Lord on those who are near his *Heart*" (Jdt 8:25-27).

Chapter Twenty

AN ATTACK ON GOD HIMSELF

"Woe to them that make wicked laws, and when they write, they write injustice, to oppress the poor in judgement, and do violence to the cause of the humble of my people: that widows might be their prey, and that they might rob the fatherless! What will you do on the day of visitation and of the calamity which cometh from afar? To whom will you flee for help? And where will you leave your glory" (Is 10-1-3).

The beginning of human life belongs to our Father, as does the end. Thus, the terrible wrong of the taking of life is no less clear in Scripture; for the end of life *too* belongs only to God: "And the Lord said, 'What have you done? The voice of your brother's blood cries to me from the ground'" (Gn 4:10), "You shall not murder" (Ex 20:13, Dt 5:17, Mt 19:18), "It is I who bring both death and life" (Dt 32:39, cf. Wis 16:13, Tb 13:2, 2 Kgs 5:7) "The Lord puts to death and gives life, casts down to Sheol and brings up again" (1 Sm 2:6). God, Scripture tells us, is always on the side of life and calls us to do the same: "I have set before you life and death, blessing and curse. Choose life then, that you and your descendants may live" (Dt 30:19).

In our times, a unique and terrible holocaust is unfolding. Through the legalization of abortion throughout the world along with other anti-life measures, a tragedy of incomprehensible proportion is taking place. It is an inhumane, demonic campaign, advanced by science and government that has permitted the greatest of evils – the taking of innocent human life – to be proclaimed as good. Tragically, the words of the prophet Isaiah ring truer in our world more than ever before:

> "Woe to those who call evil good, and good evil: that put darkness for light, and light for darkness: that put bitter for sweet, and sweet for bitter" (Is 5:20).

THE CULTURE OF DEATH

The Church has boldly responded to this crisis. During his remarkable and heroic papacy, St. John Paul II shined a bright light on the darkness of this modern plague by branding it as the "culture of death."[1] However, over time, this tragedy has continued to elevate to new heights. Through the ongoing advances of science – our age's "pride of the heart" (cf. Ob 1:3) – it is apparent that now man seeks to remove all of God's authority over every stage of life and essentially to replace God with himself. On October 16, 2008, Pope Benedict XVI commented on this misguided direction, "Science is risky when overtaken by its desire to play God."

Indeed, beyond homicide, genocide, and world wars, the culture of *science induced death* through the obstruction of life – through abortion, infanticide, euthanasia, and an array of contraceptive and genetic assaults – is deceitful and sinister, trampling consciences and institutions, celebrating a triumph over any fear of God and any *fear of divine retribution*. It is, as David wrote in his *psalm*: "Sin directs the heart of the wicked man; his eyes are closed to the fear of God" (Ps 36:1).

AN ATTACK ON GOD

In the fullness of this epic injustice, we see that this holocaust has brought death to tens of millions, perhaps hundreds of millions of innocent lives, prompting the question, "What will be the price of this great tragedy?" Clearly, "our guilt reaches up to heaven" (Ezr 9:6). Our guilt and our shame reaches to heaven because, St. John Paul II wrote in *Evangelium Vitae*, the attack on life is essentially an attack on God, "...life, especially human life, belongs only to God: for this reason whoever attacks human life, in some way attacks God himself."[2] Centuries ago, in his book, *City of God*, St. Augustine wrote, "When anyone tramples on anything, he tramples on God; when he kills any living thing, he kills God. I refuse to set forth all conclusions which thinking men can draw, but which they can express without shame." On November 15, 2014, Pope Francis denounced the Right To Die movement stating it was a "false sense of compassion" to consider euthanasia as an act of dignity when in fact it's a sin against God and creation. Speaking to the *Association of Italian Catholic Doctors*, he also condemned abortion, in vitro fertilization and embryonic stem cell research. "This is playing with life," Pope Francis said, "Beware, because this is a sin against the Creator, against God the Creator."

All of this is because civilization has obscured its "sense of God," according to St. John Paul II – and where there is no sense of God, there is no sense of man, of his divine roots, of the gift of life that is *from* God.[3] Today, moral law in regards to life is more than violated; it is blackened beyond visibility, creating a frightening vacuum of the discernable presence of the light of divine truth so traditionally seen, recognized, and necessary in understanding creation and human dignity. This is a truth that historically provides balance and answers to the mystery of man and to the mystery of life and death.

Because of international cooperation between nations that promote and export population control methods – along with organized efforts to deconstruct the institution of marriage and the sanctity of the family – a greater part of civilization now upholds laws that tolerate, foster, and promote efforts that are contrary not only to life, but to *all* moral living and to all of the sacred laws of God.

THE WARNINGS OF ST. PAUL

The international *culture of death* constructs actual "structures of sin,"[4] St. John Paul II writes in the *Evangelium Vitae* as he describes the attempt to build an earth without God and to live as "as if God did not exist."[5] More recently, over the last two decades, nations that have been historically Christian have succumbed to this *organized sin*, calling to mind St. Paul's words to Titus: "They claim to know God, but by their deeds they deny him" (Ti 1:16).

These actions are numerous, complex, and intertwined in our culture today; they paint a picture of man that Scripture reveals has been seen before and defined in a clear and revealing spiritual profile. Once more, St. John Paul II tells us that it is in St. Paul's words that we can best understand our world of today. It is a world, St. Paul wrote in his *Letter to the Romans*, comprised of men and women "who suppress the truth by their wickedness" (Rom 1:18) because their "senseless hearts [are] darkened," (Rom 1:21) and "claiming to be wise, they became fools" (Rom 1:22), carrying out "works deserving of death" (Rom 1:32). And, St. Paul concludes, "they not only do them but approve those who practice them" (Rom 1:32).

All of this has its roots in the "Spirit of Darkness" who deceives man into a false peace by attempting, since the Fall in Eden, to show God the Father as a "source of danger and threat to man," according to St. John Paul II in his encyclical letter, *Dominum et. Vivificatem*: "[T]hrough the influence of the 'Father of Lies,' through the history of humanity there will be constant pressure on man to reject God, even to the point of hating Him: 'Love of self to the point of contempt of God,' as St. Augustine puts it."[6]

Thus, in the end, man becomes inclined to see God as a limitation of himself, and not the source of freedom and the fullness of good. We see this more than ever in the new millennium, where science and politics endlessly challenge faith and religion; they deny God, and in many ways declare the *death of God* while seeking to lead man to be free of the Creator, his loving Father.

Showing great foresight, the *Second Vatican Council* contemplated this question over a half century ago and concluded: "Without the Creator, the creature would disappear…when God is forgotten the creature itself grows unintelligible. The ideology of the 'death of God' easily demonstrates in its effects that on the 'theoretical and practical' levels it is the ideology of the 'death of man.'"[7]

"No one has seen God at any time; the only begotten Son, who is in the *Bosom of the Father*, He has declared Him. The Deity is, therefore, ineffable and incomprehensible."
—St. John Damascene

Chapter Twenty-One

THE GRANDEUR OF THE FATHER'S LOVE

> *"I will give the victor the right to sit with me on my throne, as I myself won the victory and took my seat beside my Father on his throne." (Rv 3:21).*

"The voice of your brother's blood is crying to me from the ground!" (Gn 4:10). In the words of the first innocent man to be murdered, we find the same sorrow and the same injustice that befalls the innocent victims of today, especially the unborn child. Whether it is a single voice, or millions of voices, innocent blood *always* cries out to the Lord. It is a cry that heaven hears and a cry that our loving Father especially knows; for His love understands the sorrows of innocent blood, especially the innocent blood which flowed from the pierced side of Christ on the Cross, poured out for the forgiveness of sins (cf. Mt 26:28), poured out for the blood of Abel and poured out for the blood of the unborn children of today.

"The blood of Christ…," writes St. John Paul II, "…reveals the *grandeur of the Father's love* and shows how precious man is in God's eyes and how precious the value of his life."[1]

Precisely by contemplating the love of the Father, the love that led to the Cross, God's children come to understand our Father's love for man, especially for the innocent. Innocent blood is precious to Him; in His plan, this blood is a powerful source of hope, the hope of life over death, the hope of the *triumph of God*, our Father's coming irrepressible victory.

It is a victory that is to come into the world, for the Father, Son, and the Holy Spirit have conquered death and will conquer it again in our times, too. This is because God promises that there is a time and a judgment for everything" (Eccl 8:6), and that justice cannot be avoided: "Woe to them! For they go to the way of Cain… 'Behold, the Lord is coming with ten thousands of his holy ones, to execute judgment on all, and to convict everyone of all the deeds of ungodliness that they have committed'" (Jude 1:11, 14-15).

Throughout Scripture, God's words provide confidence in this approaching outcome, as we know and trust that the Cross has put "enmity to death" (Eph 2:16), that "death shall be no more" (Rv 21:4), that "death is swallowed up in victory" (1 Cor 5:4), for the Cross is truly the *Tree of Life*.

THE SPIRIT POINTS TO LIFE IN THE HEART OF THE FATHER

Love of God to the point of self-contempt is the path to the victory of God, to the *Triumph of the Immaculate Heart*, and to the coming demise of the great evil in our world. Now, through a coming change of hearts, the Father's divine will is to prevail.

"God is Spirit," and those who worship the Father must "worship the Father in Spirit and truth" (Jn 4:23), Christ told the Samaritan woman. According to Scripture, this worship is also what "the Father seeks" (Jn 4:23), for He desires to "pour out [his] Spirit" (Prv 1:23) on the world. It is the Spirit which the *Cate-*

chism of the Catholic Church refers to as the "finger of the Father's right hand."[2]

Throughout the history of the Church, the Holy Spirit renews mankind through love and grace in the Church's life and, consequently, in mankind and the world. These meetings *with the Spirit* always come when conflict and rebellion on the ethical plane, "by reason of that sin that takes possession of man's heart", must be "convicted by the Spirit." Scripture reveals that the desires of the flesh are against the Spirit, and the desires of the Spirit are against the flesh, but the fruits of the Spirit—love, joy, peace patience, holiness, goodness, faithfulness, gentleness, and self-control – possess the truth, which is always an exhortation to good, to life, to God, and to the promise of hope in life, something today's *culture of anti-hope* can never give in this world, yet alone forever.

Against this background, contemporary civilization is no different. The desires of the flesh always lead to suffering and defeat for humanity. Therefore, hope—brought by the Spirit who "blows where it will" (Jn 3:8), who "convicts" sin (cf. Jn 16:8), who "dwells within us" (2 Tim 1:14)—breathes life into man and renews him; the *life* of the Incarnation, the *life* of the Paschal Mystery, and *now* "the *life* of the living God, the Father of all men", as Pope Paul VI proclaimed in *Humanae Vitae*. Yes, for the Father, who is *Life*, grants and restores *life*, the life emanating from His victorious Paternal Heart.

A NEW SPRINGTIME

Seen in this light, the whole of Christian history, according to St. John Paul II, needs to be in preparation for that *new springtime* of Christian life which will be revealed through the action of the Holy Spirit; for the signs of the times reveal the God of love and mercy comes now to the aid of His Church and His children.

Indeed, God the Father – who sent His own Son in the likeness of sinful flesh and for sin, for He condemned sin in the flesh (cf. Rom 8:3) – now sends the Spirit of help to God's people in their weakness (cf. Rom 8:26), in this trying time for humanity. Along this path and through Mary, the "woman clothed with the sun" (Rv 12:1), who is the new "mother of all the living" (cf. Gn 3:20), a process of true change and growth in humanity – in both the individual and the world – is coming and can be seen at the doorstep of the world.

As can be discerned in the prophetic writings of St. John Paul II and Pope Benedict XVI, the Lord God now sounds the trumpet (cf. Zec 9:14) and the Paraclete comes; He is sent to us at this close of the age in order to bring a new epoch in time, an *Era of Peace*, as Mary promised at Fatima in 1917. In every way, the Spirit tells us now to "take courage" (Hg 2:4), for God has heard the cry of "the innocents" of our time (cf. Mt 2:16), "Rachel bewailing her children" (Mt 2:18), and will surely "turn our sorrow into joy" (Est, III, 4 C:10).

Moreover, He tells us it is time for "the hearts of God's people to be refreshed" (cf. Phlm 1:7) to be made "new" (Ez 36:26-28). And so, He now brings with Him the good news of the Lord in order to shape minds and hearts and to extend history in communion with its Father, the Creator, Lord, and Redeemer, the Father who longs to be reunited with His children, who loves us and in His mercy gives us "everlasting encouragement and good hope through his grace" (2 Thes 2:16). Thus, the Spirit invites all in their heart to cry "ABBA, Father!"

Our cry to our Father invites Him to take action to help free our hearts from our sin, and His call to us in return invites us to take action to do the same. Like Daniel, who "rejected the religion of the king" (cf. Dn 6:11), our heavenly Father calls His children to reject the lies and the deceits of this world and to "[h]ear… the

Commandments of life" (Bar 3:9), to be *alive* and to "live in the sight of God only" (1 Tim 6:33).

The majority of the world has abandoned our Father, as Jesus was abandoned in the *Garden* by the Apostles, but now with faith and trust, along with confidence in our Father and in ourselves, we are invited to return to Him, to fall into His mighty arms and "to feel our "Father's presence" (Jn 8:38), who is with us and who calls *the hearts* of His prodigal children to return to the love of His Paternal Heart.

It is the pure love of a Father that God's children will now see in a new way, the thundering movement of a mighty storm, one that will bring down the illusion of deceit that maintains the *culture of death* in order to "bring about…restoration" (Zep 2:7) in the *kingdom of life*, in the Creator of heaven and earth (cf. Rv 14:7); for through the *"living Father"* will now come the *triumph of life!*

202 *The Mystery of the Divine Paternal Heart of God Our Father*

"As a child the Father lifted me from the ground up to His *Heart*."
—St. Faustina Kowalska

Chapter Twenty-Two

THE LIVING FATHER

"Just as the Father who has life sent me and I have life because of the Father, so the man who feeds on me will have life because of me" (Jn 6:57)

*I*n our times, a growing recognition of and devotion to the Paternal Heart of God the Father holds for us a treasure of spiritual graces and blessings that the world needs in order to find a true and lasting peace, for our Father's Heart is truly a *tabernacle of peace*. Conversely, in recognizing our Father's Paternal Heart, the faithful are led to better understand that our Heavenly Father is not only *Love*, but *Life*—true *Life*, the greatest antidote for a world that has adopted a *culture of death*.

Through the Paternal Heart of the Father, the Church can find a perfect way for Christ, who is the *Way*, the *Truth*, and the *Life*, to shower His mercy and peace upon all hearts and to lead God's wayward children back to their *living* Father, who is the Father of all mankind. It is a peace, St. John Paul II wrote, that comes from the Paternal Heart of the Father, the source of the divine life from whom the Son proceeds, the Son who sits at His Father's *Right Hand*.

In his general audience of April 19, 1989, St. John Paul II explained this spiritual epiphany: "The full right to judge definitively human actions and consciences belongs to Christ as Redeemer of the world. He 'acquired' this right through the Cross. Therefore the Father "has given all judgment to the Son" (Jn 5:22). The Son, however, did not come precisely to judge, but to save; to bestow the divine life that is in him. 'For just as the Father has life in himself, so also he gave to his Son the possession of life in himself. And he gave him power to exercise judgment, because he is the Son of Man' (Jn 5:26-27). It is therefore a power that coincides with the *mercy* that flows into his *Heart*, from the *Bosom* of the Father, from whom the Son proceeds and becomes man 'for us men and for our salvation.' Christ crucified and risen, Christ who 'ascended to heaven and sits at the *right hand* of the Father.' Christ who is therefore the Lord of eternal life, towers above the world and above history as a sign of infinite love surrounded with glory, but desirous to receive from every man a reply of love in order to grant him eternal life."[1]

"ABBA," FATHER!

The Church teaches that it is through love, through the Sacraments, and through intimate conversation with God in prayer that man prepares to return to His heavenly Father (cf. 1 Pt 1:3-5). However, Scripture says that our Father seeks not only for a soul to desire to return to Him in the next life, but also *now*, in the present life, in answer to the Spirit's call for mankind to denounce sin and abide in the peace and love of the Creator. "For those who are led by the Spirit of God are children of God. For you did not receive a spirit of slavery to fall back into fear, but you received a spirit of adoption, through which we cry, 'Abba, Father!' The Spirit itself bears witness with our spirit that we are children of God, and if children, then heirs, heirs of God and joint heirs with Christ, if only we suffer with him so that we may also be glorified with him." (Rom 8:14-17).

In St. Paul's words, therefore, our Father calls His children on earth to know Him, to trust Him, to love Him, and to seek Him. In Jesus, our Father shows us Himself. Like the angels, we should desire to see the Father's face (cf. Mt 18:10). Through *Jesus' Heart*, as Pope Pius XII, St. John Paul II and Pope Benedict XVI write, humanity is shown the way to the *Father's Heart*. Moreover, through imitating and possessing Christ in our heart, we discover that we are obliged to not only seek our Father's Heart, but to know our Father's Heart, to love our Father's Heart, and to be "in" our Father's Heart. Thus, acknowledgement, belief, and action, in that order, will move us and all mankind into the Heart of the Creator.

We do this first and best by trusting Him, especially His unconditional love for us, through a deep and personal life of *prayer*, which is a genuine *dialogue of love* with the Father. St. John Paul II writes in His apostolic letter, *Novo Millennio Ineunte*, that prayer, most importantly, is the way to the Father's Heart: "Is it not one of the 'signs of the times' that in today's world, despite widespread secularization, there is *a widespread demand for spirituality*, a demand which expresses itself in large part as *a renewed need for prayer?*... The great mystical tradition of the Church of both East and West has much to say in this regard. It shows how prayer can progress, as a genuine *dialogue of love* [italics added], to the point rendering the person wholly possessed by the divine Beloved, vibrating at the Spirit's touch, resting filially within the *Father's Heart* [italics added]. This is the lived experience of Christ's promise: 'He who loves me will be loved by my Father, and I will love him and manifest myself to him' (Jn 14:21)."[2]

A LIVING FATHER

With this understanding, according to Fr. Galot, if we penetrate the Heart of Jesus in all its desires and glory, we truly realize that Christ's most ardent desire is to glorify the Father—the One who sent Him and the author of mankind's Redemption. In Scripture, we discover that "[t]he Father made himself known in his Son who came into our midst and became one of us."[3] In this way, our Father gave us "a portrait of Himself in the human face of Jesus."[4] Through Christ, while thought of as remote, we see in the truth of these words a considerable understanding of our Father. As with His Son on the Cross, the truth of our Father is to discover His proximity—the proximity of a most loving, living, and authentic Father, who is close to all His children. This is because, although possessing supreme transcendence, the Father's paternal love for us brings Him near to mankind, and is especially manifested in His providence, as He intervenes in His children's lives for all their needs."[5]

It is particularly in the Sacrament of life that "the Father gives" (Jn 6:32), that we realize everything concerning us is a concern of our Father; when we come to accept this, we discover that the Father does not dwell in an unceasable distance.[6] Rather, the Father is *truly alive*, and participates in all the events that occur in people's lives while responding to all their anxieties.[7] Yes, our Father is truly a "living Father" (Mt 26:15), a Father who "loves the living" (cf. Wis 11:24-26), a Father whom we are drawn to know, love, and adore, like Daniel, who proclaimed, "I worship the Lord, my God, for he is the living God" (Dn 14:25) and like David who confessed "my soul thirsts for God, the living God" (Ps 41:3).

Seeking to know our "living Father," then, is seeking to know the depths of Him as St. Paul wrote (cf. 1 Cor 2:10), and to know the depths of our Father is to know His passionate Heart, His living and life giving Paternal Heart. Quoting the *Catechism*, St. John Paul II writes of this truth: "Only the *Heart* [italics added] of Christ who knows the depths of his Father's love could reveal to us the abyss of his mercy in so simple and beautiful way."[8]

And only the Immaculate Heart of Mary, therefore, can best show us how much our Father now calls mankind *to* this *Abyss* of mercy, how much He calls His children to His Heart; for it was Mary that was the first to give her total fiat to the Paternal Heart of God our Father.

"The plan of the Lord stands forever, the design of his *Heart*."
(Ps 33:11)

Chapter Twenty-Three

FAVORED DAUGHTER OF THE FATHER

> *"The angel said to her, 'The Holy Spirit will come upon you, and the power of the Most High will overshadow you; therefore the child to be born will be holy; he will be called Son of God" (Lk 1:35).*

"The Holy Spirit will come upon you, and the power of the Most High will overshadow you" (Lk 1:35). With these words, Scripture reveals that the entire Trinity intervenes in the Incarnation. The word *overshadow* is part of the Old Testament vocabulary and refers to the divine presence in the tent of the assembly, rendered visible by means of a cloud which filled the tent (Ex 40:34, Nm 9:15-23).[1]

The consequence of this divine action is something still more extraordinary—the divine-virginal maternity of Mary, and the quintessential of wonders, the Incarnation of the Father's only begotten Son: "Therefore the child to be born will be called holy, the Son of God" (Lk 1:35).[2]

Mary gave her complete and free consent to this divine intervention: "Behold, I am the handmaid of the Lord. May it be done to me according to your word" (Lk 1:38). This was a consent that inspired St. Francis to proclaim Mary as "daughter and handmaid of the highest King, the Father in heaven." And with this statement, the new Eve had spoken, explicitly giving the willing participation of man, of humanity, of her humble self in the work of salvation. Her *yes* to the will of the Father was an act of love, faith and obedience. This perfect faith would be revealed and confirmed in the inspired declaration of Elizabeth, who confirms Mary is the "Mother of my Lord" (Lk 1:43).[3]

In his genealogy of Jesus, St. Matthew affirms that Jesus is the fulfillment of the promises made to Abraham and David by his use of vocabulary. Each ancestor is introduced by the verb *begot*, ending with "Jacob begot Joseph, the husband of Mary, and of her was *born* Jesus, called the Christ." Thus, St. Matthew's use of the word *born* versus *begot* refers directly to the mystery of Mary's virginal maternity and implicitly to the very divinity of Christ, whose conception is attributed to the Holy Spirit and the "Most High."[4]

In 431, the *Council of Ephesus*, summoned by the emperor, accepted the Second Letter of Cyril of Alexandria to Nestorius as its foundation, defining the mother of Christ for all time:

> The Word is said to have been begotten according to the flesh, because for us and for our salvation he united what was human to himself hypostatically and came forth from a woman. For he was not first begotten of the Holy Virgin, a man like us, and then the Word descended upon him, but from the very womb of his mother he was so united and then underwent begetting according to the flesh, making his own the begetting of his own flesh. ...So shall we find that the Holy Fathers believed. So have they dared to call the holy Virgin, Mother of God (*Theotokos*), not as though the nature of the Word or his Godhead received the origin of their being from the holy Virgin, but because there was born from her his holy body rationally ensouled, with which the Word was hypostatically united and is said to have been begotten in the flesh.[5]

THE MYSTERY OF MARY

All of this speaks of the *mystery of Mary*, who finds her significance in the light of the life and mission of Christ, who from His pre-existence in the Heart of the Father to His death on the Cross, is God and man in one Person; for this reason, Mary must be recognized as Mother of God.[6]

Mary's role as God-bearer is relevant as per the human generation of Jesus, but not the divine. The "Word" is born from Mary "according to the flesh." But Mary is the mother of God's Son, not of the Trinity. The term "God" refers only to the person of the divine Word. Mary is not considered "Mother of the Godhead." But God the Father chose her, God the Holy Spirit descended upon her, and God the Son dwelt in her. As we can see, the Holy Trinity is ever present in the mystery of Mary.[7]

It is a mystery of the *heart*, for the Immaculate Heart of Mary is at the heart of the Church, beginning with the Annunciation: "Behold, I am the handmaid of the Lord. May it be done to me according to your word" (Lk 1:38), through the Incarnation: "And Mary kept all these things, reflecting on them in her heart. Then the shepherds returned, glorifying and praising God for all they had heard and seen, just as it had been told to them" **(Lk 2:19-20),** to Calvary, foretold by the words of Simeon: "And you yourself a sword will pierce" (Lk 2:35), and ultimately fulfilled when Jesus saw His mother at the foot of the Cross and uttered the most tender and consoling words to her and His disciple, "'Woman behold, your Son.' Then he said to the disciple, 'Behold, your mother'"(Jn 19:26-27).

The anguish at Calvary possesses a dual meaning. Jesus' Redemption of mankind is undertaken and completely consummated. He is mankind's Savior and Redeemer with the works accomplished in the mysteries of the flesh. Christ's glorious death seals His coming victorious Resurrection.[8] And God permitted Mary to know and ponder these mysteries, for she "kept all these words… in her heart" (Lk 2:19).

MARY: PREDESTINED BY THE FATHER

Mary's collaboration in suffering, via all the mysteries of her life, climaxes in a series of events carried out and executed during the confusing moments of pain and sorrow on Calvary.[9] But her hope and ardent love, wholly singular by her compassion and union with her Son, is through her *faith* and *obedience* to God the Father, the foundation of a mystery that more unlocks the truth of the mystery of Mary—especially her most intimate possible bond with God the Father's saving will that is so inseparable from His divine paternal love for all mankind and, in essence, from His Divine Paternal Heart.

As was God's intention, the mystery of Calvary brings the three Hearts together. In spirit, Mary's Heart is nailed to the Cross with her Son's and the Father's Hearts. The three Hearts – united in the Son's fiat, in His pains, in His sufferings, and in His death – give birth from the Father of all mankind's Heart a new spiritual truth: Mary, the Mother of God, is the spiritual "Mother of Mankind."[10] In his encyclical letter, *Mystici Corporis*, Pope Pius XII illuminated this great truth of the faith:

> "It was she, the second Eve, who, free from sin, original or personal, and always most intimately united with her Son, offered him on Golgatha to the Eternal Father, for all the children of Adam, sin stained by his unhappy fall, and her mother's rights and her mother's love were included in the holocaust. Thus she who, according to the flesh, was the mother of our Head, through the added title of pain and glory, became according to the Spirit the Mother of all his members."[11]

OBJECT OF THE FATHER'S FAVOR

It is a "Motherhood" conceived and born at the foot of the Cross in and through Mary's Immaculate Heart, a Heart that through her powerful intercession is working to bring forth one of God's greatest triumphs: the establishment and recognition of God the Father's Divine Paternal Heart in the world – the infinite, true source of all life and peace that the world is to receive from Christ, who leads mankind back to the Father through His Mother, who leads all out of the *culture of death* into the *civilization of life*.

Mary, the new Eve, is the foretold triumphant enemy of the Serpent (cf. Gn 3:15). The New Eve is above all immaculate, predestined in her maternal mission of universal salvation. Mary is Virgin; she is Mother. She is the one whom Isaiah foretold would "conceive, and bear a son, and his name shall be called Emmanuel" (Is 7:14). He would enjoy divine attributes: "Wonder-Counselor, God-Hero, Father-Forever, Prince of Peace" (Is 9:5). It is to He whom "The Lord God" will give...the throne of his father David, and he will reign over the House of Jacob forever, and his kingdom will be no end" (Lk 1:30).[12]

God the Father, the Most High, the Lord God is He who allows Mary, the object of His favor (cf. Lk 1:30), to understand the eternal pre-existence of the Word, His origin in time, and, in essence, the truth of the trinitarian God. St. John describes the mission and nature of the Word in his Gospel, alluding to the virginal conception of Jesus "born not of blood" (cf. Jn 1:13). St. John knows the Father of Jesus is "His own Father" (Jn 5:18), and not St. Joseph.[13] Chapter twelve of *Revelation* also presents a "woman" who is about to give birth, without mentioning a father.[14] In *Galatians* 4:4, St. Paul refers to the dual origin of Jesus, the eternal origin from the *Heart of the Father*, as it is seen in the theological meaning of the word "sent" ("God *sent* His Son.").[15]

At the Annunciation, the angel "sent by God," speaks of the Trinity, a mystery, as stated, that Mary's faith did not deny. Therefore, Mary's holiness and faith—she who had been created and chosen by the Father to do His will—reflects at the Annunciation Mary's relation to the Holy Trinity, *especially* her relationship to God the Father.

FAVORED DAUGHTER OF THE FATHER

The Second Vatican Council delivers an exact summary of Mary's relationship to the Most Holy Trinity: "Redeemed by reason of the merits of her Son and united to him by a close and indissolvable tie, she is endowed with the high office and dignity of being the Mother of the Son of God, by which account she is also the beloved Daughter of the Father and the Temple of the Holy Spirit." The title *Daughter* is the most frequent title used to explain Mary's relation to God the Father.[16] It is prefigured in the Old Testament theme "Daughter of Zion." In this setting, St. Paul speaks of this divine maternity of Mary: "God *sent* His Son, born of a woman" (Gal 4:4).[17]

In the early Church, an awareness of a "bridal" relation of Mary to God the Father is recorded.[18] St. John Damascene, as cited in Pope Pius XII's encyclical letter that defines the Assumption, *Munificentissimus Deus* (1950), writes: "It was fitting that the *Spouse* whom the Father had taken to himself should live in divine mansions." Some Middle Age theologians also referred to Mary as the "Spouse of the Father" in order to illustrate that the Father chose Mary as His spouse so that she would become, together with Him, the *principal* of the Word's temporal generation – the Father's helper in the Incarnation.[19] This title was uncommon due to fear of misunderstanding that it meant Mary eternally generated the Son of God, contradicting the fact that her role remained in the temporal realm.[20]

But Mary and God the Father continued to find theological reflection. St. Louis Marie-Grignion de Montfort writes: "God the Father communicated to Mary his own fecundity in the greatest measure possible for a creature in order to give her the power to generate his Son and all the members of his Mystical Body."[21]

Through the twentieth century, Mary's spiritual relationship with God the Father was cited by numerous popes in papal records. St. John Paul II especially underlined the Trinitarian character of Marian devotion and, indeed, emphasized her title "Mother of God." He noted that it was appropriate she be understood as "Favored Daughter of the Father."[22]

THE MOTHER LEADS TO THE FATHER

The predestination of Mary to be the Mother of God – of the Incarnate Word, before the foundation of the world by the Father's will – reflects her role in the economy of salvation. It pertains to her as no other person to the order of the Hypostatic Union, for she lived in the Father's will. The grace of predestination is found in the writings of St. John that reflect her virgin birth of God (cf. Jn 1:13), her prior love of God (cf. 1 Jn 4:10), and her grace with God (cf. Lk 1:30). She is, the Second Vatican Council teaches (*LG* 61), "Mother in the order of grace." In Mary, the Holy Spirit fulfills the plans of the Father's loving goodness.[23] In her *Canticle*, Mary lifts up the thanksgiving of the whole people of God, and thus of the Church, to the Father in the Holy Spirit while carrying within her the Eternal Son.[24] Most significantly, the mystery of Mary reveals that she was chosen by God the Father before the world to be the Immaculate Virgin, Mother of the Savior God. St. Augustine, St. John Damascene, and St. Bernard all cite this reality.[25]

As the Church moved through time, the mystery of the Immaculate Conception and the Church's upholding of this truth in the

Dogma, it confirmed the glory of Mary's predestination. It is a predestination that, because of Mary's virginal maternity, makes possible the virginal body of a divine Person. Through the body of this divine Person, the critical mystery of the Redemption unfolds, along with that of the Paschal Mystery and even the unfolding plan of salvation that the Church is to embark upon in history.[26]

As it can be seen, the interconnection of the mysteries all involve the *Body of Christ*, the divine body that holds the key to so many mysteries of the faith. Through Mary's fruitful virginity, the birth, life, and death of Christ all bring the Kingdom of God upon the world; while living His words bring the truth of man's divine origin and calling, and upon death, insures that God's children can return to the *House of the Father.*

Accordingly then, it is *in* Christ's body that we *further* understand Mary's extraordinary role in fulfilling the Father's will, especially the profound mystery of the Divine Paternal Heart of God the Father.

"I need nothing but God, and to lose myself in the *Heart of God.*"
—St. Margaret Mary Alacoque

Chapter Twenty-Four

OUR LADY OF THE PATERNAL HEART

"For the Almighty has done great things for me. Holy is his name" (Lk 1:49).

As with so many of the mysteries in Christ's life, Mary's role in this mystery of the Father's Paternal Heart involves several divine truths of the faith, beginning with the Eucharist.

The key to God being with us and remaining in us is in the mystery of the Eucharist. Christ's Body and Blood become our spiritual meal, and therefore, the surest and safest way to conduct our pilgrimage in this life back to our Father. The Church has long understood that nothing could underscore the significance of Mary's virginity and how it shaped her body to be the worthy dwelling place of the Incarnate Word—whose body we celebrate and enjoy fully in the fruits of that mystery as Sacrifice and Sacrament.

As Marian theologians note, Mary made the holy Eucharist possible because she brought Christ into the world and into people's lives in the Sacramental Blessing.[1] In Christ's body, the faithful are called to share the invisible divine nature of the Eucharist.

This is a truth made possible only by Mary's fiat,[2] from which emerges a second truth in this regard that is perhaps not as visible.

As noted, the Father's divine paternal love for His Son and for His people is an essential truth to the mystery of the Eucharist, as is how the *life* contained in the Eucharist is also a life in our Father—a life emanating from His Paternal Heart that we are invited to share through the Sacrament: "Just as the living Father sent me and I have life because of the Father, so also the one who feeds on me will have life because of me" (Jn 6:57). Moreover, Christ emphasized: "[M]y Father gives you the true bread from heaven. For the bread of God is that which comes down from heaven and gives life to the world" (Jn 6:32-33). Thus, this truth of the Father and the Eucharist also bears the truth of the role of Mary in accomplishing through her body the bringing of this *Bread of Life* into the world, and the *fulfillment of the Father's will* to have His children "live forever" (Jn 6:58). For without Mary's fiat, the Father's desire to give the real *Heavenly Bread* (cf. Jn 6:32), to send the Son who "has life" (cf. Jn 6:57) because of the Father who "has life" (cf. Jn 6:57), would not have occurred and, consequently, it is evident that Mary plays an essential role in the mystery of the Eucharist in fulfilling the Father's will in this regard.[3] In truth, Mary's fiat to the Father's will is a *dual fiat* because it allows the coming of Christ into the world, in addition to permitting the coming of the Eucharist – the coming of the Father's *Sacrament of Life* into the world.

Additionally, this truth provides a more profound understanding to the words of the *Our Father*. For when we pray to the Father "to give us our daily bread," we are asking for not only earthly replenishment, but also the *Bread of Life* that our Father gives the world in the Sacrament of Life, the Eucharist, which is his *life* sent into the world through Christ, the *stamp of the Father* formed *in* and born *of* the Virgin Mary.

MARY AND "SEEING THE FATHER"

"Whoever has seen me has seen the Father" (Jn 14:9). With these words, Christ explains that we can see His Father, our Father, in Him, as He said in reply to St. Philip's plea to "show us the Father" (Jn 14:8). Subsequently, Scripture reveals that Christ repeatedly asserts this truth:

-"If you know me, you will also know my Father" (Jn 14:7).

-"I am in the Father and the Father is in me...The Father who dwells in me is doing his works" (Jn 14:10).

-"[Y]ou, Father, are in me and I am in you" (Jn 17:21).

These Scriptural passages reveal a subtle, yet undeniable truth of this mystery. And like the truth of the mystery of the Eucharist, it is found in Mary. In the Incarnate Christ, both human and divine, lies again the reality that because of Mary's virginal maternity—which makes *possible* the virginal body of a divine Person—we are able to recognize the Person of the Father *in* the Son. St. John Paul II stated, "He who sees me sees the Father. The New Testament is completely marked by the light of this Gospel truth. The Son is the reflection of the Father's glory, and he is 'the very imprint of his being' (Heb 1:3). He is the "image of the invisible God" (Col 1:15).[4] He is the "epiphany of God" (*the Father*).[5]

This means that within the Incarnate Christ, conceived and born of Mary, lies the *"complete revelation of the Father"* that, according to Christ, allows us to *"see"* the Father, for He is "one with the Father." Seeing the Father through Christ, whom Mary conceived and bore, is not an inconsequential truth. It is an essential expression of the revealed unity of the Father and the Son, a unity only made possible by Mary's role in the mystery. This truth appears to be noted by St. Francis de Sales, who in his book, *Intro-*

duction to the Devout Life, writes, "Honor, reverence and respect with a special love for the sacred and glorious Virgin Mary. She is the Mother of our sovereign Father and consequently she is our own mother in a special way."[6]

Indeed, this epiphany of the Father, this reality of the image of the Father in Christ, finds its conception and fulfillment in Mary. This is because Mary's fiat allows us *to see* the Father in the Incarnate Christ; without the role of Mary, this truth would not have been manifested. In an indirect, but nevertheless profound way, this truth additionally emphasizes and illuminates Mary's dignity as *Mother of God*, our *Theotokos*.

THE MYSTERY OF THE IMMACULATE HEART, THE SACRED HEART AND THE PATERNAL HEART

Through Mary's role in the Incarnation of Christ, we also come to contemplate her undeniable participation in our understanding and recognition of the truth of God the Father's Divine Paternal Heart.

Like many mysteries of the faith, Christ's Sacred Heart would be impossible without Mary, whom through her fiat, brought the Incarnation of the Son and therefore the Incarnation of His Sacred Heart. The enormity of this reality is *twofold*.

The Church has long maintained that the mystery of the Father's great love and mercy is symbolized and understood through the Sacred Heart. Thus, from a theological perspective, can a divine Heart be attributed to the Father without the Son's Incarnation, which brought forth the full truth of His Sacred Heart?

As previously stated, according to the Fathers and Church doctrine, the Son cannot possess a divine attribute unless the Father *first* possesses a divine attribute, since the Church holds that they are of the same divine nature and that "all divine attributes must first be possessed in the divinity of the Father, who derives nothing outside of himself." As St. John Damascene writes, "unless the Father possesses a certain attribute, neither the Son nor the Spirit possesses it."

Therefore, the Father's Divine Paternal Heart, though *completely divine* in nature, essentially owes its *recognition* to Mary's unique role. If Christ's Sacred Heart had not become Incarnate, His Heart's *divine nature* would not be seen, understood, and acknowledged; therefore, it would not be possible for *the Father's* Divine Heart to be seen, understood, and acknowledged.

Assuredly, this does not mean that Mary in any way contributes to the *divine nature* of the Father's Heart anymore than she does to the divine nature of the Son's Heart. However, it does assert that because of Mary's pure Immaculate Heart—which rendered her humble fiat to the Father's will—the faithful are able *to discover, understand, and see the truth of Our Father's Paternal Heart*, made visible in the recognition of the Son's Sacred Heart, which the Church holds is both human and divine. As St. Irenaeus expressed concisely, "The invisible reality of the Son was the Father, and the visible reality of the Father was the Son" (Adv. Haer. IV, 6, 6).

Thus, for our purposes, if to see the fullness of Christ is to see the fullness of the Father, then to see the Sacred Heart is to see the Paternal Heart; for one cannot be without the other and neither could be apprehended without the role of Mary, *Our Lady of the Paternal Heart*, who affected the perfect union of the two natures by her fiat, and therefore made visible to us the invisible Heart of the Father through the visible Heart of her Son, Jesus.

"Eternal Wisdom began to manifest Himself outside the *Bosom of His Father* where He dwelt from eternity, when He made light, heaven and earth.."
—St. Louis de Montfort

Chapter Twenty-Five

THE TRIUMPH OF THE IMMACULATE HEART

"Now a great sign appeared in heaven: A woman adorned with the sun standing on the moon, and with twelve starts on her head for a crown (Rv 12:1).

For centuries now, the most Holy Trinity has been sending the Virgin Mary to prepare for the approaching times. This is because the dream of the ages is the restoration of the Father's children through Christ to Him in the fullness of time, and Mary has prepared her children for this step.

At Guadalupe, at Rue du Bac, Lourdes and Pontmain, and especially at Fatima and many places around the world, Mary's name is heard.[1] She calls to her children to see if they are ready to come home to their Father. Peace, prayer, fasting, penance and a conversion of heart are her words of encouragement to her children.[2] She talks to them, and she prays with them. She cautions, she nudges, she warns – all in hope, and all in her preparation for mankind to come to her Son, who is ready to lead all back to the Father.

Her plan is the Father's plan, the plan for God's lambs to graze in the pasture of their Father and for them to feed upon His love (cf. Is 5:17). Thus, Mary gathers and prepares all of God's children to reconcile with their Father. No longer should humanity be wandering in the dark, lost forever. Like a bridal bouquet of bright, vibrant colors and scents, we are called to come ready, fully blossomed, to the wedding feast. We are called to be transformed in God's light and love, immersed in His powerful mercy and brought into a new time – into the paradise of the Father's *Divine Will*, when heaven and earth will touch. It is to be the *time of the Father* – the fulfillment of the promise of *Our Lady of Fatima*.

FATIMA

Fatima – the Triumph of the Immaculate Heart of the Mother foretold there in 1917 – descends upon the world. Fatima, and its great miracle of the sun, leads to a renewed world according to many writers. As St. John Paul II so boldly proclaimed in his message of hope, "the threshold to the Father" is to now be crossed.[3]

Mary, the Queen of heaven and earth, is preparing for mankind to return to God both individually and collectively through Fatima. The graces and the words of hope she brings are an ocean of mercy that will permit mankind to be subsumed in the love of God, in His dawning *civilization of love*. Through such love, the *culture of death* cannot survive. That which is *of* the Father is *in* the Father. That which is not remains separated. But it is God's plan, through Mary's Immaculate Heart, to now invite all to Him, and for all her children to move in the direction of their Father.

The Church is the light which pierces the darkness in these times; it forever stands high and above the crowds, the chaos, and the din of the world. The Church is there to be seen – ready to release all from the vice, which is the culture of the world today. Mary's words then are given by heaven to seep into the hardest of hearts in order to lead God's children back home – back to the Heart of their Father – through the Church and its many gifts. But each must embrace the great pearl, which is the wonderful gift of choice.

JOSHUA CHOSE GOD

"But as for me and my household, we will serve the Lord" (Jos 24:15).

The words of Moses' successor, Joshua, are immortal and relevant for every generation of believers; they stand before us again today as bold as the man who uttered them centuries ago. They reveal to us not only God's call and our need to answer, but also the fact that our answer is immersed in our gift of free will – our constant invitation by God to choose the priceless gift of choice to return to Him.

Like Joshua, we must now choose God, our Father. We must say *yes*, in our minds and our will, to His will and reverse forever the mistake in Eden: the wrong choice that Christ already has paid for on the Cross by opening the Kingdom of our Father to us.

In Eden, the *choice* preceded the act; we recall how our first parents, deceived by the enemy, separated themselves through their own free will from the Father's will and thus separated us too from the fullness of our Father and from His original plan for all His children. Since then, life on earth for every human being has been contained and guided in a series of choices, some right and some not. And as with Adam and Eve, our choices are always subject to the influence of the *Deceiver* as we try to make our way back to our Father and His Kingdom safely.

As with Joshua, who God always prepared for battle, Mary and all of heaven have prepared and guided the moment at hand – the moment of the great choice for mankind. In essence, we must say *no* to the enemy in our lives in a sure and safe way. We must say no to him as individuals, as nations, and as people of God. And we must say *yes* to God, to our Father, in the way He desires to hear the most.

Returning to our Father, we see then, is a two-fold process. It is to be a duel effort on our part: First, we must continually rebuff and reject the efforts of the Evil One, stop his influence in our life and our choices, and grow in the divine life through prayer, Mass and the Sacraments.

Second, we must recognize our need to lovingly call and invite our Eternal Father back into our personal lives and our world. We must invite Him back into our lives through an individual act of consecration to Him, and we must invite Him back into our world in a special way by honoring Him.

THE LAST CRUSADE

Like David's sling shot and the five stones kept in his bag, the greatest weapon to defeat the enemy in our lives is Mary's *Rosary*, which contains the twenty mysteries of Christ's love for mankind as revealed in His life. Each of these mysteries begins with an *Our Father*, followed by ten appeals to Mary for her to step on the enemy's head, five stones to be fired at the "Father of Lies;" and ten declarations of faith in our Queen of Peace that give her the power to form and tighten the chain that is to bind him forever.

Indeed, a worldwide *Rosary Crusade*, the last crusade, is now needed by mankind to crush the evil in our lives and the world.[4] For the Rosary is heaven's preferred weapon, given to us for our protection and for our deliverance from the powers of darkness. This call to the Rosary is not to exclude the many other divine gifts the Church provides for our spiritual safety to help us win the war that mankind has been immersed in since Eden. All prayers, as well as other spiritual gifts – holy water, medals, scapulars, and acts of consecration and deliverance – are sacred possessions to aid in this crusade too. But the Rosary, Our Lady of Fatima's chosen prayer that will bind the Evil One forever, is her weapon "of choice" to bring God's victory.

And perhaps a famous painting tells us why.

MICHAELANGELO'S LAST JUDGEMENT

On the wall of the Sistine Chapel, Michelangelo's *Last Judgement* is an awe-inspiring yet intimidating painting of the power and glory of God. Completed in the year 1541, its newly refurbished finish proclaims the story of salvation like no other.[5]

Coming at a time of crisis in the Church, the painting was a message from Michelangelo to the Bishops and Cardinals who first met at the Council of Trent in 1545. Their task was to initiate the counter-Reformation which would solidify the Church's doctrines and teachings. And all around them, they found in Michelangelo's work the inspiration to do so.

Most significantly, the *Last Judgement* incorporated in its visual message those doctrines that forever imprinted the Church's position on Mary, the Mother of God and the honor given to her as such. Indeed, Michelangelo's great fresco showed that Mary is forever at the side of her Son, reigning as heaven's Queen and earth's model of discipleship. Michelangelo's painting expressed the depth of this message; he painted a huge Rosary hanging down over the ramparts of heaven, on which two souls can be seen grasping and pulling their way into Paradise. No message through word or image better tells us how important the Rosary is in the lives of the faithful. Heaven has been calling souls to understand and implement this mystery of salvation for centuries.[6]

THE MIRACULOUS WORKS OF THE ROSARY

The prayer of the Rosary is said to have begun in the year 1214, when the Virgin Mary appeared to St. Dominic and presented it to him as a powerful means of converting the Albigensians and others in need of grace.[7]

While some dispute the origination of the Rosary with St. Dominic, five Popes have credited him with its founding.[8] Although its full history is somewhat a mystery, the accounts of its numerous successes are not. Just thirty years after the Council of Trent's initial meeting, a greatly outnumbered force of Christian defenders held off a Turkish invasion on October 7, 1571.[9] It was considered a miraculous victory brought about specifically through the Rosary, for St. Pius V's Rosary Crusade united all of Europe in prayer. From this, the *Feast of the Most Holy Rosary* was established in 1573 and is still celebrated to this day on October 7th.

Even before the battle of Lepanto, the Rosary was credited with bringing a miraculous victory in 1474 to the city of Cologne, which was under attack by Bergundian Troops.[10] After Lepanto, another victory over the Turks at Peterwarde in Hungary by Prince Eugene on August 5, 1716 – the Feast of Our Lady of the Snows – led Pope Clement XI to extend the Feast of the most Holy Rosary to the Universal Church.[11]

By the nineteenth century, the miraculous favors credited to the Rosary were so numerous, that Popes began to recognize the Rosary as an institution within the Catholic Church. During his twenty-five year reign (1878 – 1903), Pope Leo XIII wrote twelve encyclicals regarding the Rosary and its devotion. Pope Leo especially attempted to use the Rosary to bring unity to the Church. His writings also "officially" credited the Rosary with the Church's victories of the past.[12]

THE TRIUMPH OF THE IMMACULATE HEART

In her last apparition at Fatima, on October 13, 1917, the Virgin Mary told the children that she was **"Our Lady of the Rosary"**. Appearing with the Rosary in her right hand and Scapular in her left, the Virgin invoked the memory of what she told St. Dominic centuries before – "one day the Rosary and Scapular will save the world."[13]

And that day is today. Beginning with her apparitions at Rue Du Bac, Paris in 1830 all the way until the present, the modern era of Mary and her "Rosary Crusade' is evident. From Lourdes in 1858 – where she called for penance and the Rosary – to Pontmain on January 17, 1871 – where the children reported the image of Mary in the sky grew when the people prayed the Rosary – Mary has continuously invoked the Rosary in almost all of her apparitions.[14]

Foretelling a troubling future for the entire world at Fatima, the Queen of the most Holy Rosary made it clear; the Rosary would be the solution to a world living in this dark and perilous age. At Fatima, she said that a critical time in the history of the world was coming, a time when "annihilation" could be just moments away.[15] But through prayer, through the Rosary, Mary also promised that "in the end her Immaculate Heart would triumph" and an 'era of peace" would be granted to the world.

A TRIUMPH OF LOVE AND LIFE

Since the time of the Apostles, there has been an intimate bond between the presence of Mary and the action of the Church. God sends Mary, the Mother of Mercy, before the judgment so that she may intercede for all sinners and carry all of the Father's children in her Immaculate Heart. As St. Anselm of Canterbury writes, "God (*the Father*) is the Father of created things, and Mary the Mother of recreated things. God is the Father of the constitution of all, and Mary is the Mother of the restitution of all. God (*the Father*) generated him through who all things are made, and Mary bore him through all things that are saved."[16] Therefore, Mary, who carried God in her womb, is connected to all His children through her divine maternity. It is a role God the Father now wishes the Mother continue and extend by bringing the truth of His Divine Paternal Heart to all His children.

As the Holy Spirit helps to bring fulfillment to the Church's recognition of a fifth dogmatic truth concerning Mary's role in our salvation, the Lady of the Rosary – through her children's fiats – continues to marshal the prayers of God's children, distributing graces throughout the world so God's will is done on earth as it is in heaven. The Holy Spirit works in and through God's chosen *remnant*, so that the Father's plan for all mankind is realized.

Mary, Daughter of the Father's Heart, leads His children home. Through her counsel and protection, Jesus' good news triumphs over the woes and sorrows inflicted by the Evil One. Mary, tucked deep inside the hearts of the Father's children, whispers and guides them along – home to their Father. She is with each always. She stands at the foot of the cross of her children as they offer their sacrifices to the Paternal Heart of the Father, where He hears their cries, their fiats, and announces that it is time; time for our Father, who is *Love*, to come down to rescue His children; time for our Father, who is *Forgiveness*, to bathe the world in His mercy; time for our Father, who is *Justice*, to end the *culture of death* and bring the *civilization of life*. It is time for the *Mother of Life* to return God's children to the *Father of Life*.

Most of all, it is time for there to be peace in this world, "the peace of God that surpasses all understanding," (Phil 4:7) the fullness of *Shalom*! It is a peace that cannot be denied by the Father, for the Mother's Heart has asked for it. Her heart is the portal of peace. As Arnold of Chartres, a disciple and friend of St. Bernard, wrote in the seventeenth century, "What the Mother asks, the Son approves, and the Father grants" (cf. *De septem verbis Doini in cruce*, 3:PL 189, 1694).

Thus, like the Sacred Heart of the Son, the Paternal Heart of the Father is, in essence, mystically revealed by the role of the Mother. It is revealed by the eternal fiat of her Immaculate Heart, by her tireless good deeds brought to light, and now by her wondrous *Triumph of Love and Life* – a triumph that will see God's prodigal children answer their Father's call to return to the peace of His Paternal Heart, His call to "rest in my Bosom" (Sg 1:13).

It is to be the crowning moment in the fulfillment of the Queen of Peace's "time of visitation" (cf. Lk 19:44), brought about by the infinite graces bestowed by God upon the world through her Immaculate Heart![17]

Part VI

Temples of God

"The Lord has sought out a man after his own *Heart* and has appointed him to rule over his people" (1 Sm 13:14).

Chapter Twenty-Six

DAVID: A MAN AFTER GOD'S OWN HEART

"But the Lord said to Samuel: "Do not judge from his appearance or from his lofty stature, because I have rejected him. Not as man sees does God see, because man sees the appearance but the Lord looks into the heart" (1 Sm 16:7).

It was known as Solomon's Temple. With construction starting around 970 BC, the Temple was one of the most impressive buildings of antiquity. For centuries, it housed the *Ark of the Covenant*, which contained the restored tablets of the *Law* given by God to Moses. But although Solomon built the Temple, God inspired his father, David, to create and design it. And David gathered the wealth of his people to build it, for it was his heart's desire that God's presence be honored in a great house of worship.

David—the shepherd, the boy who slew Goliath and "tens of thousands," who played his harp and was anointed by the prophet Samuel as King of Israel—is today viewed as a biblical figure of almost mythical proportions. His Hebrew name means "prince," or "beloved one." His ancestry places him as an Ephrathite of Bethlehem in Judah, the youngest and eigth son of his father, Jesse. Among his noted accomplishments include unification of the twelve tribes of Israel into one nation, the establishment of Jerusalem as the capital, and the conquest of the Philistines, Edomites, Moabites, and Ammonites.[1] Along with being King of Israel for forty years, David is known as a deeply religious man, a shrewd politician, a brave soldier, a skillful musician, and a prophet, as he foretells the Messiah in his acclaimed *Psalms*, or "hymns of praise."[2] But most of all, he is heralded as God's *"chosen"* one, whose lineage lead to Christ. He was *"chosen,"* according to Scripture, because he was a "man after God's own Heart."

From Abraham and Moses to Peter and Paul, the Old and New Testaments present many chosen souls who fulfilled God's will in their lives through great faith. They were souls who answered the call of the Lord to take action. All are remembered and celebrated for their love of God and obedience to Him. But only David is called a "man after God's own Heart." Samuel told the insubordinate King Saul after God decided to replace him with David, "The Lord has sought out a man after his own *Heart* [italics added] and has appointed him to rule over his people…" (1 Sm 13:14).

What does it mean that David was a man after God's Heart? Theologians conjecture that David was chosen by God because the Lord knew his heart (cf. 1 Sm 16:7), a heart filled with a great love for his God and fellow man. It was a heart that followed the ways of God's Heart, one that was faithful, merciful, and humble. We find proof of this truth in David's actions and his words.

THE HEART OF DAVID

David's life reflects his understanding of God. Confronted with the giant Goliath, the young David knows the Lord is trustworthy and will protect him: "The Lord who delivered me from the paw of the lion and the paw of the bear, will deliver me from the hand of this Philistine" (1 Sm 17:37). Given the opportunity to kill King Saul, his betrayer and nemesis, David knows that only God has the right to determine the fate of a chosen one: "I will not raise a hand against my lord, for he is the Lord's anointed and a *father* [italics added] to me" (1 Sm 24:12). And when crushed by guilt from his own adultery with Bathsheba and the murder of her husband Uriah, David repents, humbles himself, and surrenders to the mercy of God in his time of disgrace: "I have sinned against the Lord" (2 Sm 12:13).

Likewise, David's words in Scripture reveal his love for the Lord. It is a love of the heart that permits him to have great faith in God's will for him and Israel, and to possess a supreme confidence in the Lord's goodness:

- " I love you, O Lord, my strength" (Ps 18:1).

- "I delight to do your will, O God; your law is within my heart" (Ps 40:8).

- "My heart and my flesh sing for joy to the living God" (Ps 84:2).

- "Towards the faithful you are faithful; toward the wholehearted you are *wholehearted* [italics added]" (2 Sm 22:26).

- "But know that the Lord has set apart the faithful for himself; the Lord hears when I call to him" (Ps 4:3).

- "I will give thanks to the Lord with my whole heart; I will tell of all your wonderful deeds" (Ps 9:1).

- "From heaven the Lord looks down and observes the children of Adam, from his dwelling place he surveys all who dwell on earth. The One who fashioned together their hearts is the One who knows all their works" (Ps 33:13-15).

A FATHER WHO HAS A HEART

David's actions and words reveal two realities. First, David knew the God of Israel was foremost a God of *truth* and *love*, and a *faithful* God that desired His chosen people to come to see His plan for them. David saw that it was a plan that came from God's *Heart*, the great symbol in Scripture of His divine love:

> "But the plan of the Lord stands forever, the design of his *Heart* [italics added] through all generations. Blessed is the nation whose God is the Lord, the people chosen as his inheritance" (Ps 33:11-12).

Secondly, David understood that God wanted His people to come to know and trust in Him like they would a Father—that is, as the divine *Head* of the family of Israel:

> "Blessed may you be, O Lord, God of Israel, our *Father* [italics added], from eternity to eternity. Yours, O Lord, are grandeur and power, majesty, splendor and glory. For all in heaven and on earth is yours; yours O Lord, is the sovereignty; you are exalted as *Head* [italics added] overall" (1 Chr 29:10-11).

MOSES AND DAVID

A father is the cornerstone of a family because of his paternal love for all its members. With this truth in mind, David knew God's faithfulness to Israel stemmed from His Fatherly love for His chosen people. David realized that Israel's God, therefore, was a different kind of God—one never seen before in the ancient world. Unlike the silent idols of stone and wood, God was a *living God* (cf. Ps 42:2) to David, whose love for His children was strong, committed, and forever.

This was not a new revelation. Moses understood that God was a Father to Israel. God's words to Egypt's pharaoh reveal this truth: "Israel is my son, my firstborn. I have said to thee: Let my son go, that he may serve me" (Ex 4:22-23). It was a divine paternity that Moses stressed to his people: "Is not he your Father, who created you, who made you and established you" (Dt 32:6)? Moses knew God's love too, the *everlasting, steadfast* love of His Fatherly Heart. As with God's paternity, Moses emphasized this truth to Israel: "The Lord has set his *Heart* [italics added] on you and chose you because the Lord loves you" (cf. Dt 7:7-11).

In examining his life closely, David's actions and words in Scripture reveal that he *personally* understood what Moses tried to get Israel to see: God was a *Father* who loved him with all His *Heart*. Thus, the God of Abraham, Isaac and Jacob, the God of Moses and his father Jesse, became David's sacred *refuge*. He became David's *intimate* Lord, forever at his side through trial, tribulation, joy, and sorrow: "You kept track of my every toss and turn through the night. Each tear registered in your ledger, each ache written in your Heart" (Ps 56:8).[3] Indeed, whether in the *valley of the shadow of death* (cf. Ps 23:4) or escaping the *deadly spear of King Saul* (cf. 1 Sm 18:10-11), David trusted in his Lord. God was his "*Rock*", as Moses described Him (cf. Dt 32:4). He is "the Rock," David wrote, "of my heart" (Ps 73:26).

David was God's *rock*, too. He was the rock God *wanted* to build upon—the rock where His house and His kingdom would "endure and stand firm forever" (cf. 2 Sm 7:16). No words describe better God's love for David than those found in the post-exilic psalm composed by different sources:

> "I have chosen David, my servant;
> with my holy oil I have anointed him.
> My hand will be with him;
> my arm will make him strong.

No enemy shall outwit him,
nor shall the wicked defeat him.
I will crush his foes before him,
strike down those who hate him.
My faithfulness and mercy will be with him,
through my name his
horn will be exalted.
I will set his hand upon the sea,
his right hand upon the rivers.
He shall cry to me, 'You are my *Father* [italics added],
my God, the Rock of my salvation!'
I myself make him the firstborn,
most high over the kings of the earth.
Forever I will maintain my mercy for him,
my covenant with him stands firm.
I will establish his dynasty forever,
his throne as the days of
heaven" (Ps 89:21-30).

Over time, David's reality of Israel's mighty God made him a man with a mission. In his heart, he became determined to find the best way to bring honor and glory to his fortress and deliverer (cf. 2 Sm 22:2), his sovereign Father (cf. 2 Chr 5:7).

This is because David lived in the Father's Heart – and the Father lived in his.

"The Son lives by the Father, because He is the Word given forth from the *Heart of the Father*, because He comes forth from the Father, because He is begotten of the bowels of the Father, because the Father is the fountain and the root of the Son's Being."
—St. Ambrose

Chapter Twenty-Seven

THE HEART OF SOLOMON

"Give your servant, therefore, an understanding heart to judge your people and to distinguish right from wrong" (1 Kgs. 3:9).

From childhood, Scripture reveals that the Lord was faithful to David and guided his life and Israel's fate forward (cf. 1 Sm 17:37). After becoming King, David's love for his God led him to want the whole world – "all the kings of the earth" (cf. Ps 138:4) – to come to know his God. This was because David believed that the *one true God* deserved honor and glory—not just from Israel, but from all mankind:

> "Sing to the Lord, all the earth!
>
> Tell of his salvation from day to day.
>
> Declare his glory among the nations,
>
> his marvelous works among all the peoples!
>
> For great is the Lord, and greatly to be praised,
>
> And he is to be held in awe above all gods. For all the gods of the peoples are idols;
>
> but the Lord made the heavens.

> Honor and majesty are before him;
> Strength and joy are in his place" (1 Chr 16:23-27).

Motivated by the fact that God's dwelling place on earth, the *Ark of the Covenant*, was woefully inadequate in a tent or pavilion (cf. 1 Chr 17:5)—and a personal embarrassment to David in lieu of the grandness of the home the Lord had given him (cf. 1 Chr 17:1)—David informed the prophet Nathan that he hoped to correct this injustice by "building a house" to "honor" the Lord (cf. 1 Chr 17:12, 2 Chr 5:7).

Through Nathan, Scripture reveals that God favors David's desire to build a home for Him: "Go, do all that you have in mind: for the Lord is with you" (2 Sm 7:3). It is a desire that God knows comes from David's heart which is entirely with the Lord (cf. 1 Kg 11:4). It is a heart consumed by the love God has for him (cf. Ps 84:3). David's words say no less of this epiphany of his soul:

> "For your servant's sake, and according to your own *Heart* [italics added], You have brought about this entire magnificent disclosure to your servant" (2 Sam 7:21).

THE GREAT TEMPLE OF JERUSALEM

United in *heart* with God, David goes forward with preparations to build God's house. From the start, the Temple is intended by David to become the focus of the worship of God throughout the entire nation of Israel and to attract the eyes of the world. Consequently, David plans an impressive and beautiful Temple in Jerusalem, one that would reflect Israel's God was the one and only true God:

> "The house that is to be built for the Lord must be exceedingly magnificent, famous and glorified throughout all lands" (1 Chr 22:5).

This story unfolds in the Books of *Samuel* and *Kings*, and the author of the *Chronicles* is especially interested in how the centralization of worship at the Temple in Jerusalem is the key to better understanding the unfolding of God's revelation to the Jews through time.[1]

The *Second Book of Chronicles* (cf. 2 Chr 3:1) speaks of the revelation to King David of the site in Jerusalem upon which the Temple of the Lord is to be constructed.[2] It is to be placed on Mt. Moriah, the spot upon which the faithful Abraham—who, like Moses and David, recognized and knew God as a Father, "I have sworn to the Lord, God Most High, maker of heaven and earth" (Gn 14:22) and who knew God's Heart, "And I will set a morsel of bread, and strengthen your Heart" (Gn 18:5)—prepared to sacrifice his son Isaac (cf. Gn 22:2).

The location had also been the threshing floor of Ornan—where David encountered the Angel who was poised to exterminate the people of Jerusalem because of David's sin—and the site of David's altar upon which he made holocausts and peace offerings to the Lord to seek relief from the plague (cf. 2 Sm 24).[3]

GOD CHOOSES SOLOMON

But although the Lord acquiesces in principle to David's longing to build a temple for Him, he instructs him that a future son to be named Solomon is who He has chosen to do so: "A son is to be born to you…his name shall be Solomon…he shall build a house for my name…" (1 Chr 22:9-10).

God chooses Solomon for a reason. Like David, God predestines Solomon, who He reveals "will be like a son," and that "He will never stop loving" (cf. 1 Chr 17:13). And as he comes of age, God acknowledges Solomon's love for Him and his desire to serve Him (cf. 1 Kgs 3:3).

The name of Solomon means "beloved by Yahweh" or "peaceful." He was the youngest son of King David and Bathsheba. In addition to his wisdom, he is remembered for his writings, including his poems and proverbs. He is also known for his wealth, wives, commercial success, and magnificent buildings, including palaces and other structures. Solomon reigned as King of Israel, like his father David, for forty years. But most significantly, Solomon is remembered for constructing the great *Temple of Jerusalem*.

THE HEART OF SOLOMON

The *Book of Kings* states that Solomon deeply desired to fulfill his father David's wishes for the Temple. This was not only because of his love for the Lord, but because he wanted to honor David's decrees: "Solomon loved the Lord, walking in the statutes of his father David" (1 Kgs 3:3). Moreover, it appears that Solomon desired to be like David in another way: to have a "heart that was entirely with the Lord" (cf.1 Kg 11:4), a heart after "God's Heart" (cf. 1 Sm 13:14), and to have his father David's "heart of wisdom" (Ps 90:12). David himself told Solomon that it was important for him to serve the Lord with "a *whole heart* [italics added] and a willing soul, for the Lord searches all hearts" (1 Chr 28:9), as he did in choosing David to be king (cf. 1 Sm 16:7).

In Solomon's memorable reply to God in Scripture, who told Solomon to ask for something of Him that would be granted (cf. 1 Kgs 3:5), he essentially asks God for a special grace, one that recalls to mind the reason God chose his father David and remained faithful to him. He asks God to anoint his *"heart"* in order for him to carry on in the tradition of David (1 Kgs 3:6).

Indeed, Solomon desired to be a good king in the eyes of God and for the sake of his chosen people (cf. 1 Kgs 3:7-8). Consequently, knowing his father's "heart" was the reason God chose David to be King (cf. 1 Sm 16:7)—as well as knowing David remained in

God's favor because he "faithfully" followed his "upright heart" (cf. 1 Kgs 3:6-8)—Solomon asks God to grace his "*heart*" too in a special way: "Give your servant, therefore, an understanding *heart* [italics added] to govern your people and to distinguish right and wrong" (1 Kgs. 3:9).

In Solomon's words, we find that the gift he requested from God is not just an enhancement of his *mind*, as often assumed, but rather a bestowment of a special grace upon his *heart*, which is the source of the love within him; this is reflected in his obedience and *faith* in God and in his desire to do *good* for his people (cf. 1 Kg 3:7-9). In God's response to Solomon, we find that He answers his prayer in a way that corresponds to this desire: "I do what you have asked," God replied to Solomon, "I will give you a wise and discerning *heart* [italics added], so that there will never have been anyone like you …" (1 Kgs 3:12).

WISDOM OF THE HEART

The greatest attribute of God is His love—the love of *His* Heart working in *our* hearts—for it breathes joy into our souls and truth into our minds. Consequently, as with both David and Solomon, it can be seen that God bestows His graces on those that He sees are led by love and those who know that God *is* love. David knew that Israel's God was a God of love (cf. Ps 37:28), as did his son, Solomon, whose words echo his father's: "O Lord, God of Israel, there is no God like thee, in heaven above or on earth beneath, keeping covenant and showing *steadfast love* [italics added] to thy servants who walked before thee with all their heart…" (1 Kgs. 8:23-24).

David and Solomon were essentially guided by *hearts* that sought to capture "divine truth" through the prism of love and to acquire a "wisdom of the heart." The *Book of Sirach* states, "Happy is the person who meditates on wisdom and reasons intelligently, who reflects in his heart on her ways and ponders her secrets" (Sir 14:20-21).

Indeed, from Joseph in Egypt—centuries before Solomon—who Pharaoh saw was gifted in a divine way, "Since *God* [italics added] has shown you all this, no one can be as wise and discerning as you" (Gn 41:39), to Daniel in Babylon—centuries after Solomon—who King Belshazzar acknowledged had "God-like wisdom" (cf. Dn 5:11), Scripture shows how numerous souls have been led by the love of God and their fellow man in their hearts.

Wisdom of the heart, in essence, is divine wisdom. The author of *Ecclesiastes* tells us that divine wisdom is acquired through love: "I applied my *heart* to know wisdom" (Eccles 8:16). It is then nurtured through obedience in the ways of the Lord: "So teach us to number our days that we may get a heart of wisdom" (Ps 90:12). Scripture teaches that this begins with a fear of the Lord (Sir 1:12, Ps 111:10) and matures into a source of happiness for the man who relishes God's truth and whose mind "ponders wisdom in his heart" (cf. Sir 14:20).

The *Epistle of James* explains why God's wisdom is based on love: "wisdom from above is first of all innocent. It is also peaceable, lenient, docile, rich in sympathy, and the kindly deeds that are its fruits, impartial and sincere" (Jas 3:17). It is a "wisdom that is vindicated," the *Gospel of Luke* states, "by all who accept it" (cf. Lk 7:3).

It is not surprising that God sought to work through Solomon's heart, like with his father, David, for it is the way God desires to work in His children. This is confirmed in Solomon's own *Proverbs*, which proclaim that God's Spirit of truth and wisdom works best through faith and love and *not* one's intelligence: "Trust in the Lord with all your heart, on your own intelligence rely not…

be not wise in your own eyes" (Prv 3:5-7), for "wisdom will enter your heart" and "knowledge will please your soul" (Prv 2:10).

WISDOM OF THE WORLD

Scripture emphasizes the folly of the mind that acts separate from the heart. This is known as the "wisdom of the world" or the "wisdom of the flesh, which is the "enemy of God" (cf. Rm 8:7). This is the wisdom that Eve first desired in the Garden of Eden; "the woman saw the food was good...desirable for gaining wisdom" (Gn 3:6).

In his *First Letter to the Corinthians*, St. Paul's words allude to how human wisdom without God can be deceiving: "My speech and my message were not in plausible *words of wisdom*, [italics added], but in demonstration of the Spirit and power, that your faith might not rest in the wisdom of men but in the power of God" (1 Cor 2:4-5). Farther on in his message to the Church in Corinth, Paul proceeds to elaborate more on the trappings of worldly wisdom: "Let no one deceive himself. If any one among you considers himself wise in this age, let him become a fool so as to become wise. For the wisdom of this world is foolishness in the eyes of God, for it is written: 'He catches the wise in their own ruses,' and again, 'The Lord knows that the thoughts of the wise, that they are vain'" (1 Cor 3:18-20).

Christ addressed this truth when He dismissed the "wise of the world" in favor of the "humble of heart," for such souls are more in imitation of Him, who St. Paul called "the wisdom of God" (1 Cor 1:2): "I give thanks to thee, O Father, Lord of heaven and earth, because thou has hidden these things from the *wise*...learn of me because I am meek and humble of *Heart*" [italics added] (Mt 11: 25-29).

THE HEART OF KING SAUL

God's desire to work in and through the hearts of David and Solomon, the second and third kings of Israel, is consistent with His approach to His chosen ones in Scripture. Even with King Saul, Israel's first king who also ruled Israel for forty years, God moved mightily to prepare his "heart" for the task at hand.

In choosing King Saul to be Israel's first King, Scripture reveals that God instituted measures to prepare Saul's "heart" for reception and knowledge of His love and His Spirit. This was in order to work better in Saul – to help lead him in the ways of God, not man.

Upon anointing Saul as God's chosen one to be the first King of Israel, the prophet Samuel tells him that he is to recognize a series of signs, all of which are to be fulfilled to him. This in turn, Samuel says, will change Saul into another man (cf. 1 Sm 10:1-6). After explaining this to him, Scripture states that as "Saul turns to leave Samuel, God gave him another *heart* " [italics added] (c.f. 1 Sm 10:9). In essence, Saul receives an infusion of God's divine love and grace within his heart. It is a grace that is *necessary* for the "Spirit of the Lord" to "rush upon him" (cf. 1 Sm 10:6).

But tragically, King Saul still despaired and perished as "the Spirit of the Lord departed [him]," (1 Sm 16:14) and "he lost heart completely" (cf. 1 Sm 28:5).

"I will appoint over them shepherds after my own *Heart*"
(Jer 3:15).

Chapter Twenty-Eight

"MY HEART SHALL BE THERE"

"And now I have chosen and consecrated this house that my Name may be there forever, my Eyes and my Heart also shall be there always" (2 Chr 7:16).

As David knew God as a Father (cf. 1 Chr 29:10-11), so too was God a Father to Solomon: "I will be a Father to him" (1 Chr 22:10). The establishment of this relationship of *Father and son*, therefore, allowed God to speak to Solomon of His concerns for His chosen people in the way He did with His father, David (cf. 1 Kgs 6:13). When examined in context with God's plan for Solomon, this truth is significant. This is because the purpose of the great Temple of Jerusalem was not just for God's name and presence to dwell within the Ark, but in an even more special way: God desired to dwell in the Temple with His love, with His Fatherly "Heart" (cf. 2 Chr 7:16).

Thus, after receiving Nathan's blessing and instruction, David draws up the plans of the Temple and prepares the means to construct it. But most importantly, he remains obedient to God's will and anoints his son Solomon as King of Israel, exhorting him before he dies to "complete all the work for the service of the house of the Lord" (cf. 1 Chr 28:20).

After David's death, God remains true to both David and Solomon in fulfilling His promises to them. God tells Solomon: "And to this temple you are building – if you observe my statues, carry out my ordinances, keep and obey all my commands, I will fulfill toward you the promise I made to your father David. I will dwell in the midst of the Israelites and will not forsake my people – Israel" (1 Kgs 6:11-13).

Solomon built the Temple employing the materials and treasures amassed by his father David. The building was rectangular in shape and constructed of stone. It was fronted by an *eight-step* staircase flanked by two pillars. According to the *Book of Wisdom*, its design was inspired by the original *Meeting Tent* erected in the desert by Moses (cf. Wis 9:8), and consisted of three main areas, including the *Holy of Holies* that enshrined the *Ark of the Covenant*.

The Temple was completed around the year 964 B.C. Scripture states that Solomon dedicated the Temple "to the glory of God" upon completion. He then called upon the Lord God, who he declared, "alone knows the hearts of men" (1 Kgs. 8:39), to "advance to his resting place" (2 Chr 6:41), so His "eyes can be open and His 'ears attentive to the prayer of this place'" (2 Chr 6:40).

When Solomon concluded his prayer, fire descended from heaven and the "glory of the Lord filled the temple" (2 Chr 7:1).

GOD'S "HEART" DWELLS IN THE TEMPLE

Enraptured in his love for God, Solomon decried, "But will God indeed dwell on the earth" (1 Kgs 8:27)? Scripture states that Solomon "consecrated the *middle* of the court" of the Temple, and commenced an *eight-day feast* of celebration. After this feast, the Lord appeared to him and answered Solomon's prayer: "Now my eyes will be open and my ears attentive to the prayer that is made in this place" (2 Chr 7:15).

But Scripture reveals that the Temple of Jerusalem was to be not only the place where the *Ark of the Covenant* was to physically dwell, but also a place where God's great love for His people – as understood in His Paternal *Heart* – was also to dwell.

As the *Psalms* show David desired, the Temple was to honor God's unique love and faithfulness for His chosen people, the love of His Fatherly Heart and the essence of His glory. Henceforth, God tells Solomon no less this truth, as not just God's name comes to dwell in the Temple, but His Divine Heart: "And now I have chosen and consecrated this house that my name may be there forever, my eyes and my *Heart* [italics added] also shall be there always" (2 Chr 7:16).

In essence, God called upon David, *"a man after his own Heart"* (cf. 1 Sm 13:14) and his son, Solomon, who He blessed with a *"wise and understanding heart"* (2 Chr 9:23), to bring forth the earthly *home for His Divine Paternal Heart* (2 Chr 7:16), the great Temple of Jerusalem. For although in human eyes the Temple was understood to hold the presence of God within the Ark, it was only through God's Heart dwelling in the Temple that He could be with His people in the way He desired the most.

In God's own words to Solomon, we see how He profoundly led His chosen people to be even nearer to His great love for them— the everlasting love held within the promises given to Israel over the centuries.

ISRAEL FALLS AWAY FROM GOD

However, Israel was still unaware of the name God desired to be known by most: Father! And in their sin—their failure to be faithful and true to God as He requested before coming to dwell in their Temple (cf. 1 Kg 9:6-9)—Israel demonstrated its ignorance of God's true love for His chosen people.

Indeed, the visible presence of God on earth, the Temple of Jerusalem, now held the invisible presence of God on earth. However, Israel's heart did not abide in the Lord's Heart, nor did Solomon's heart maintain his father David's steadfast love for God, even though God had warned him not to "lose heart" (cf. 1 Chr 22:13). Like King Saul, Solomon allowed his love to stray from God: "For when Solomon was old his wives turned away his heart after other gods; and his heart was not wholly true to the Lord his God, as was the heart of David his father" (1 Kg 11:4). As a result, Solomon's and his people's sins lead to difficulties and disaster, as Israel, along with its great Temple, is pillaged and plundered over time.

But the purpose of the Temple was served. The glory of the *living God* filled not just the Temple of Solomon in a visible way, but also the entire world; Israel's God now dwelled among His children and became renowned before all mankind.

A COVENANT OF THE HEART

Over the centuries, the words of the great prophets Isaiah, Jeremiah, Ezekiel, and Daniel, as well as the lesser prophets, move the story of Israel forward. Through their efforts, the prophets call God's people to oppose sin, for it separates man from God. They also emphasize the three main features of Israel's religion: monotheism, morality, and future salvation. The prophets proclaim that God's people must *love Him* and keep *His Commandments* in order to remain faithful to Him. They emphasize that the Covenant with Him must come from the people's *hearts*.

We see this in the major prophets' words. Isaiah teaches that Jerusalem enjoyed special privileges from God, because "Yahweh rules from the Temple" in Jerusalem.[1] But, he bemoaned, the people's "hearts are sluggish" (Is 6:9, Mt 13:5), and are far from Him." Jeremiah speaks of a circumcision of the heart and of a "new covenant that God will write on the tablets of the heart" (Jer 31:33).[2] Ezekiel is also focused on the Temple and its return to glory, all in striving for God's chosen people to attain "a new heart and a new spirit" in order to be acceptable to Him (Ez 36:26).[3] Daniel prepares for the coming triumph of the Church, the ultimate *mystery of God's love* which will arrive with the foretold Messiah of mankind (Dn 7:13-14). It is a mystery of His Heart, waiting to be revealed. For God seeks to reveal such mysteries, says Daniel: "There is a God in heaven who reveals mysteries" (Dn 2:28).

The words of the minor prophets are in the same light. The prophet Joel speaks of the coming of the Spirit (cf. Jl 3:1-5) and tells the people to "render their hearts, not their garments, and return to the Lord" (Jl 12:13), for "near is the day of the Lord" (Jl 11:15). Zechariah foretells the Messiah and that the people's "hearts shall rejoice in the Lord" (2 Ec 10:7).

Finally, the *Book of Malachi,* the last book of the Old Testament in most bibles today, concurs with the words of Joel, as Malachi declares Elijah the prophet is to be sent "to turn the hearts of fathers to their children and the hearts of the children to their fathers." Once again, it is to be before "the coming of the day of the Lord" (Mal 3:23-24).

A FATHER TO ISRAEL

As with David and Solomon, the prophets played an essential role in continuing to shine light on the unfolding mystery of the God of Israel, especially His Paternal love.

Because God is a Father who is faithful to His children, the prophets teach that He alone deserves "all" glory, for He is holy, just, and true; He never abandons His people but always remains with them. He is Immanuel—"God with us" (cf. Is 7:14). He is "our Father" (cf. Is 64:7-8).

Most of all, God remains true to Israel because he is a *Father* who loves them. Over the centuries, the prophets' words illuminate this truth:

> -"But it is your providence, O Father, that steers its course, because you have given it a path in the sea, and a safe way through the waves (Ws 14:3).
>
> -"I cried out, 'Lord, you are my Father; do not forsake me in the days of trouble'" (Sir 51:10).
>
> -"Yet O' Lord, thou art our Father" (Is 64:8).
>
> -"And I thought you would call me, my Father, and would not turn from following me" (Jer 3:19).
>
> -"Have we not all one Father" (Mal 2:10)?

A HEART FOR HIS PEOPLE

As the New Testament is to reveal, "Father" is the one *name* that God longs for Israel to come to know. This is so God's paternal Heart can truly live in His people's Temple forever. This time though, it is the temple of *their* hearts that He seeks to dwell.

And so, regardless of Israel's infidelity and regardless of its violations of His laws, God's Heart remains with His chosen people: "How can I give you up, O Ephraim! How can I hand over you, O Israel...My *Heart* [italics added] recoils within me, my compassion grows warm and tender" (Hos 11:8).

In the words of the prophet Jeremiah, who uttered the great "Oracle of the New Covenant," sometimes called the "Gospel before the Gospel" we find a fitting summary of the end of the age and the approaching times of fulfillment. Jeremiah's words reveal, as David and Moses had conveyed, that God was a *Father* who loved His people with all His *Heart*:

> "For I am *Father* to Israel...

Is Ephraim not my favorite son?

Is he my darling child?

For as often as I speak against him,

I do remember him still;

Therefore my *Heart* [italics added] yearns for him,

I will surely have mercy on him, says the Lord…

I will make a new covenant with the house of Israel, and the house of Judah…

I will put my law within them,

and I will write it upon their *hearts* [italics added];

I will be their God,

And they shall be my people…

For I will forgive their iniquity,

and remember their sin no more (Jer 31:10, 20, 31, 33, 34).

In the remaining centuries before the coming of Christ, God's plan for Israel continued to manifest, for the stage was being set for the coming of the Messiah. Indeed, God told His chosen people to recognize Him in their *hearts* as their Father, for Israel is still his "firstborn" (cf. Sir 36:11), and that He would shepherd them forward with His *own* loving Heart: "I will give them a heart to know that I am the Lord" (Jer 24:7), and "I will appoint over them 'shepherds after my own *Heart*'" [italics added] (Jer 3:15).

"'No one has ever seen God; it is the only Son, who is nearest to the *Father's Heart*, who has made him known' (Jn 1:18). This fundamental saying – it now becomes plain – is an explanation of what comes to light in Jesus' prayer in his filial dialogue. At the same time, it also becomes clear what "the Son" is and what this term means: perfect communion in knowledge, which is at the same time communion in Being. Unity in knowing is possible only because it is unity in being."
—Pope Benedict XVI

Chapter Twenty-Nine

CHRIST: THE NEW TEMPLE

*"Destroy this Temple and in three days
I will raise it up" (Jn 2:19).*

That first Shepherd is to be the "Good Shepherd" (Jn 10:11) – Jesus Christ – the only begotten Son of the Father. He will completely bring God's people to know the Father as He does, which is the way God desires to be known, as a divine Person who is a *Father*: "I am the good shepherd; I know my own and my own know me, as the Father knows me and I know the Father" (Jn 10:14-15).

With the coming of Christ—the long awaited Messiah of the House of David—the glory of God is brought to fulfillment. *Through* and *in* Christ, man's "sins" are to be blotted out and a new dwelling place of God is established forever, fulfilling *Ezekiel's* promise: "My dwelling shall be with them; I will be their God, and they shall be my people. Then the nations will know that I the Lord sanctify Israel, when my sanctuary is in the midst of them for evermore" (Ez 37:27-28).

It is a new covenant, in essence, of the *heart*. For as with David (cf. Ps 89:27), God is truly a Father to Jesus. And like David (cf. Acts 13:22), Jesus is truly of the Father's Heart – His Paternal Bosom – the infinite, divine Temple the Father and Son dwelled together before all creation (cf. Jn 1:18).

THE NEW TEMPLE

The Presentation of Jesus in the Temple of Jerusalem, forty days after His birth, brings this truth upon us swiftly. Brought to Jerusalem, Mary and Joseph fulfill the dictates of the law as the Old and the New converge in a visible way. Christ, the *new Temple of the Father's Heart*, is offered to His Father in the *old Temple of the Father's Heart*.

In the Temple resides Simeon, who led by the Holy Spirit, holds the Christ child in his arms, and therefore, near his heart (cf. Lk 2:28). Apart from Mary and Joseph, and later the Apostle John, Simeon is the first to rest his heart near God's Heart, as a new era dawns upon the world—the *era of the heart* foretold by prophets Isaiah, Jeremiah, Ezekiel, Malachi, and others.

Simeon then informs Mary that her heart is to *co-suffer* with her Son's Heart, the Sacred Heart that will be pierced on Calvary: "And you yourself will be pierced by a sword – so that the thoughts of many hearts may be laid bare" (Lk 2:35). Likewise, there comes forward Anna the prophetess, who lives constantly in the "Temple, worshipping day and night while thinking about and praying to God (cf. Lk. 21:37). Again, the symbolism is clear: the new worship is not to be just a visit to the Temple in an annual celebration, but a perpetual reality of God living in His people's hearts day to day, as they are invited to live in the Father's Heart day to day.

THE PRESENCE OF THE FATHER

By age twelve, Christ's first words in Scripture acknowledge the Temple of Jerusalem as the *Temple of the Father*: "Why were you searching for me? Did you not know that I must be in my Father's house" (Lk 2:49)? Now the old Temple and the new Temple are understood in a similar way. Both contain the divine presence of the Father's love, *His Heart*, and are intended to bring Him glory in a *visible* way. And as Samuel went ahead and anointed David while Saul remained King, so comes Christ, the new Temple, who the Father "dwells within" (cf. Jn 14:11), even though the Temple of Jerusalem still stands.

Indeed, as David sought the great Temple of Jerusalem to be a light for the world to bring glory to the God of Israel, Christ, too, is now "the light of nations" and the "glory of Israel,"[6] bringing honor to God His almighty Father!

A LOVE FOR HIS FATHER'S HOUSE

After the finding of Jesus in the Temple by Mary and Joseph, Jesus continued to go to the Temple during His *hidden Life*, at least for Passover.[1] The Gospels reveal that His public ministry was patterned by these pilgrimages to Jerusalem, where the great Jewish feasts were held every year.[2]

According to the *Catechism*, Jesus went up to the Temple as the privileged place of encounter with His Father.[3] For Him, the Temple *was* not only the House of the Father (cf. Mt 21:13, Jn 2:16), but His *House of Prayer*: "It is written, 'My house shall be called a house of prayer'" (Mt 21:23). However, Jesus became angered when the Temple's outer court was turned into a place of commerce,[4] a place of sin, and a "den of thieves" (cf. Mt 21:13). The *Catechism* states that Christ drove the merchants out of the temple because of a jealous love for His Father:[5] "You shall not make my Father's house a house of trade"⁶ (Jn 2:16-17). This was in reference to David's *Psalm*: "Zeal for your house that has consumed me" (Ps 69:9).⁷

WORHIPPING THE FATHER IN TRUTH

Most of all, the profound significance of the Old Temple in relationship to Christ, the New Temple, is completely revealed. Jesus foretells that the Temple is to be replaced *forever* by Him: "Destroy this temple and in three days I will raise it up" (Jn 2:19). The *Gospel of John* further explains, "He was talking about the temple of his body" (cf. Jn 2:21, Mt 12:6).

In the fullness of this revelation, Christ's words concerning His bodily death and His glorious resurrection are intended to presage the total destruction of the Temple, which is to come by the Romans.⁸

The Temple of Jerusalem had been plundered by the Babylonias in 586 BC and again in 169 B.C. by Anteochus Epiphanes. It was further profaned in 167 B.C. by the worship of Zeus Olympios (cf. 1 Mc 1:44-59). King Herod the Great rebuilt the Temple in 20 B.C., the eighteenth year of his rule, expanding its base and surrounding it with courtyards, annexes, and secondary structures. But in AD 70, following the Jewish revolt against Roman rule, the Temple and its surrounding areas were totally destroyed by the Roman Emperor Titus. It was a destruction Christ foretells: "Your temple will be abandoned" (Lk 13:35), "Truly, I say to you, there will not be left here one stone upon another, that will not be thrown down" (Mt 24:2, cf. Lk 21:5).

Now in no uncertain terms, Christ's words manifest the dawning of a new age in the history of worshipping and glorifying the one revealed God. Now through Christ, "true worshippers" are to depart forever the Temple of Jerusalem and come to dwell in Him. This is because Christ is the everlasting, imperishable Temple of the Father's Heart who is to be *forever* the focal point of all worship to God our Father – the forever, unchanging *Truth*. The *Gospel of John* reads: "Believe me woman, an hour is coming when you will worship the Father neither on this mountain nor in Jerusalem. You people worship what you do not understand, while we understand what we worship; after all, salvation is from the Jews. Yet an hour is coming, and is already here, when authentic worshipers will worship the Father in Spirit and truth. Indeed, it is just such worshipers the Father seeks" (Jn 4:21-23).[9]

The new form of worship of the Father through Christ, the *Gospel of Matthew* reveals, is because Christ is "greater than Solomon" (Mt 12:42), "something greater than the Temple" (Mt 12:42).

According to the *Catechism*, "Christ identified himself with the Temple in order to present Himself as the Father's definitive dwelling place among men."[10]

"You (*the Father*) have given us the Spirit and *Heart* of Your Son, which is Your own Spirit and Your own *Heart*; and You have given them to be our Spirit and our *Heart* according to the promise that You made by the mouth of Your prophet in these words: 'I will give you a new heart and I will put a new spirit within you.'"
—St. John Eudes

Chapter Thirty

TEMPLES OF GOD

> *"You are the temple of the living God, just as God has said: I will dwell with them and walk among them. I will be their God and they shall be my people. Therefore, 'Come out from among them and separate yourselves from them' says the Lord; and touch nothing unclean. I will welcome you and be a Father to you and you will be my sons and daughters, says the Lord Almighty" (2 Cor 6:16-18).*

The mystery of the "Temple" does not end with Christ. Scripture reveals the Father seeks to dwell not only in His Son, but with Him and His Spirit in all His children – in the *temple* of their hearts. As we read in St. John's Gospel, the ultimate end of the whole divine economy is the entry of God's creatures into the perfect unity of the Father and of the Blessed Trinity: "If a man loves Me," said Christ, "he will keep my word and my Father will love him, and *we will come to him and make our home within him.*"[1]

Not long after the *Ascension*, St. Stephen and the early Christian community had already begun to reflect upon the religious significance of Christ's prophecies concerning the abandonment and destruction of the *Temple in Jerusalem*. According to the *Acts of the Apostles*, Stephen saw that God could not be confined to the Temple, and with the coming of Christ, the new age of the Holy Spirit was at hand:

> "So it was until the days of David, who found favor in the sight of God and asked leave to find a habitation for the God of Jacob. But it was Solomon who built a house for him. Yet the Most High does not dwell in houses made with hands; as the prophet says, 'Heaven is my throne, and earth my footstool. What house will you build for me…or what is the place of my rest? Did not my hand make all these things?'" (Acts 7:45-50)!

The *Letters* of Sts. Peter, Paul and John emphasize this unfolding truth of the faith. St. Paul, known as Saul at the time, had been in the crowd that day and heard Stephen's words before he was stoned to death. In his *Epistles*, Paul emphasizes that God's children should see that they are "temples of the living God," in imitation of Christ and in fulfillment of St. Stephen's words:

> "Do you not know that you are God's temple and that God's Spirit dwells in you? If any one destroys God's temple, God will destroy him. For God's temple is holy, and that temple you are" (1 Cor 3:16-17).

> "Built upon the foundation of the Apostles and prophets, Jesus Christ himself being the chief corner stone: In whom all the building, being framed together, growth up into a holy temple in the Lord. In whom you also are built together into a habitation of God in the Spirit" (Eph 2:20-22).

In his first Epistle, St. Peter ascribed to this truth too,

> "Come to him, a living stone, rejected by men but approved, nonetheless, and precious in God's eyes. You are living stones, built as an edifice of spirit,Into a holy priesthood, offering spiritual sacrifices Acceptable to God through Jesus Christ. For

Scripture has it: See, I am laying a cornerstone in Zion, an approved stone, and precious, He who puts his faith in it shall not be shaken.'" (1 Pet 2:4-6)

Likewise, St. John concurs in his first *Letter* that through love we are all invited to be ever lasting temples of God,

> "No one has ever seen God. Yet if we love one another, God dwells in us, and his love is brought to perfection in us. The way we know we remain in him and he in us is that he has given us of his spirit. We have seen for ourselves, and can testify, that the Father has sent his Son as savior of the world. When anyone acknowledges that Jesus is the Son of God, God dwells in him and he in God. We have come to know and to believe in the love God has for us. God is love, and he who abides in love abides in God, and God in him" (1 Jn 4:12-16)

CONSECRATION OF OUR TEMPLES

The Temple of Jerusalem—the first Temple of the Father's Heart—continues to symbolize the unfolding truths of our faith. As God our Father was to no longer dwell in a temple of stone, He also refuses to dwell in hearts of stone. So, God gives us "new hearts," taking our "stony hearts" and replacing them with "natural hearts" (cf. Ez 36:26). In essence, our heart is to be our "Meeting Tent" with God's Heart, and like Christ's Heart, our hearts are to be indestructible and imperishable in our love for God.

But first, like Christ did in the Temple of Jerusalem, we must *drive out* the evil and cleanse our temples, we must *reconcile* and *purify* them. This is so we can properly receive our God, and so that He may see our obedient and faithful love for Him at work, preparing for His arrival in us.

Then, we must consecrate the *middle* of our temples—our hearts—like Solomon consecrated the *"middle of the Temple"* to God (cf. 1 Kg 8:64). This solemn act unifies us with God our Father, unifies our heart with His Heart, and gives the Father all glory and honor. In this, we find the fulfillment of Christ's words:

> "I have given them the glory you gave me that
> they may be one, as we are one – I living in them,
> you living in me – that their unity may be complete.
> So shall the world know that you sent me, and that
> you loved them as you love me" (Jn 17:22-23).

Indeed, a solemn act of consecration invites God to give us new and pure hearts, giving the Father all glory and honor, and allowing Him to dwell in us. Moreover, in a special way, it continues to mend the separation from our Father that began so long ago in the Garden of Eden.

ENDING THE SEPARATION FROM OUR FATHER

From the beginning, Scripture reveals the separation of man from its Father was a matter of the *heart* for both man and God:

"When the Lord saw how great was man's wickedness on earth, and how no desire that his *heart* conceived was ever anything but evil, the Lord regretted making human beings on the earth, that he had made man on the earth, and his *Heart* [italics added] was grieved" (Gen 6:5).

Henceforth, from *Genesis* through *Revelation*, the essential theme of God's call to His people to return to Him can be seen as a call not just to man's mind, but to man's *heart*. Ancient Israel, Scripture reveals, understood this need: "Create in me a clean heart, O' God" (Ps 50:12), King David beseeches the Lord after the prophet Nathan came to him because of his sin with Bathsheba. In confessing his sin and examining his actions, David understood he needed a *new heart*, a deep interior change of his inner being to correct his errant ways: "Who shall ascend the hill of the Lord"...he who has clean hands and a *pure heart*" [italics added] (Ps 24:3-5).

To affect change in people, the prophets demanded behavior in conformity with God's will, which presupposed a *conversion of heart*, or a *complete rightness* before God, an *interior obedience* to the Lord. This, the prophets understood, was the only path to true change in man, because they knew that man in his pride repeatedly withdrew his heart from the Lord: "The beginning of pride is man's stubbornness in withdrawing his heart from his Maker" (Sir 10:12). As we read in Scripture, conversion of the heart was their relentless cry:

> "Less their eyes will see, their ears hear,
> their heart understand, and
> they will turn and be healed" (Is 6:10).
>
> "Cleanse your heart of evil
> O Jerusalem, That you may be saved" (Jer. 4:14).
>
> "For wisdom will enter your heart,
> knowledge will please your soul" (Pr 2:10).
>
> "The just man is glad in the Lord
> And takes refuge in him, in him glory
> All the 'upright' of heart'" (Ps 64:11).

In the New Testament, Jesus continued in many ways the message of the prophets, confronting the ways of the heart, *both towards evil*, "Hypocrites, well did Isaiah prophesy about you when he said, "This people honors me with their lips, but their hearts are far from me, (Mt 15:7-8), "for out of the heart comes evil thoughts, murder, adultery, fornication, theft, false witness, slander, these are what defile a man..." (Mt. 15:19-20); *and towards good*: "Blessed are the pure in heart for they shall see God" (Mt.

5:8), "where your treasure is there will your heart be also" (Mt 6:21).

As is so clear in the Beatitudes, Christ's words are directed towards His listeners' hearts, for He teaches His followers that it is in the *heart of man* where a sense of truth is to be discovered and reawakened, where a new temple for the Lord must be made ready and welcome.

MAN'S HEART IS UNIQUE

As we read in both the Old and New Testaments, although Scripture speaks of the soul and spirit, it most often speaks of the heart.[2] In Hebrew Scriptures, the word heart (*leb*) is the most common term used for the deepest reality of a person and is cited 814 times, more than the Hebrew word for soul (*nepes*), which occurs 755 times.

The *Catechism of the Catholic Church* reveals the heart is cited more than one thousand times in the Bible,[3] and is the place where all of God's people find the truth of who they are. The *Catechism* states: "The heart is the dwelling place 'of where I am, where I live.'"…the heart is the place "to which I withdraw". The heart is our hidden center, beyond the grasp of reason and of others; only the Spirit of God can fathom the human heart and know it fully. The heart is the place of decision, deeper than our psychic drives. It is the place of truth, when we choose life or death. It is the place of encounter, because as "image of God" we live in relation; it is the place of Covenant[4]…it is the heart that "prays" and if "our heart is far from God, the words of prayer are in vain."[5]

The Bible tells us that God's laws are written in man's heart (cf Jer 31:33) and the full expression of this gift is acquired when man's heart is opened by love, for love helps the heart to achieve its deepest aspirations. In his general audience of December 3, 1980,

St. John Paul II reflected on this truth of the ethics of man being rooted in the love found only in his heart: "Referring in this case to the heart, Christ formulated his words in the most concrete way. Man is unique and unrepeatable above all because of his heart, which decides his being from within. The category of the heart is, in a way, the equivalent of personal subjectivity. The way of appeal to purity of heart, as it was expressed in the Sermon on the Mount,...purity is a requirement of love. It is the dimension of its interior truth in man's heart."[6]

THE FATHER'S LAW OF LOVE

In these words the truth becomes apparent: love is the answer and the path to rediscover man's *new* and *pure* heart. Through grace, our hearts are to come to see and know the limits and errors of sin. Through the nourishment of love, a new vision of life emerges, one that allows our hearts to clearly distinguish the call of our Father, for now we can truly *see* and *hear* Him in Christ. We can see Him with the *eyes of our soul* and hear Him with the *ears of our heart*. In this context, the words of St. Augustine are called to mind: "All our striving in this life consists in "healing the eye of the heart" in order that it may see God (Serm. 88,5).

Scripture tells and shows us that our models and teachers on this path to a conversion of heart, are to be Mary, our Mother, and Jesus, our Savior. They – through their love for us – can teach us to love our Father and to love each other, with our whole heart; to love with the eyes of faith, which is the true foundation of the soul's life. They, more than anyone or anything, can teach us that love sustains, and is patient, that love provides all. They can teach us that *love* is *life* and *life* is *love*, that to love is to live, that to love is to obtain life.

Most of all, they alone can demonstrate that true love, *God's love*, is doing what is best for others, that true love is doing for others even when we do not want to, that true love is sacrificial, often painful, that true love is *truly unconditional*, and permits us to love, as Pope Benedict XVI tells us, "even the person whom [we] do not like or even know,"[7] even as Scripture says, "our enemies" (Mt 5:44).

Our Lord and Our Lady, in their love for us, can help us to realize that love is not love unless it is shared, unselfishly and endlessly shared. This is because sharing energizes love, because shared love is dynamic and creates good, endless good – because love that is not shared is *not* love. In life, we give and we take in a rhythm and balance that evolves through our love. Life, each moment, is love lived, expressed, shared. Each day is an opportunity for love – for love shared! Over time, shared love becomes a divine harmony, a *choir of hearts*, and that is the music of God! Yes, *love* is the music of God. While the notes are not always perceptible, the rhythm and harmony of God's music is love, *the fruit of the Tree of Life.*

Compassionate love becomes a refuge, an anchor, and not a weapon. The human condition is feeling and thinking in the context of love. Love realigns what one feels and thinks and does in the Father's will. And this all starts with love for our God, our heavenly Father – in our hearts, in the hearts of our souls, and then for one another.

Thus, we come to see that the Father works out of love, the Son *judges* out of love and the Spirit *inspires* out of love. We come to realize that Mary *lived* by love, the angels sing out of love and the Saints' *joy* is love. Yes, all life, in this world and the next, exists because Life is Love – blessed and holy Love – the resurrecting Love that lives, flourishes and seeks to rise in us every day, as Christ rose on the third day!

This is our Father's *Law of Love* and a cornerstone of the Holy Spirit's *New Evangelization*. We should love the Lord God with all our heart, and remember that when we love Him, we love all others and ourselves for love of Him, for we are attracted through the heart, and not the senses. Moreover, a heart expanded by such total love for God and one another then becomes *a universe* that contains the presence of God – our Father, a temple for Him to dwell in forever.

A NEW "ERA OF THE HEART"

Our world today suffers from what can no less be described as a "hardness of heart" (Mt 19:8), a *poverty of love* for one another, for our heavenly Father, for our God. But for ages a *new era of the heart* has been foretold, one in which God, "who is the searcher of hearts and minds" (cf Rev 2:23) and "who knows the hearts of all men" (Acts 1:24), brings a new beginning to man's heart through His infinite paternal love by stripping him of his old heart and giving him a new one. In this regard, the prophet Jeremiah delivered God's words to His chosen people, "I will give them a heart with which to understand that I am the Lord. They shall be my people and I will be their God, for they shall return to me with their whole heart" (Jer 24:7). In *Ezekial*, God's promise to His children is the same, as He will give to them a "new" heart: "I will give you a new heart and place a new Spirit within you, taking from your bodies your stony hearts and giving you natural hearts. I promise to put my Spirit within you and make you live by my statutes, careful to observe my decrees…you shall be my people and I will be your God" (Ez 36:26-28).

In our time, we are called to turn our hearts in love toward the Father.

We are called to give Him our simple and beautiful *fiat* while seeing the infinite grace and love the Father wishes to bestow upon us through His Paternal Heart; thus, the words of Jeremiah and Ezekial come to fulfillment.

Furthermore, from Christ's words in His *Sermon on the Mount*, we are invited to understand that our hearts are called not only to become *new* but to remain *pure*, 'Blessed are the pure of heart for they shall see God" (Mt. 5:8). It is purity of heart that leads to a purity of *mind*, *soul* and *body*, Scripture reveals. It leads us to desire a Christ-like purity, "Everyone who has this hope based on him makes himself pure, as he is pure" (1 Jn 3:1-3)

With this profound understanding and hope, we are called to pray that the power of the Father's Paternal Heart, more radiant than a million suns, will bring to man's heart the dawning of his divine destiny. It is a destiny that calls us to see with the eyes of our soul the Father's true face, to hear His true voice, and to touch His true *Heart*. It is a destiny foretold to "turn the hearts of the fathers to their children, and the hearts of the children to their fathers" (Mal 3:24).

Yes, God's prodigal children need to say to their Father – like David in his broken and humbled moment of truth – what He most desires to hear in His Paternal Heart from each of His children: "Create in me a clean heart, O' God (Ps 51:10), "for the clean of hand and pure of heart…will receive blessings from the Lord" (Ps 24:3-5).

Part VII

THE COMING OF THE FATHER

"The religion which originates in the mystery of the Redemptive Incarnation is the religion of dwelling in the *Heart of God*, of sharing in God's very life. Saint Paul speaks of this in the passage already quoted: 'God has sent the Spirit of his Son into our hearts, crying, "Abba! Father!"'" (Gal 4:6).
—St. John Paul II

Chapter Thirty-One

THE ARK OF THE FATHER

"But the hour is coming, and now is here, when the true worshipers will worship the Father in spirit and truth, for the Father seeks such as these to worship him" (Jn 4:23).

From the time of Sts. John and Paul, the Church has held some form of devotion to the love of God.[1] In the early Church, this effort focused on God the Father, as He loved the world and He gave to it His only begotten Son. The early Church also focused on the love of Jesus – who gave the world His *Commandment of Love* – and how His great love for mankind led to His death on the Cross. While the open side of Christ and the mystery of His blood and water being shed were meditated upon and contributed to the birth of the Church and the Sacraments, devotion to the Sacred Heart of Jesus did not develop until around the tenth century.[2]

THE VISION OF ST. GERTRUDE

As noted, there is documented evidence of devotion to the Sacred Heart in the eleventh and twelfth centuries. Out of the Benedictine and Cistercian monasteries, a fervent atmosphere of prayer emerged around the "Wound of Love," Christ's wounded Heart as represented in His pierced side on Calvary. In the recorded histories of some of the Saints from this period, it is seen that the devotion to the Sacred Heart was well known.[3] From these accounts, we can find beautiful prayers and spiritual exercises within these histories.

However, there is a special acknowledgement in St. Gertrude's life of a vision she reportedly had on the Feast of St. John the Evangelist, which forms sort of an epoch moment in the growing devotion to the Sacred Heart.

In her account, she reports being allowed to rest her head near the wound in Christ's chest, where she heard aloud His Divine Heart beating. She then asked St. John if on the night of the *Last Supper*, he too had experienced such a moment of delight and, if so, why he had not recorded it in his Gospel. St. John reportedly responded by saying that this mystery of Christ's love had been "deliberately withheld" by God and reserved for subsequent ages when the world, having grown "cold in love," would rekindle its love for Christ by the revelation of His Sacred Heart.[4]

St. Gertrude's words, which report that devotion to the Sacred Heart was reserved for later ages, is revealing and significant, for the Church has always recognized God's *timely will* in all matters. It is noted that St. Gertrude's explanation is very similar to one found in the revelations given to the Venerable Mary of Agreda, who according to her book, *The Mystical City of God*, was told that "the Eternal Father's wisdom is found at work in the *timely appearance* of the revelations." Like St. Gertrude, she reports that God the Father told her that until that point, mankind was not prepared to be introduced to the "mystery of Mary," since the mysteries were so great that the faithful in the early Church would have been "lost in the contemplation and admiration of them at a time when it was more necessary to establish firmly the law of grace and of the Gospel."[5]

A DIVINE TIMELINE

Scripture upholds this divine approach in revealing the mysteries of the faith in Christ's own words to the Apostles at the *Last Supper*: "I still have many things to say to you, but you cannot bear them now" (Jn 16:12). Likewise, St. Paul speaks in *Corinthians* of how the faithful are brought to understand God's mysteries in the proper time: "Brothers, I could not talk to you as spiritual people, but as fleshy people, as infants in Christ. I fed you milk, not solid food, because you were unable to take it" (1 Cor 3:1-2). In these passages, we see God's ways always involve a "divine timeline," emanating from His perfect will and wisdom.

This truth is especially apparent in the divine pedagogy of the Scriptures, with the New Testament hidden in the Old, and the Old Testament made manifest in the New, all of which have gradually unfolded and blossomed over many centuries. Most significantly, God's Divine Revelation was to be centered around the birth of Christ, who we are told came "in the fullness of time" to dwell among us. Thus, with the Incarnation, God finally established His Kingdom on earth and fulfilled the messianic prophecies of the Old Testament. And for our purposes, the *manifestation of the Father* in Christ was finally revealed to the world.

Now, the time has arrived for a fuller and more profound manifestation of our Father and His mysteries, especially the mystery of His love for us as revealed in His Paternal Heart, the great symbol of this infinite love. Through the call of the Holy Spirit, we are being led to better understand His love and the many graces that His Heart represents in calling us to come to better know, love, and honor Him.

Moreover, it is our Father, the *Father of Life*, in which the Spirit is telling us we need to turn to now, as life and the mystery of its sacred origin are under attack, as the Herods' of today seek to destroy again the Christ Child, *the Christ in every child the Father's Heart conceives in love.*

As with past crises in the world in which the Church saw that sinful man needed to come closer to Christ—whose love and mercy were clearly understandable in the symbol of His Sacred Heart—we need to recognize through our spiritual instincts that the uniqueness of our times calls us to turn to our Father, who is *Love*, who is *Life* itself, and who is the giver of all life through His everlasting love for all His creation. Our Father, therefore, is inviting us to turn to His Paternal Heart in order to find the answers we need to heal our broken world.

THE WAY TO THE FATHER'S HEART

In *Haureitis Aquas,* Pope Pius XII wrote that by revealing His Sacred Heart, Our Lord Jesus Christ especially wanted to invite men to consider and worship God's merciful love for the human race. Contemplating "the bitter hardships" of his pontificate during the Second World War and the emerging Cold War, Pope Pius XII turned to the Sacred Heart, seeking to again stir devotion to Christ. However, the Holy Father also wrote in his letter that the Son's Heart was the *"way"* to the Father's Heart, reminding us that Christ Himself said, "I am the way, the truth and the life. No one comes to the Father except by me" (Jn 14:6).[6] Pope Pius XII further writes of how Jesus spoke of a time when devotion to God the Father would come alive, for it was what His Father sought from His children: "But the hour is coming, and now is, when true worshipers will worship the Father in Spirit and in truth, and indeed, the Father seeks such people to worship him" (Jn 4:23).[7]

Almost fifty years later, Pope John Paul II contemplated in *Tertio Millennio Adveniente* the Father's merciful love for man and described it as being a love moved "by His Fatherly Heart."[8] It is the Father, he implied, that will prepare the Church to move into the new millennium; a time St. John Paul II foresaw to be a new "springtime" in the Church[9], and a more "definitive coming of the kingdom" on earth.[10]

Indeed, the Father's Paternal Heart is where God's children need to turn, where we need to lay our head – for the time has come for the world to see this merciful Heart, this great symbol of our Creator's goodness and infinite love for His children. In essence, it is a time of *presentation*; a time when *the Father of lights* presents to us the perfect gift, His Paternal Heart, now unwrapped for the whole world to see. It is a timely present from the Father of all mankind, and it is to be used to replenish souls with the dew of His divine grace that is present in this great gift.

Today, at such a pivotal point in the affairs of men, God's mystery to reshape history anew is revealed in the form of the Father's Paternal Heart, the symbolic revelation of His great, undying paternal love for His children, whom He longs to save and to be reunited with in a special way. Thus, as we move forward into the new millennium, our Father, through love and devotion to His Heart, is now "coming" to take mankind out of the turbulent waters of our world. His Heart, His Divine Paternal Heart, needs to be seen as a divine lifeboat propelled by the grace and mercy of His paternal love. In this time, we are called to board this life-saving ship, this *Ark of the Father*, to huddle in it for protection, and to leave the shores of the *culture of death* in order to make our way upstream to the *civilization of life*.

It is to be a journey where the fruits of our Father's great love for His children will be made manifest. It is to be a journey where His Spirit will lead us, like with Noah, to build a new life, an eternal life in our Father's love.

"*My Heart* is overwhelmed,
My pity is stirred.
I will not give vent to my blazing anger,
I will not destroy Ephraim again;
For I am God and not a man,
the Holy One present among you.
I will not come in wrath" (Hos 11:8-9).

Chapter Thirty-Two

THE COMING OF THE FATHER

"Those who love me will keep my word, and my Father will love them, and we will come to them and make our home with them" (Jn 14:23).

"Behold, I am coming soon" (Rv 22:12). In the final chapter of *Revelation*, St. John tells us that in these words, the promise of the ages is held as Christ assures believers that He will return in power and glory. As if to erase all doubt, the Lord again emphasizes His promise at the very end of *Revelation*, "Yes, I am coming soon" (Rv 22:20).

In the Church today, *Come, Lord, Jesus* is used as a liturgical refrain, similar to the Aramatic expression, *Maranatha*, "Our Lord, come!", that is written in St. Paul's *First Letter to the Corinthians* (1 Cor 16:22). The early Christians were believed to have used it as a prayer for the second arrival of Christ, or as an expression of hope in the proximity of the *Parousia*, the coming of Christ in glory.

The Church solidified the belief in doctrine. The *Apostles Creed* confesses, "From whence he shall come again to judge the living and the dead." The other Creeds concur with this, with the *Nicaeno-Constantinople Creed* adding the words "in glory."

During His ministry, Christ repeatedly spoke of His Second Coming at the end of the world (cf. Mt 16:27, Mk 8:38, Lk 9:26): "The Son of Man shall come in the glory of his Father with his angels: and then will render to every man according to his works" (Mt 16:27). Many of the Epistles also contain references of the Second Coming of Christ, contemplating the manifestations of His majesty and the reward to be conferred by Him in judgment. The early Church held the *Parousia* to be imminent, although the Apostles taught the uncertainty of the time. Both Sts. Peter and Paul are ascribe to the delay of the *Parousia*; they advise of seeing the wisdom of God, who in "patience" wishes to give sinners time to repent.

A THIRD COMING

While the end of the world and its renewal, therefore, is well defined within Scripture and the Church, *Tradition* also recognizes a "Third Coming" or an ongoing "Coming of the Lord" in individual lives. This is the process within a soul that unfolds in life as it moves toward God through prayer and the Sacraments. In essence, God comes to live in the soul, in His temple, and the soul comes to live in God, as described in the writings of the many Saints.

The Church also is open to the long-held belief found in *Tradition* that there remains a grace-filled era of time, one that is to be marked by a *Triumph of the Church* on earth; an era of time before the Second Coming of Christ. This "Third Coming", as it is also known, is seen as a highpoint in history of the ongoing coming of the Father's Kingdom "on earth as it is in heaven" (Mt 6:9-10). It is foretold to be a period in which God lives in so many of His children's hearts that the whole world is changed for the better in a unique and visible way.

Many of the Saints, Doctors of the Church, and popes have written over the centuries of both of these realities regarding a "Third Coming."[1] The fourth century works of St. Cyril of Jerusalem (313-386) contain letters of his catechetical lectures that allude to the three comings.[2]

Acknowledging the First Coming of Christ in a birth from the Virgin in the fullness of time, St. Cyril writes, "There is a hidden coming, like that of rain on fleece, and a coming before all eyes, still in the future."[3] Also calling it the "hidden coming" that spans from the first coming of Christ to the end of the world, the understanding of a "Third Coming" was rediscovered in the writings of St. Bernard of Clairvaux.[4] A Church Doctor, St. Bernard reiterated St. Cyril's nomenclature regarding its reality:

> "We know that there are Three Comings of
> the Lord. The Third lies between the other two.
> It is invisible, while the other two are visible. In the
> First, he was seen on earth, dwelling among men;
> he himself testifies that they saw him and hated him.
> In the Final coming, 'all flesh will see the salvation of
> our God, and they will look upon him who they pierced.'
> The intermediate coming is a "hidden one"; in it only
> the elect see the Lord within their own selves, and
> they are saved. In his First Coming, Our Lord came
> in our flesh and our weakness; *in this Middle Coming,
> he is our rest and consolation.*"[5]

"A SABBATH REST"

A "Third Coming" is for all "souls" who open their hearts to the actions of God in their lifetime; since Mary's apparitions at Fatima in 1917, however, there has been an increase in curiosity over whether or not her words there, which foretell an *Era of Peace*, are in keeping with the belief of a coming grace-filled time of peace on earth, a period that many see is alluded to in the Old Testament and in the writings of the Church Fathers.[6]

St. Augustine (354-430) is attributed to referencing this foretold period as "a Sabbath Rest" on earth, one he accredited to being necessary to fulfill God's planned stages of history over thousands of years. The Church in the medieval period adopted this presentation, but over the centuries through efforts to repel the erroneous teachings of Millenarianism, Augustine's "Sabbath Rest" fell into obscurity.[7]

After this period, for a long time academics chose to avoid discussing the possibility of a historic era of the Church for fear of being seen as teaching Millenarianism. Although the Church never condemned the Apostolic Father's doctrines on this era, the Church did condemn "even modified forms of this falsification of the Kingdom to come under the name of millenarianism, especially the 'intrinsically perverse' political form of secular messianism."[8] This position further led to setbacks for such a view as Augustine's. However, many theologians over the centuries have persisted, citing Old and New Testament sources they believe portray a period on earth that is to come that will be "a renewing of the face of the earth," a *Second Advent* or a *Second Pentecost*, as it is often defined.

In the past three decades, the Virgin Mary's words at Fatima of a coming "Era of Peace" have especially vitalized this discussion, as have the writings and words of St. John Paul II and Pope Benedict XVI. According to some commentators, St. John Paul II's encyclical letter, *Tertio Millennio Adveniente*, especially seemed to allude to a renewed humanity in Christ when he wrote of a "new springtime in the Church," and a more definitive coming of the Father's "Kingdom."[9]

As Prefect for the *Doctrine of the Congregation of the Faith*, Pope Benedict XVI, the former Cardinal Joseph Ratzinger, stated his views concerning such an era, *"The question is still open to free discussion as the Holy See has not made any definitive pronouncement in this regard."*[10]

A COMING OF THE FATHER

In his book, *Jesus of Nazareth*, Pope Benedict XVI entertains what he also writes of as being a "threefold" coming of the Lord.[11] The Pope describes it as an "intermediary coming in Spirit and power" in the lives of the faithful, referencing St. Bernard of Clairvaux. Pope Benedict XVI writes that St. Bernard bases his thesis on the Gospel of St. John: "If a man loves me, he will keep my word, and my Father will love him, and *we* will come to him and make our home with him" (Jn 14:23).[12]

It is this "Coming of the Father," alluded to in John 14:23, that Pope Benedict XVI especially calls to focus; for he sees it as "an eschatology of the present" that St. John was aware of in his understanding of the definitive coming of Christ.[13] Pope Benedict XVI writes that this awareness of a "Coming of the Father" is preempted in Scripture.[14] After the *Miracle of the Multiplication of the Loaves and Bread*, Jesus dismisses His Apostles, who go by boat to their destination while Jesus goes "up on the mountain: to pray and be with the Father." Because He is with the Father, He sees them and comes to them in their turbulent moments on the lake during the storm, calming the waves while getting in the boat and making is possible for them to continue to their destination. The Pope concludes that because Jesus is with the Father, *He comes with the Father* to restore peace and calmness, and to remain close in times of trouble so that the danger is put to rest.[15] In our lives, and in history, it is the same. Both the Church and the world, the Pope explains, travel against the headwind of history through the unpredictable ocean of time. Many times, it looks as if we are about to sink. But at the right moment, our Father is there, "He comes to us," to the world, to save it.[16]

Like previous moments in the history of the Church that marked a "coming," an expectation of a definitive change in the world, the world has entered such a time. It is not the time of Christ's coming, but a change that shows, Pope Benedict XVI says, "that interim time is not empty, it is marked by *adventus medius*, the middle coming."[17] According to the Pope Benedict, this middle coming takes place in a number of ways. God comes to souls through His Word, the Sacraments – especially in the most Holy Eucharist –and into the lives of His children through words and events that redirect lives.[18] Moreover, He intervenes in a manner that clearly can reshape history. Pope Benedict writes: "Yet he also comes in ways that change the world. The ministry of the two great figures Francis and Dominic in the twelfth and thirteenth centuries was one way in which Christ entered anew into history, communicating his word and his love with fresh vigor. It was one way in which he renewed his Church and drew history toward himself. We could say much the same of the saints of the sixteenth century. Teresa of Avila, John of the Cross, Ignatius of Loyola, and Francis Xavier all opened up new ways for the Lord to enter into the confused history of their century as it was pulling away from him. His mystery, his figure enters anew – and most importantly, his power to transform men's lives and refashion history becomes present in a new way."[19]

"God's search for man is 'the mysterious design of His wisdom and goodness…[a] plan born in the *Father's Heart.*'"
—The Catechism of the Catholic Church

Chapter Thirty-Three

THE OUR FATHER

"Your Heavenly Father knows all that you need. Seek first his Kingship over you, his way of holiness, and all these things will be given you beside" (Mt 6:33).

"The "middle coming" in the lives of both individuals and the world that Pope Benedict XVI writes of is essentially given to us in the words of the *Our Father* prayer; for truly the *Our Father* invites us to contemplate the *coming* of God, our Father, in our lives and in the world, a coming for both individuals and mankind.

The **Our Father** is the quintessential prayer of the Church. Over the ages, millions have prayed the *the Lord's Prayer* as the Spirit comes into hearts crying, "ABBA! Father!" In their wisdom, the Fathers, Doctors, and elders of the faith, firmly fixed the prayer in liturgical tradition. They understood the *Our Father* to be "truly the summary of the whole Gospel" and that Christ desires the prayer to help the Church hold fast to its mission of bringing the final coming of God's reign.

Today, Christians of every denomination embrace the *Our Father*; it remains our common patrimony, as it is recognized as being the words that the Father gave to Jesus – who, because He embraced our human condition, knew the needs of His brothers and sisters in His Heart.

Considered the perfect prayer, the *Our Father* contains seven petitions that address our desires and needs in beseeching God to help us on our earthly pilgrimage. According to St. Thomas Aquinas, the *Our Father* fulfills Jesus' words "Ask, and it shall be given to you" (Mt 7:7) and "teaches us not only to ask for things but also in what order we should desire them."[1] Of the seven petitions in the *Our Father*, the first petitions are compelling: the pleas for our Father's "Kingdom to come, His will to be done on earth as it is in heaven."[2]

Although the *Catechism of the Catholic Church* states the petitions refer *primarily* to the final coming of God's reign through Christ's return, by discernment Catholics recognize that the Father's Kingdom has been coming since the *Last Supper*; in the Eucharist, it is in our midst. Therefore, in every Eucharistic celebration, in praying the *Our Father*, in praying for fulfillment of the words of the Lord's Prayer, we help to bring the Kingdom of Our Father within "our hearts", as Christ taught: "For behold, the Kingdom of God is in your midst." (Lk 17:21) and this, then, allows us to also help to bring the Kingdom of the Father "on earth as it is in heaven": "Thy Kingdom come. Thy will be done on earth as it is in heaven" (Mt 6:9-10).

THE KINGDOM OF THE FATHER

To be specific, the *Our Father* teaches us that the inward reality (*the Kingdom within*) is shown in the outward expression (*the Kingdom on earth*) and the outward expression (*the Kingdom on earth*) illustrates the inward reality (*the Kingdom within*). In essence, they are one in the same. The one (*the Kingdom on Earth*) is the outer action of the inner reality (*the Kingdom within*). Both are necessary and both are needed in this time; the more people allow God into their hearts, the more they allow our Father to manifest His Kingdom in the world.

Most importantly, the outer expression (*the Kingdom on earth*) is not only for those of God's children who have come to know and love Him, but also for those who will learn from such souls and who will be drawn to Him by observing this reality lived out in others. Consequently, in our time, the words of *Our Father* help us to see more than ever the light of the path that is before us.

It is the way of Christ, who did God's will through prayer and perfect obedience, and who came to lead us to our Father and His Kingdom. Thus, it is the way we must now follow, too.

Indeed, we must take action, we must turn back towards our Father; we must thank Him, praise Him, and adore Him! We must love Him! Through persistent prayer, loving obedience, and His divine gifts of life, we must be consecrated witnesses of His love and be ready to battle for Him. Most of all, we must be like Our Lady and the Saints, striving and longing to do His will. The rhythm of the universe is the *Heartbeat* of the Father. Thus, we must be one—united in praying the *Our Father* and united in our loyal hearts to our Father's Divine Paternal Heart—in order to bring greater love, devotion, and honor to Him. It is then that He may come to us, pouring out His blessings and His merciful intercession upon our world and all mankind.

This is our Father's will for us, the Church, and the world. It is the path to the kingdom **"within."** It is the path which brings the Kingdom **"on earth."** It is the path to holiness and to peace that is within us and the world—*the peace of Shalom*—a peace that is the reconciliation of the world to God's holy will. It is a peace where life is lived in God, and each child has a home within Him; for it will be true peace, one in which man abides in God and God abides in man; the Creator filled with His creation, and creation filled with its Creator – its loving and glorious Father!

As our faith teaches us, for every hope there is the power to make it so. Now, the hope of our heavenly Father is that His love for us and our love for Him will plant the everlasting seeds of a new beginning for our world that is to have no end.

It is to be a world filled with the peace of Jesus Christ, bathed in the love of the Holy Spirit, and basking in the radiant glory of the *Family of God* [3] – all while living together in the rhythm and harmony of the Divine Paternal Heart of God our Father.

Part VIII

TO KNOW, LOVE AND HONOR GOD OUR FATHER

"...Man is invited to meet the Father toward whom He moved in the journey of faith and love during life, and into whose arms he threw himself with holy abandonment at the hour of death. It is an abandonment which, like that of Jesus, implies a total gift of self on the part of a soul which accepts to be despoiled of the body and of earthly life, but in the knowledge that it will find in the arms and *Heart of the Father* the new life, a participation in the very life of God in the Trinitarian mystery."
—St. John Paul II

Chapter Thirty-Four

CONSECRATION TO OUR FATHER

"Consecrate them by means of truth—'Your word is truth.' As you have sent me into the world, so I have sent them into the world; I consecrate myself for their sakes now, that they may be consecrated in truth" (Jn 17:17-19).

Love is the inspiration for all that is done and beheld in heaven and on earth. It is God's legacy to us. It is what binds us to Him and to each other. It is what constitutes the Family of God.[1]

God's children, therefore, are of consequence in His eyes. We are His beloved. We come from Him and are to return to Him—to His Divine Paternal Heart. Unfortunately, the true meaning of this truth has remained hidden. But now, its full importance must be realized; for our hearts are ready, as our world is ready, to return to the Father. And He is leading us to return to Him, to His home—*His Heart*—where He desires to delight in us for His holy purpose.

Now and always, our Father in heaven is but a heartbeat away from all His children. For our hearts are joined with His—and with that, His Fatherly love. His desire then, for our daily lives, is for each of His children to make the "choice" to be reunited with Him. This is His holy and ordained will. This is His plan for us.[2]

Thus, with the Rosary as our spiritual weapon to defeat the power of the Evil One in our lives and in the world, we must also continue to mend our separation from the Father and move towards His loving arms and Paternal Heart.

This can be better achieved by individuals giving themselves, through personal consecration to the Father, back to His Paternal Heart—where each and every soul is conceived in the Father's love.

Adam and Eve's choice to disobey God's will in the Garden was first and foremost a decision in both their *minds* and *wills* before an action was undertaken. In essence, their wills rejected the Father's will. Thus, we can do what they did not: we can say "yes" to our Father's will, individually and collectively, in order for *us* to truly turn toward Him in a meaningful way.

While there are many ways to give ourselves to our Father, a personal act of consecration to Him is perhaps the best way to demonstrate such love for our Creator.

WHAT IS CONSECRATION?

Consecration is a solemn dedication to a special person, place, or thing. In religious terms, it signifies one's total giving, the placing aside of all else in order to be completely in the service of God.

Moreover, to consecrate oneself means to set oneself apart from *evil,* to turn to the Lord, and be prepared to be used by Him. It means to associate with the *sacred* in order to grow towards God and His will for us. The Bible tells us, "Consecrate yourselves therefore, and be holy; for I am the Lord your God" (Lv 20:7).

There are two parts to the process of consecrating ourselves to God: our part and God's part. Our part is first the practical side of removing ourselves from sinful living. We especially need to resist the temptation of "serious sin." We do this by applying our minds and hearts to what is *good, pure, and of God*. In essence, we try to become "less" of this world, although we still live in and must be a part of it.

Through consecration, we then draw near to God and His design for our life. And, with the help of the Sacraments, consecration helps become a spiritual roadmap for holy living—the drinking in of God's presence—every moment of our life. Thus, once on this path, we become even less attracted to this world and its charms. In this way, we seek God and His will, for as God's presence increases, sin and unwanted behavior are replaced by the joy and happiness that comes from greater purity of mind, body, heart, and soul.

Finally, consecration also helps find within us the desire to be righteous in the eyes of God, for it inspires a yearning to please Him like all children wish to please their earthly parents.

God's part in our consecration to Him is inherent in His desire to dwell in us; He wishes to draw near to our hearts, so that His love is something we can feel more and never want to be separated from again. God knows that His presence cleanses us and makes us holy, as He is holy, giving to us new life in every way. This is what God desires for every soul. Thus, through consecrating ourselves to our Father, He sees we desire Him too. Therefore, He knows that He is permitted to act in us, to change us, and make us more like Him.

THE OLD TESTAMENT

The Old Testament is clear that God had desired consecration from His chosen people:

- "Consecrate to me all the first-born; whatever is the first to open the womb among the people of Israel, both of man and of beast, is mine" (Ex 13:2).

- "And the Lord said Moses, "Go to the people and consecrate them today and tomorrow, and let them wash their garments" (Ex 19:10).

- "So Moses went down from the mountain to the people, and consecrated the people; and they washed their garments" (Ex 19:14).

- "You shall be men consecrated to me; therefore you shall not eat any flesh that is torn by beast in the field; you shall cast it to the dogs" (Ex 22:31).

- "And he poured some of the anointing oil on Aaron's head, and anointed him, to consecrate him" (Lv 8:12).

- "And he said, 'Peaceably; I have come to sacrifice to the Lord; consecrate yourselves, and come with me to the sacrifice.' And he consecrated Jesse and his sons, and invited them to the sacrifice" (1 Sam 16:5).

- "O Lord, God of heaven, behold their arrogance, and have pity on the humiliation of our people, and look this day upon the faces of those who are consecrated to thee" (Jth 6:19).

Moreover, while Scripture speaks of God's people consecrating themselves to the Lord, it also speaks of God Himself taking the initiative and consecrating His chosen ones, preparing them to undertake His holy plan for their lives:

- "For they had afflicted him; yet he had been consecrated in the womb as prophet, to pluck up and afflict and destroy, and likewise to build and to plant" (Sir 49:7).

- "Before I formed you in the womb I knew you, and before you were born I consecrated you; I appointed you a prophet to the nations" (Jer 1:5).

- "Be silent before the Lord God! For the day of the Lord is at hand; the Lord has prepared a sacrifice and consecrated his guests" (Zep 1:7).

Indeed, from Samson to Samuel to Solomon, there are many chosen souls in the Old Testament who were consecrated by God in the womb or in early childhood—much like David, the anointed of God's Heart. This was God's way of establishing a special relationship with souls, so they could better come to know, love, and honor Him in their lives.

THE NEW TESTAMENT

In the New Testament, we especially take note that Scripture reveals how the Father "consecrated Jesus" before He came into the world:

> "Do you say of him whom the Father
>
> consecrated and sent into the world,
>
> 'You are blaspheming,' because I said,
>
> 'I am the Son of God'" (Jn 10:36)?

Likewise, Jesus consecrated Himself to His Father and encouraged the need for consecration. In what Scripture calls Christ's *Last Discourse*, He prayed to His Father for His Apostles to be consecrated:

> "Consecrate them by means of truth –
>
> 'Your word is truth.' As you have sent
>
> me into the world, so I have sent them
>
> into the world; I consecrate myself for
>
> their sakes now, that they may be
>
> consecrated in truth" (Jn 17:17-19).

To consecrate ourselves to the Father, therefore, is to consecrate ourselves in truth to His Heart. In essence, it is the path to unifying our heart with His Heart, so that like the Apostles, we can be totally of God.

OUR CALL TO CONSECRATION

As we see in the lives of God's Saints, individual consecration to our Father is the path to a new life in Him. It is the path that each of God's children should be encouraged to take, for it allows us to know our Father personally and to walk with Him in our daily life. It allows us to take His hand in trust, and escape a culture God did not desire for man to live in.

As life in ancient Rome was for the first Christians, our culture today breeds despair and crushes hopes and dreams. It is a culture that removes peace. Through consecration, therefore, God intervenes and holds us in the palm of His hand. In this way, though still in this world, we become closer to the Father's Heart, where He can cleanse us of the culture and bless our lives with goodness, hope, and love. In this way, we begin to make our way back home to Him and to find His will for our lives.

To know, love, and honor our Father is our calling. *Through* and *in* our Father, we are each called to His truth. Deep within our hearts, He will show us this truth when we are consecrated to Him and when we seek His divine will for our lives.

A BETTER WORLD

Warm and welcome in the Heart of our Father, our consecration to Him is a ladder to our Father's heart and brings miracles into our lives and families. This is because we are filled with a brilliance that glimmers in the eyes of the souls of all who meet us. It is a spark of the divine, a *sign* of our Father's presence, in which those who meet us wish to possess and experience in their lives too.

Thus, consecration is an awakening, a time of personal renewal that can then lead us to a better world. The Father, strong and vital, is *Life*, the life inside us. When we choose to step into our Father's will, this *life* of His transforms us. We see and feel His glory and we take joy in our efforts to be part of Him. Like Jesus, who is *the Way, the Truth, and the Life*, we allow the life of Christ to take us into the Heart of our Father; here, there is only love and peace, a oneness with Him that is priceless and incomparable to anything else the world has to offer.

"*Seek and ye shall find*," Jesus tells us. Through consecration, we find our Father. We find His love for us, for all His children. Thus, we begin to lead the world back to Him. Together, united *to* and *with* Him, mankind can then begin to enter a new era, the *Era of Peace* promised at Fatima.

Past the pain, past the darkness of our times, an angelic army seeks to lead us into the new times, to help bridge for us the future that has been promised to mankind. It is a future where, comforted by Mary, we are no longer separated from our Father but sealed and carried in His love for us—secured safely in the Ark of our Father's Heart—where all darkness succumbs to His light and mankind is in more intimate union with its Creator.

A SPECIAL CONSECRATION PRAYER

How then should we consecrate ourselves to the Father?

Although there are prayers of consecration to God the Father that are good and acceptable, a beautiful eight-day octave prayer, one that includes meditations of both the Old and New Testament's mysteries, appears to have been inspired by the Holy Spirit for the times at hand.

Because of its exceptional content, I believe it is a devotion to the Father that perhaps the Church should examine and, if found worthy, encourage and promote some day. This is because it is a prayer that allows the faithful to say "*yes*" to our Father, to begin individually, one person at a time, to end our separation from Him in a special way.

The octave prayer entitled *God Our Father, Consecration and Feast Day for the Father of All Mankind (see Appendix A at the end of the book)*, outlines a path that a soul can undertake in a deliberate, meditative action. It permits the consecration of one's self to God the Father over an eight-day period, culminating with a final day—a feast day in the Father's honor.

While the Church in its wisdom may seek to study and recommend changes to its present format, the eight-day consecration prayer has been acclaimed by theologians[3] and is perhaps a spiritual window into better understanding our need to return to God the Father in a meaningful, prayerful way—a way that is a purposeful step along the Church's path to the fulfillment of its mission in salvation history.[4]

CONSECRATION TO GOD OUR FATHER

The most compelling precedent for consecrating ourselves to God Our Father over an eight-day feast, or octave, is found in the *Gospel of St. John*, Chapter 10:22-39. This passage describes how Jesus, during the eight-day *Feast of Dedication*, reveals how He had been consecrated to God our Father (Jn 10:36).[5]

Jesus explains that He consecrated Himself to our Father so we, too, could be consecrated to Him in truth (cf. Jn 17:19-21).[6] The concept of consecration to God our Father is crucial because, as Jesus tells us, "the hour is coming, and now is, when the true worshipers will worship the Father in spirit and truth, for such the Father seeks to worship him. God is a spirit, and those who worship him must worship in spirit and truth" (Jn 4:23-24).[7] Thus, if we follow Jesus, if we model ourselves after Him, shouldn't we also consecrate ourselves to God our Father during an eight-day feast, so that we, too, can adore Him "in spirit and in truth?"[8]

Therefore, if we choose to consecrate ourselves to God Our Father, how should this be done? The concept of an "octave," or eight-day feast, has been significant in our relationship with God since the beginning of our Salvation history.[9] It is not by coincidence that Jesus chose to reveal His consecration to God our

Father on the eight-day *Feast of the Dedication*. Clearly, the octave symbolizes a designated period of time in which God's children grow and His relationship with them changes or is transformed.[10]

Unlike other consecration methods, *The Holy Octave of Consecration to God Our Father* views the "big picture" of our salvation history.[11] It involves the entire process of our spiritual journey that progresses towards Our Father, which includes the most prominent figures in our faith: Mary, our Mother; Jesus, our God and our Savior; and the Holy Spirit, our God and our Sanctifier—with progression always toward God our Father.[12]

God's Word, in both the Old and New Testaments, provides us with extensive Scriptural support for an eight-day, or "octave," format. From the *Book of Genesis* to the Gospels and Epistles, the number "eight" is used to signify salvation, covenant, purification, and dedication.[13] Perhaps, more importantly, it is used to indicate the end of one era and the beginning of another in which God the Father is revealed, manifested, and is presented to His children in a special way.

Holy Scripture illustrates that in the past, these periods of transformation always involved a time of our turning away from God, a time of purification and cleansing, a time of re-dedication, and a time of regathering and renewal.[14]

The octave or eight-day period is significant, then, in representing a divinely ordained process that involves a shifting from one period to the next. Often the process that propels us from one period ino the next has involved seven days of praise, thanksgiving, offering, and repentance, followed by an eighth day of solemnity and assembly of God's children.[15] This process can work on two levels to purify and dedicate us: individually and as a body. Therefore, *The Holy Octave of Conseration to God Our Father* is necessary and much needed in these times – for each of us individually and for the Church as a whole.[16]

To place the need for a consecration feast to God our Father in proper perspective for the times we live in, we should remember that at the turn of the last century, Pope Leo XIII dedicated the world to the Sacred Heart of Jesus.[17] Again in 1925, Pope Piux XI ordered a formal consecration of mankind to the Sacred Heart of Jesus, to be publicly recited and renewed annually on the Feast of Christ the King.[18]

Finally, *The Holy Octave of Consecration to God Our Father* prayer, in its present format, is intended as a formal eight-day feast for God our Father culminating with the feast day on the first Sunday of the "eighth" month, August.[19] The solemn eighth day is celebrated under the title, *The Feast of the Father of All Mankind*, a special day that not only the Church could celebrate but the whole world, for there is only one Father of all mankind,[20] only one Father whose Heart the world must come to see and know, to love, and honor in a special way!

"O' Eternal Word, my Savior, You are the Eagle I love and the One who fascinates me. You swept down to this land of exile and suffered and died so that You could bear away every soul and plunge them into the *Heart of the Blessed Trinity*, that inextinguishable furnace of love."
—St. Therese of Lisieux

Chapter Thirty-Five

THE SOLEMNITY OF THE DIVINE PATERNAL HEART OF GOD OUR FATHER

"A son honors his father, and servants their master; If, then, I am a Father, where is the honor due me?" (Mal 1:6)

Each of us is conceived in the Paternal Heart of God Our Father, and each of us is called to return to His Heart. Returning to our heavenly Father, to His love and to His Paternal Heart, is therefore what every soul desires and is inspired by grace to discover.

Fr. Jean Galot, SJ, in his book, *ABBA FATHER, We Long to See Your Face*, writes that this is a deep desire, placed in our heart by God:

> "Only such knowledge of God the Father can fulfill the deepest yearnings of the human heart. As long as God is seen simply as God without a Father's face, an essential aspect is lacking in the vision of the one who hopes to encounter him. The human soul needs the revelation of the Father, and its deepest desires which are inspired and quickened by grace are satisfied only when it discovers God as a Father...for every repentant sinner has the privilege of *'rejoicing the Father's Heart.'*"[1]

The desire to return to our Father is His gift to us, a *perfect gift*, for "[e]very best gift, and every perfect gift, is from above, coming down from the Father of lights" (Jas 1:17). But the call to know the Father, to know the Heart of the Father, is more than just a call to experience a greater personal relationship with Him. In truth, it is a call to the Church, the world, and mankind to come home to the Father. It is a historic passage of faith and time, intended to bring hope to men and nations that they may live in peace and security along the path of salvation. It is the long awaited fulfillment of the Church's call to make the Father known just as He is – so that mankind may increase its trust and love for its heavenly Father, a Father who desires to watch over and delight in His children like a painter contemplating the picture He has painted, for mankind is the masterpiece of our Father's creation.

In essence, the Spirit's call in the *New Evangelization* is a call for each soul to return through Christ to its Father so that He can shower His love upon all and heal our wounds and so we then can pay homage to our Father in a way that is deserving of Him, for He is "one God and Father of all, who is above all and through all and in all" (Eph 4:6).

But there needs to be more. The Church needs to acknowledge the cry of God's children – their cry of love in response to the Spirit's invitation – by proclaiming *a Feast for God our Father*. It is to be the *Feast of Life*:

The Solemnity of the Divine Paternal Heart: The Feast of the Father of All Mankind

According to theologians, such a feast would lead to many positive benefits for all of humanity and would fulfill *Lumen Gentium's* prophetic words: "In Christ, the head of all things, all honor and glory may be rendered to the Creator, the Father of the universe."[2]

Indeed, the *Feast of the Father of All Mankind* would most of all fulfill the need to bring honor and glory to God our Father, and to finally answer the cries of God's children that have echoed throughout the centuries. It is a cry that will go on until this need is fulfilled, for such honoring of our Father is long overdue; it is an honor that is encouraged and presaged in many passages in Scripture, such as in the *Book of Sirach*:

> "For the Lord sets a father in honor
>
> over his children
>
> and confirms a mother's authority over her sons.
>
> Those who honor their father
>
> atone for sins;
>
> They store up riches who respect their mother.
>
> Those who honor their father will
>
> have joy in their own children,
>
> and when they pray they are heard.
>
> Those who respect their father
>
> will live a long life;
>
> Those who obey the Lord honor their mother…
>
> Kindness to a father will not be forgotten;
>
> it will serve as a sin offering—it will take lasting root" (Sir 3:2-6,14).

"The chorus of the Church Triumphant and those of the Church Militant are united to our Lord in this divine action, so that with Him, in Him and through Him, they may ravish the *Heart of God the Father* and make His mercy all our own."
—St. Francis de Sales

Chapter Thirty-Six

THE FEAST OF THE FATHER OF ALL MANKIND

"'Father, glorify your name.' Then a voice came from heaven, 'I have glorified it and will glorify it again'" (Jn 12:28).

In the crucifixion, death, and resurrection of Christ, a great mystery of His teachings emerged. A new form of worship and a new Temple was to be built, replacing the old form of worship and the old Temple. In Jesus' words, "Destroy this sanctuary, and in three days I'll raise it up" (Jn 2:19), the promise of the ages reveals its coming fruition.[1]

Christ's Resurrection assures us that His Father, the Father of creation and mankind, is finally to be recognized, praised, and honored as the one, true God; replacing centuries of pagan worship and even the monotheistic form of Jewish worship. The most Holy Trinity, revealed by Christ as the real God, now would have real followers who worship in *truth*. And the risen Savior's words to Mary of Magdala centered this worship on the Father: "I am going to my Father and your Father, to my God and your God" (Jn 20:17).

Thus, this new, divine worship is to be forever addressed and focused on the Father, for it is the *path of truth* as "commanded by the Father" (2 Jn:4), who Christ sought to lift all mankind towards, by way of His Ascension, to the *Father's right hand* [2] (Mk 16:19).

THE NEW WORSHIP

This higher truth had already been foretold, in no uncertain terms, to the Samaritan woman at the well. Christ had assured her that "the hour is coming, and is now, when *true worshipers will worship the Father 'in spirit and truth,'* for the Father is seeking such people to worship him" (Jn 4:21-23).[3] With Christ's reply to the Samaritan woman, the age of the past is forever over, the past the woman spoke of and believed was centered on the teachings of "our ancestors who worshipped on this mountain" (Jn 4:20). Now, the Trinity was revealed. Jesus spoke of "God Himself, our Father" (1 Thes 3:11), the one Father of all mankind, who was truly our Father, who *loved* His children, and who, therefore, deserved to be worshiped not out of fear or out of *tradition*, but out of love in return.[4]

The new worship, addressed to the Person of the Father, inspired by the Holy Spirit, and revealed by Christ, implies a newly perceived relationship between creature and Creator. It is a relationship founded on love, as the humble obedient creature, God's friend (cf. Jn 15:15), has found "love in God the Father" (cf. Jude 1:1) – a love so great and transforming that it causes the creature to have desire to not only love the Creator with a heartfelt need, but also have desire to honor and glorify Him, for it finds no better way to fulfill this *heart to Heart* relationship. Like the ancient Israelites, the creature desires to stand before his God, his heavenly Father and cry:

"Blessed be your glorious name, which is exalted above all blessing and praise" (Neh 9:5).

In no uncertain terms, this *honoring of the Father*, this "work of truth" (Jn 3:7), is already addressed in the Holy Liturgy. From the beginning, the Church had established that all liturgical worship must be directed to the Father. The *Catechism of the Catholic Church* states the Father is the source and goal of the Liturgy.[5] In the Liturgy, God the Father is blessed and adored as the *origin* of all the blessings of creation and salvation, with which He has given us in His Son in order to give us the Spirit of filial adoption.[6] In the New Covenant, all prayer is the loving relationship of God's children with their Father—who is good beyond measure—with His Son, Jesus Christ, and with the Holy Spirit.

Some may ask, if all liturgical worship and all Christian prayer either directly or indirectly is addressed to the Father, is there truly a need for the inauguration of a special feast in honor of God Our Father? And is this need not already met with the *Feast of the Blessed Trinity*?

These questions and objections, along with others, have been pondered since the seventeenth century, when documented efforts to establish a liturgical feast for God the Father first began to be recorded.[7]

EARLY EFFORTS TO INAGURATE A FEAST OF THE FATHER

In 1657, Pope Alexander VII received a petition from Leige, Belgium, requesting approbation of a Divine Office and Mass in honor of the Eternal Father. The Sacred Congregation of Rite refused to grant it on December 1, 1657.[8] In 1684, King Charles II of Spain pursued the same efforts with no success. Over the next two centuries, similar efforts produced the same results. Pope Leo

XIII, in 1897, was the last Pope to note the cause, briefly alluding to it in his encyclical letter on the Holy Spirit, *Divinum Illud*, although not attempting doctrinal examination of the issue.[9]

For the most part, the objections have emphasized the lack of precedent in regards to feasts intended to venerate the individual Persons of the Holy Trinity. In addition, there became a concern for the potential excessive multiplication of feasts that would come if a feast of the Father was implemented, as well as potential theological problems—such as confusion over the divine essence of the Trinity, or the false assumption of each divine Person with their own feast having several divine natures attributed to them. Some argued that since no such feast for the Father has ever been inaugurated, the example of the "wisdom of the ancients" needs to be followed.[10]

Nevertheless, throughout the twentieth century, efforts to promote a feast for the Father have continued to surface.[11] Various petitions have been attempted and, in the latter part of the century, eminent theologians, religious, and laity have taken up the cause by lending their authoritative voices through writings and lectures.[12] Collectively, these individuals believe that the objections of the past, for the most part, are not insurmountable and that the time has come for the Church to inaugurate a feast in honor of God Our Father.

They especially emphasize that the Church, now two thousand years old, does not in any way honor the Creator, *God Our Father*, with a special day. And this, they argue, is in itself most surprising and unacceptable, and that it should be addressed at this time in history.[13]

HONORING THE FATHER'S HEART: THE SOURCE OF HIS PATERNAL LOVE FOR ALL MANKIND

Although the need for the Church to confront the inauguration of separate feasts in honor of the individual Persons of the Trinity is perhaps a matter to be taken up and addressed at some point—considering the breadth and depth of the theological questions involved in such an undertaking—any action forthcoming can be seen as most probably in the future.

However, in lieu of the Church's institution of many feasts in honor of the attributes, traits, and divine actions of both the Son and the Spirit—such as the Feasts of *Pentecost*, the *Sacred Heart of Jesus*, the *Precious Blood* and most recently Christ's *Divine Mercy*—an effort to inaugurate a feast in honor of the Father's divine paternal love as seen in His Paternal Heart presents sound reason for immediate action, acceptance, and approval in both theological and practical terms. Moreover, it would uphold and be consistent with the precedent established by existing feasts that honor the divine traits and characteristics of Christ and the Holy Spirit; at the same time, it would be the easiest way to confront and place aside the objections of the past.

Let us, therefore, consider the many reasons why it is time to honor and glorify our Father's Divine Paternal Heart in a special way, why it is time to "rejoice in the Lord" (Heb 3:18), and why it is time "to sing the to the glory of his name" (Ps 66:2), as we read in Scripture that God's faithful are called to do:

> -"A son honors his father, and a servant his master; if, then, I am a Father, where is the honor due to me?" (Mal 1:6).
>
> -"Blessed art thou, O Lord the God of our fathers; and worthy to be praised, and glorified, and exalted above all forever: and blessed is the holy name of thy glory: and

worthy to be praised, and exalted above all in all the ages" (Dn 3:52).

-"Worthy are you, Lord our God, to receive glory and honor and power" (Rv 4:11).

-"Worship him who made heaven and earth and sea and springs of water" (Rv 14:6-7).

-"Father, glorify thy name. A voice therefore came from heaven: I have glorified it, and will glorify it again" (Jn 12:28).

"O' Lord, for thy servants sake, according to thy own *Heart*, thou has shown all this magnificence, and would have all the great things to be known" (1 Chr 17:19).

Chapter Thirty-Seven

THE CELEBRATION OF LIFE

"Fear God and give him glory...Worship him who made heaven and earth"(Rv 14:6-7).

First and foremost, a feast in honor of God our Father's Paternal Heart would express homage to His Fatherhood, especially His paternal love as expressed in Scripture (Eph 1:3-5) and manifested in the works of creation and salvation. Moreover, such a feast would invoke the words of Christ, who called upon us to *know* God the Father was *His* Father and *our* Father. A feast would truly do this, thereby renewing in a special way the faithful's confidence in the *Lord's Prayer*—particularly the prayer's essential theme of loving our Father, the echo of Scripture's words as heard in the teachings of the prophets and recorded in the *First Commandment*: "To love God with all our heart, mind and strength."[1]

Equally important, a feast for our Father would especially call to mind His *divinity*, His holiness, His awesomeness as God, and the giver of all gifts to His children through His omnipotent will and loving Paternal Heart. Indeed, a feast would "proclaim to all God's great power" (2 Mc 3:34).

Some have argued in the past that this is accomplished in the liturgical *Feast of the Blessed Trinity*. However, theologians today point out that this feast calls for homage to the Trinity's *unity in nature*, and does not express homage to the Father or the divine Fatherhood—especially His divine paternal love as is manifested in the work of creation and salvation in relation to the members of the human race. For the most part, a feast in honor of the Paternal Heart of the Father would truly commemorate that our Father is a loving Father, the *Giver of Life*, whom we attribute our existence to in a loving and thankful way.

In essence, it would be the *Celebration of Life*. In turn, the mystery of the Son's Incarnation would be renewed too, as Christians see the need to be united with the Father, just as was the Son in the flesh. Similarly, it would renew our relationship with the Holy Spirit, for in honoring our Father, the Spirit imparts in our souls that the image of the Son we are called to see is *one with the Father*.[2]

Especially for the laity, a feast in honor of our Father would emphasize our need to see and glorify His name in a more enlightened way; this would cause the faithful, some of whom that may have had a *fear of the Father*, to deeply penetrate through meditation the truth of Father of all mankind and His great love for each and every soul.[3] Through such meditation, the call to seek heaven and be with our Father forever would fill people's hearts, giving greater reality to life's most important purpose and calling.[4] Indeed, it is a calling to our "ABBA" in trust and not fear, as we reach up to take His hand in order to be led into his Kingdom forever, and to return to His Divine Paternal Heart, where we first were conceived.[5] This is the mystery of Himself the Father is calling us to know. St. John Paul II writes, "Did not Christ say that our Father who 'sees in secret,' is always waiting for us to have recourse to him in every need and always wanting for us to study his mystery: the mystery of the Father and his love?"[6]

Finally, in the tradition of the many feasts in honor of Christ, Mary, and the Saints, a feast for our Father would celebrate an important phase in the mystery of salvation in each year of the liturgical cycle.[7] The Father's plan, which leads the Church and governs the Liturgy, would be expressed with greater clarity each year. This would mean that the solemnity of the mystery of the Father and His paternal love, as symbolized in His Divine Paternal Heart, would be similar to the cultural development of *Father's Day* (a celebration that occurs in many nations around the world) and would become a highlight of the liturgical cycle, casting great light on divine Fatherhood in relationship to the significance of human fatherhood and its deserving of honor.[8] In this light, we would consider heaven and earth to be more closely united and seen with a new strength of bonding through the fullest meaning of the virtue of fatherhood, which contains mercy and forgiveness in its love.[9] In addition, today's families would be enhanced through such a celebration with not only the greater ongoing reality of the Fatherhood of God, but of motherhood and the love between the spouses. This is because the example of the Father's paternal love would also have a profound influence on the home and the need for authority, respect, and love in all situations; in addition, the example of the Father's paternal love would reinforce the idea that a family must persevere in hope and faith.[10] According to St. John Paul II, all of this is "fundamental to… the *civilization of love*…[because] the family is organically linked to this civilization."[11]

PROFOUND ECUMENICAL IMPLICATIONS

From a strictly theological perspective, a feast for God our Father's Paternal Heart contains many ecumenical implications because of its sound Scriptural roots. The fundamental truth emphasized at the beginning of the *Letter to the Ephesians* (Eph 1:2-14) is that salvation is governed by the Father's intention, in and through

Christ, to establish His universal Fatherhood.[12] This implies that our Father is not only to be understood as a *universal Father*, but also as the *individual Father* of each and every human being. Such a feast would express this awareness with clarity.[13]

Furthermore, Catholics and Christians of every denomination throughout the world could relive the mystery of salvation in its various stages and in its most important events each year. This is because our Father is at the beginning and at the conclusion of this mystery.[14] Therefore, the entire process of sanctification results from our Father's paternal love and His Paternal Heart, which is primordial and decisive; therefore, deserves to be recognized and honored by a special feast.[15]

Finally, such a feast would be also more than a celebration on the Catholic liturgical calendar. The creation of a feast in honor of God our Father's Paternal Heart would espouse profound ecumenical implications and be a basis for unity of all Christians and all human beings, for our Father—the one and only Father—embraces all His children in His Fatherly love and in His Divine Paternal Heart.[16] Consequently, like common Christian celebrations, including Christmas and Easter, and also like our common patrimony in the *Our Father* prayer, a feast for our Father could come to be shared by all Christian denominations and wherever the sanctity of human fatherhood is held in respect and honor. This is because the joy of finding God, manifested in many religions *as one common Father*, would be an inspiration for every person and for every heart everywhere.[17] Once more, we are reminded of the prophetic words of Pope Benedict XVI: "Christians long for the entire human family to call upon God as 'Our Father!'"[18], an echo of St. John Paul II's call in his apostolic letter, *Euntes in Mundum*, for there "to be one family of God on earth."[19]

AN OCTAVE CELEBRATION

With all of this in mind, such a great and glorious feast, as I already noted, deserves to be inaugurated and celebrated in the tradition of an *octave*, the practice of celebrating a major feast on the feast day itself and for seven days preceding or seven days thereafter.[20]

This practice began in the Old Testament tradition of prolonging a feast day such as the feasts of *Passover and Tabernacles* (cf. 1 Mc 4:56). Today, it is continued in the Church, primarily at Christmas and Easter. For all Christians, an octave celebration would involve eight days of prayer, Scriptural readings, meditation, and (*for Catholics*) participation in the Holy Mass, the Eucharist, and Sacrament of Reconciliation; this period of time is culminated with the feast day, which could also be a day of individual consecration (*and then each year a renewal of such consecration*) to the Father and His Paternal Heart.[21]

In this tradition, *The Solemnity of the Divine Paternal Heart of God Our Father: The Feast of the Father of All Mankind*, would be an annual eight-day celebration beginning and ending with complete attention to our Father; we note that this occurred in the life of Christ Himself, whose first recorded words in Scripture focused us on the Father: "[D]id you not know, that I must be about my Father's business?" (Lk 2:49) as were those among the last from His lips on the Cross, "Father, into your hands I commend my spirit" (Lk 23:46).

This glorious tradition of honoring God our Father has already been adopted annually by many in the Catholic Church in the Philippines, where an octave of celebration with individual consecration culminating on the feast day, the *Feast of the Father of All Mankind*, is celebrated on the first Sunday in August every year.[22]

RAISING OUR VOICES

Therefore, through the powerful intercession of Mary, *The Mother of All Mankind*, "who prays for the unity of the Family of God,"[23] the world is called to return to its Father, *The Father of All Mankind*, who is supreme good, who is our fortress and deliverer, who is the giver and keeper of all *life*, and who is *our Father*.

Now, in reflection of their Mother's total *fiat*, Mary's children unite in their total *fiat* to their Father's Paternal Heart, saying *yes* to *life* and giving the Father what He desires most: the praise, honor, and glory that is rightfully and deservingly His, so that He can cover the world with His grace and mercy, so He can *come down* to rescue His children from their errant ways, and so He can reveal His great love for His children at this moment in time by bringing the *civilization of life* into the world with one sweeping wave of His mighty hand!

Through consecration of ourselves, our nations, and our world by the bishops and the Pope to the Divine Paternal Heart of God the Father, through the declaration of a solemn feast day in the universal Church in honor of our Father, humanity can build a new world, departing forever the shores of today's dark age and arriving at last in a new and glorious epoch of human history.

Thus, in St. John Paul II's prophetic words, the prayer of our hearts storms heaven like the crashing peel of the rams' horns upon the walls of Jericho: "[W]e raise our voices and pray that the love which is in the Father may once again be revealed at this stage of history, and that, through the work of the Son and Holy Spirit, it may be shown to be present in our modern world to be more powerful than evil: more powerful than sin and death."[24]

Indeed, the time has come for our blessed Father, the comforter of man, to help His children carry their crosses of redemption so that the world will see the era of reconciliation with God and the coming of the foretold *Era of Peace* promised by Mary at Fatima.

It is to be an era of love, joy, and peace on earth—delivered from the Immaculate Heart of Mary to the Divine Paternal Heart of God Our Father.

> "It is not so much the length of prayer, but the fervor with which it is said which pleases almighty God and touches His *Heart*."
> —St. Louis de Montfort

Chapter Thirty-Eight

ST. PHILIP AND THE APOSTLES OF THE FATHER

> *"Just Father, the world has not known you, but I have known you, and these men have known you sent me. To them I have revealed your name, and I will continue to reveal it, so that your love for me may live in them, and I may live in them" (Jn 17:25-26).*

"'Lord,' Philip said to him, 'show us the Father and that will be enough for us.'
'Philip,' Jesus replied, 'after I have been with you all this time, you still do not know me?'
'Whoever has seen me has seen the Father. How can you say, 'Show us the Father'? Do you not believe that I am in the Father and the Father is in me?
The words I speak are not spoken of myself; it is the Father who lives in me accomplishing

his works.
Believe me that I am in the Father
and the Father is in me,
or else, believe because of the works I do.
I solemnly assure you, the man who has faith in me
will do the works I do, and
greater far than these.
Why? Because I go to the Father,
and whatever you ask in my name I will do.
so as to glorify the Father in the Son.

Anything you ask me in my name
I will do.
If you love me
and obey the commands I give you,
I will ask the Father and he will
give you another Paraclete –
to be with you always:
the Spirit of truth..."[1]

In 1994, I traveled to Mt. Tabor in the Holy Land. It was a highly anticipated and deeply profound experience for me. This is because I had always wondered what it must have been like for the three Apostles – Sts. Peter, John and James – to be there to witness the Transfigured Jesus, to behold the extraordinary vision of Moses and Elijah, and to hear the voice of God the Father: "This is my beloved Son on whom my favor rests. Listen to him."[2]

The experiences of these three individuals come to mind when contemplating which Saint is best associated with God the Father. Who would be a shining and powerful example of devotion to our Father?

As we know, the Father inspired St. Peter to voice His public affirmation that Jesus was the Messiah, the "Son of the living God." St. John the Baptist, like the three Apostles on Mt. Tabor, heard the Father's voice at the Jordan River. There are, of course, numerous holy men and women worthy of consideration. From St. Irenaeus – the *Father of Christian Theology*, whose writings on the Father reveal his profound devotion to "the uncreated, beyond grasp, invisible, Maker of all"[3] – to St. Catherine of Sienna – whose mystical *Dialogue* with God the Father is a classic in Christian literature – there are many Saints that have expressed their strong devotion to God the Father.

But while many names come to mind, I believe that St. Phillip best shows us the way to the Father. For his very words in Scripture ask Christ to do just that:

"Lord, show us the Father and that will be enough for us" (Jn 14:8).

Needless to say, if St. Peter's declaration of Christ being "the Son of the living God" was a result of the Father's revelation to him, St. Phillip's desire for Jesus to "show us the Father" appears to be no less a moment of divine prodding.

THE LAST DISCOURSE

There is a reason for this belief. In the annals of time, few words may be found to have contributed as much to man's quest to find its Father than Phillip's heartfelt plea to Jesus. This is because Christ, in responding to Phillip, uses the moment at hand to unfold for us what is known as the *Last Discourse*; these were His departing, immortal words to the Apostles in the *Gospel of St. John* that emphasized His mission to lead all back to the Father, so all may be "one" in the Father as He is "one" in the Father.

Jesus explains to His Apostles that through love of the Father, man is invited to intimately know and share in the very *life in God*. In the *Last Discourse*, which runs from Chapter 14 through Chapter 17 of John's Gospel, Christ speaks of the Father by name, or refers to Him, a total of 122 times.[4] Clearly, the truth of the Father and His love is the essence of the *Discourse*, especially the part known since the sixteenth century as the *"High Priestly Prayer"* of Jesus.[5]

In His prayer, Christ's words are addressed directly to the Father rather than to the disciples, who overhear.[6] Although still present in the world, Jesus considers His earthly mission as a thing of the past.[7] Whereas He had previously stated that the Apostles could not follow Him, He now wishes for them to be in union with the Father too,[8] especially through the Father *consecrating* them in truth. Thus, as Jesus passes into eternity the world is now to be challenged by the mission of His disciples.[9] It is a mission to call mankind to the Father through the Son and the Spirit, the *Paraclete*, who Jesus promises to send to them.[10] In essence, their challenge is more fully revealed to them; they are now *Apostles of the Most Holy Trinity*. They must take to the world the *complete truth* of the revealed God, the truth given to them by Christ, the only begotten Son who was with His Father "before the world began" (Jn 17:24).

Sparked by St. Phillip's request to see the Father, the *Last Discourse* is instrumental in understanding the mission of the Church. Jesus tells the Apostles that the truth of the Father's love for mankind needs to be heralded loud and clear and spread far and wide throughout the world. To this very day, it has been His message to us.

APOSTLES OF THE FATHER

As Christ called His Apostles, so must we answer the call of our Father. We must, quite simply, tell the world of the Father's love and the depository of graces that God wishes to dispel upon mankind through His Divine Paternal Heart. We must become *Apostles of the Father*. We must be filled with love and zeal for our Father and consecrated in truth to Him. Indeed, although divine, Jesus would probably humbly declare Himself an Apostle of His Father too. This is because His love and zeal for the Father was present in His every word and deed until His *Ascension* into heaven.

In our world today, the *Father of Life* is truly the answer to the *Culture of Death*. Therefore, our Father – the *one* and *only* Father – is ready to help us confront and defeat this great crisis of our time. And He will bring this victory through His children. We need merely to *consecrate* ourselves to Him and let Him work in and through us. We need to hold the Father's standard high and go into battle with Him leading the way.

But more importantly, the time has come for mankind to realize it has been separated from its Father for too long and needs to return to Him. This truth, this reality, must become visible in the world through those who are ready to become His special followers and lead the world back to Him. We must lead the Father's children back to Him through His Word and His Spirit – through His one, holy, Catholic and Apostolic Church.

This is a call not only to the religious, but especially to the laity, who through inspired efforts must take the truth of the Father to their friends and neighbors, to all they know and meet in their daily lives. While religious orders for priests and nuns in the Father's name will arise, along with holy and blessed Sacramnetals such as such as medals and scapulars of Him, so must come new conferences, organizations, schools and Churches in the Father's name. These are efforts the laity must work hard to bring into existence in the tradition of our Catholic forefathers, those who filled the world with Churches and Church institutions in Christ's name and the names of the great saints of the past.

Moreover, we must also take to the highway, especially today's super highway of information, which is more than capable of communicating the reality of our Father to an infinite number of people. Using today's technology and social media prowess, there is no reason why the truth of the Divine Paternal Heart of God our Father cannot be brought into the homes of millions of believers and non-believers alike. In essence, a concentrated and determined effort to make the *Face of the Father* visible to all mankind must come.

With confidence, we can trust the Father Himself will answer the prayers of those who seek His creative guidance and divine assistance in this work. Thus, in just a short period of time, I believe such efforts will bear great fruit.

After this, the *deluge* will then come; billions of God's children will seek their Father in order to know, love and honor Him in a greater way than ever before in history.

THE FAMILY OF GOD

From my faith and experience, I suspect that many of the Father's chosen disciples are already in the world. Through His divine plan, God has seeded the ground and is already watering it with His tears of love for the work at hand.

Over time, all has been working towards this end. The Father's appeal to His children, to all Israel, has remained constant. 'Come home,' He says, 'realize and be enlightened of My presence in your HEART and in the world. Hear the words of My Shepherd,

My Son Jesus, who calls to you from the Cross, to follow Him home to Me, back home to My HEART.'

Much awaits the *Family of God* in and through the Divine Paternal Heart of its Father. The call of the ages has been sounded again in these times. The *peace of God* descends on the *Apostles of the Father*, who are now called to lead mankind forward to claim its true inheritance.

"The eternal Word descends on earth to save man: and whence does He descend? *His going out is from the end of Heaven.* He descends from the *Bosom of His divine Father,* where from eternity He was begotten in the brightness of the Saints.
—St. Alphonsus de Liguori

Epilogue

BACK TO THE GARDEN

> "*I am the Alpha and the Omega, the first and the last, the beginning and the end. Blessed are they that wash their robes in the blood of the Lamb: that they may have a right to the tree of life, and may enter in by the gates into the city*" (Rv 22:13-14).

The Church possesses not only its ministerial structure, external and visible, but simultaneously and above all, an interior capacity belonging to an invisible, yet real sphere – where there is the source of every bestowal of the divine life, and of the sharing in God's Trinitarian nature.[1]

The Sacraments are visible signs of this capacity to transmit the "new" life, a new life that pertains to the invisible mystery from which the supernatural vitality of the faithful derives from the Church.[2] This invisible dimension of the life of the Church draws from Christ's life and from Christ Himself. It is undepleting and inexhaustible for Christ is the "Vine":[3] "I am the vine and you are the branches. He who abides in me, and I in him bears much fruit…" (Jn 15:5)[4] This divine life that we draw from Christ belongs to Him by means of the Paschal Mystery, His victory over sin and death; the fruits of the Cross.[5]

In sending the Apostles to preach the Gospel and to administer Baptism, Christ made it clear that Baptism in Him is the Sacramental beginning of a new life and the sharing of the divine life (Mt 28:19).[6] Likewise, the Sacrament of Penance is also essentially connected with the mystery "of the vine and branches."[7] St. John Paul II writes that to forgive sins means, "in effect, to restore to man the sharing in the life which is Christ."[8]

But it is in the "Bread of Life," the Eucharist, that the full expression of this *communion of life in Christ* is found. For the Eucharist is the lasting sign of the presence of Christ's Body and Blood, the fraternal meal connected with the promulgation of the *Commandment of Love* (Jn 13:34; Jn 15:12).[9] It is the communication of "'life' from the vine to the branches," a communication that holds a Trinitarian unity formed by the Son together with the Father, as is evident in Jesus' words, "As the living Father sent me, and I live because of the Father, so he who eats of me will live because of me" (Jn 6:57).[10]

The call to "abide in [him], and I in you" (Jn 15:4), from the *Parable of the Vine and the Branches*, holds even deeper significance with the Father through the Eucharistic meal, for it is our call to perfection in the divine life—a perfection modeled after our Father. "You therefore must be perfect, as your heavenly Father is perfect" (Mt 5:48).[11] Moreover, it is a perfection that we are called to in imitating Christ, for He is the "perfect" reflection of the Father, "He who has seen me has seen the Father" (Jn 14:8-9).[12]

In light of this truth, we can see that it is the path laid out at the well to the Samaritan woman, who was told by Christ that worshiping the true God—God the Father—needed to be done "in spirit and truth" (Jn 4:23). Christ tells her that this may only be done by drinking the "living water" (Jn 4:10) that "provides eternal life" (cf. Jn 4:14).

NEW LIFE IN THE GARDEN

This "living water" and "living food" that the Church avails us in the Sacraments, are the sacred stepping stones along our path back to God. The Sacraments, in essence, are the key to the invisible part of mankind's journey back to the *life* that was offered to us in the Garden – back to *life* in our Father.

In the Garden of Eden, there were two special trees: the *Tree of the Knowledge of Good and Evil* and the *Tree of Life* (cf. Gn 2:9). Adam and Eve ate the fruit of the tree that they were told to avoid—the *Tree of the Knowledge of Good and Evil* (cf. Gn 3:7). They did not eat of the *Tree of Life* and after their sin, Scripture states, they were removed from the Garden by God (cf. Gn 3:24) so that they would *not* eat of this *Tree* (cf. Gn 3:22-24). From that time, through the coming of Christ until the present, Scripture tells us that man continues to experience pain, falsehood, wickedness, and turmoil; these are the consequences of the *Fall* in the Garden.

With Christ's Crucifixion and Resurrection, the way was opened by the Father through the Son and the Holy Spirit to return to our Father, to return to the Garden, and to partake in the *divine Fruits* of the *Tree of Life*. St. John's Gospel records the subtle mysteries that point to this truth in a symbolic way.

After Jesus died, after blood and water flowed from His Heart, St. John wrote that Christ is taken to a "garden" where a sepulcher is, and from where He will be resurrected from the dead: "Now in the place where he had been crucified there was a *garden* [italics added], and in the *garden* [italics added] a new tomb, in which no one had yet been buried. So they laid Jesus there because of the Jewish preparation day; for the tomb was close by" (Jn 19:41-42).

It is in this *garden*, therefore, where Jesus is resurrected and where the fullness of His life in the Father is restored; Jesus, the new

Adam, comes forward to *new life* in the Garden, to new life in the Heart of His Father.

Christ's Father, our Father, invites us also to return to His Garden and receive *new life* in Him. And, like Christ, to access the Father's Garden, we too need to die to our old self and be resurrected to new life. We do this through the Church's Sacramental mysteries that find their source in our Father. Thus, Christ invites us to drink from the "fountain of eternal life" (cf. Jn 4:14) and to "eat of the food that remains unto life eternal" (cf. Jn 6:27) that our Father gives through Him and the Holy Spirit to the world, so mankind might have life and to "have it abundantly" (Jn 10:10).

Like Jesus, we are resurrected in our Father's Heart, the mystical *Garden of Life*; we come to share in the fruit of the divine life in order to "bear the image of the man of heaven" (1 Cor 15:49).[13] In truth, we are "one" with the Father, Son, and Holy Spirit, "that they may all be one. As you, Father, are in me and I am in you" (Jn 17:21), and we "bear fruit," giving the Father all the glory: "By this is my Father glorified, that you bear much fruit and become my disciples" (Jn 15:8).

Indeed, in returning to our Father's divine Heart, we are like the Samaritan woman. We now worship our Father in truth and spirit, as the time for such worship is truly at hand. Like her, there is new *life* in us and, therefore, we feel the Spirit of our Father *in us* and want to tell all those who will listen. Like her, we are ready to leave our possessions at the well, ready to leave our old lives, and announce to everyone how our Father knows us, has forgiven our sinful past, and called us to His mercy and love. Through the "Father's mysterious plan," through "*His Fatherly Heart*," we come to know and see Him clearly, as He desires to reveal Himself. In the Heart of our Father, we "have the right to the *Tree of Life* [italics added]" (Rv 22:14), we have our "share" in it (Rv 22:19). It is the continued unfolding of the enlightened vision that St. Paul tells us of in Ephesians, "May the God of Our Lord Jesus Christ, the Father of glory, grant you a spirit of wisdom and insight to know him clearly" (Eph 1:17).

THE FAMILY OF GOD

From the *Garden* to the *Well*, and back to the *Garden*, mankind's road to salvation and eternal life is part of the mystery of our Father and the mystery of His paternal love for us as revealed in Christ. St. John Paul II writes, "It is precisely thanks to this likeness that Christ, the final Adam, by revelation of the mystery of the Father and his love, fully reveals man to man himself and makes his supreme calling clear" (*GS* 22).[14]

In giving our *fiat* to our Mother Mary's call, in walking in the footsteps of our Lord and Savior, Jesus Christ, all of mankind is called to help build a new world—a new *Paradise*. Through the Catholic Church's proclamation of a feast day in honor of the paternal love our heavenly Father, the Church can lead the whole world to come to share in this vision of great hope.

It is to be a new world where the *love* and *life* contained in our Father is ours to possess and ours to share in a more profound and richer way; for we are *one* with and in the Father, Son and Holy Spirit; a *Family of God*,[15] dwelling together in the *Garden*, the Divine Paternal Heart of God our Father, as it was meant to be – *in the beginning*.

Consecration Prayer *to* God Our Father

My Dearest Father, please accept this offering of myself—my body, mind, and soul:

I *praise* You for Your Creation—all Your works and wonders.

I *thank* You for giving me life and for all that You have done for me.

I *offer* up to You all that You have so generously given me.

I am sincerely *sorry* for not knowing, loving, serving, and honoring You as I should.

I embrace my *inheritance* as Your child, both the joy and the responsibilities.

I give you my *"Yes"* so that I may be an instrument of Your Will.

I pledge my *fidelity* and I ask for the grace of steadfastness and perseverance in my Faith.

Most loving, caring, and merciful of Fathers, in Your Divine Presence, I sincerely proclaim my love for You; I give myself (and my family) to You; and I solemnly *consecrate* myself (and my family) to You—now and forever.

Dearest Father, as Your child, I ask—

That You send Mary to guide me to Jesus, and that Jesus sends me the Holy Spirit so that they may all bring me to You.

That You dwell with me and in me—a living temple prepared by Mary, dedicated by Jesus, and purified by Your Holy Spirit. And may I always be with You and in You.

That You permit me, as Your child, to be Your true and intimate friend—one who loves You above all things.

And that You come for me when I die, to bring me home to You.

I further ask You, Father, for the sake of all mankind:

To have mercy on all Your children—past, present, and future.

To bring peace to the world and to gather all Your children to Yourself.

And that Your Kingdom comes and Your Will is done on earth as it is in heaven.

Amen.

NOTES

THE MYSTERY OF THE DIVINE PATERNAL HEART OF GOD OUR FATHER

INTRODUCTION – FINDING OUR FATHER

1. J. Bainvel, (1910) *Devotion to the Sacred Heart of Jesus, The Catholic Encyclopedia*, New York: Robert Appleton Company. Retrieved August 19, 2012, from New Advent: http://www.newadvent.org/catlen/071/163a.h+m.
2. Dr. John Magee, D.D., *The Two Hearts in Papal Teaching*. Dublin, Ireland: The Marian Centre of Resource and Information, 1997, pg. 5.
3. Ez 36:26-27.
4. John Paul II, *Tertio Millennio Adveniente*, I, N. 7.
5. Raniero Cantalamessa, O.F.M. Cap., *Life in the Lordship of Christ: A Commentary on Paul's Epistle to the Romans,* New York: Sheed & Ward, 1990, pp. 96-97.
6. John Paul II, Apostolic Letter, *Tertio Millennio Adveniente,* (10 November 1994), IV, N. 52.
7. Ibid.
8. Ibid., III, N.18.
9. Ibid., IV, N. 46.
10. Benedict XVI, Encyclical Letter, *Caritas in Veritate*, (29 June 2009), II, N. 33.
11. John Paul II, Encyclical Letter, *Dives in Misericordia*, (30 November 1980), VIII, N.15.
12. Ibid., I, N.1.; 2 Cor 1:3.
13. Michael O'Carroll, C.S. Sp., *Trinitas, A Theological Encyclopedia of the Holy Trinity*, Collegeville, Minnesota: The Liturgical Press, 1987, pg. 17.

14. Johannes Quasten, *Patrology, Vol I, The Beginnings of Patristic Literature,* Allen, Texas: Christian Classics, 1952, pg. 240.
15. John R. Willis, S.J., *The Teachings of the Church Fathers*, San Francisco: Igantius Press, 2002, pp.172-173.
16. St. Basil the Great, *On the Holy Spirit*, 3rd Printing, Westwood, NY: St. Vladimirs, Seminary Press, 1997.
17. John R. Willis, S.J., *The Teachings of the Church Fathers*, pg. 185.
18. Michael O'Carroll, C.S. Sp., *Trinitas*, pg. 35.
19. Pius XII, Encyclical Letter, *Haurietis Aquas,* (15 May 1956), N. 65.; Registr. epist., lib. IV, ep. 31, ad Theodorum medicum: P.L. LXXVII, 706.
20. John R. Willis, S.J., *The Teachings of the Church Fathers*, pg.112.
21. St. Thomas Aquinas, *Summa Theologica – Vol. I*, Warminster Maryland: Christian Classics, 1981, pg. 175.
22. Paul Milcent, *Saint John Eudes*, Glasgow, England: John S. Burns & Sons, 1963, pg. 130.
23. Ibid.
24. John K. Ryan (ed.), *Introduction to the Devout Life – St. Francis de Sales*, Garden City, New York: Image Books, 1972, pg. 104.
25. St. Alphonsus de Liguori, *The Incarnation Birth and Infancy of Jesus Christ*, Brooklyn, New York: Redemptoris Fathers, 1927, pg. 265.
26. St. Louis de Montfort, *The Love of Eternal Wisdom*, Bayshore, New York: Montfort Publications, 1960, pg. 13.; This meditation is the same as Meditation V., for the first Thursday of Advent, p. 182.; "A summo cœlo egressio ejus."— *Ps.* xviii. 7."; "Non horruisti virginis uterum."
27. John Beevers, *The Autobiography of Saint Therese of Lisieux, The Story of a Soul*, New York, New York: Image Books, 1957, pg.158.
28. *Divine Mercy In My Soul, The Diary of Sister M. Faustina Kowalska*, Stockbridge, Mass.: 1987, N. 1279, pg. 461.
29. Pius XII, *Haurietis Aquas*, N. 106.; Jn 14:6.
30. John Paul II, General Audience, August 19, 1987.
31. Joseph Ratzinger, Pope Benedict XVI, *Jesus of Nazareth, From the Baptism in the Jordan to the Transfiguration*, pg. 7.
32. *Vatican Insider, CA, La Stampa It*, 04/24//2013, News.VA, *The Vatican Today*, Vatican Radio 2013-24-24.

33. *Catechism of the Catholic Church*, New Hope, Kentucky: Urbit et Orbi Communications, 1994, N. 758, LG 2.
34. Robert Moynihan, *The Antichrist, Inside the Vatican*, Rome. Italy: August- September, 2002, pg. 5.
35. Ibid.
36. Ibid.
37. Ibid.
38. Ibid.
39. Ron Rosenbaum, *How the End Begins, The Road to a Nuclear World War III*, New York, Simon & Shuster, 2011, pp. 6, 24-30.
40. Jean Galot, S.J., *ABBA, Father, We Long to See Your Face – Theological Insights into the First Person of the Trinity*, New York: Alba House, 1992, pg. 9.
41. Ibid., pg. 226.
42. Raniero Cantalamessa, O.F.M. Cap., *Life in the Lordship of Christ: A Commentary on Paul's Epistle to the Romans*, pp. 96-97.
43. Jean Galot, S.J., *ABBA, Father, We Long to See Your Face, Theological Insights into the First Person of the Trinity*, pp. 205-232.
44. Ibid.
45. Ibid.

PART ONE – THE THRESHOLD OF THE FATHER

CHAPTER ONE – ORIGINAL SEPARATION

1. Austin Flannery (ed.), *Dogmatic Constitution of the Church, Lumen Gentium, The Mystery of the Church* from *Vatican Council II, The Conciliar and Post Conciliar Documents*, Northport, New York: Costello Publishing Company, I, N.2.
2. *Catechism of the Catholic Church*, N. 758, 759.
3. Ibid., N. 391.
4. Ibid.
5. Ibid.
6. Ibid., N. 392.
7. Ibid.
8. Ibid., N. 397.

9. His Holiness Pope John Paul II, *Crossing the Threshold of Hope*, New York: Alfred A. Knopf, 1994, pp. 225-228.
10. Benedict XVI, Encyclical Letter, *Deus Caritas Est*, (25 January 2006), I, 1.
11. *Catechism of the Catholic Church*, N. 403.
12. Ibid., N. 404.
13. Dr. Ludwig Ott, *Fundamentals of Catholic Dogma,* Rockford. Illinois: Tan Books and Publishers, Inc. 1974, pg. 107.
14 *Catechism of the Catholic Church*, N. 404.
15. Ibid., N. 405.
16. Ibid., N. 400.
17. Ibid., N. 400, 401.
18. Ibid., N. 408.
19. Ibid., N. 409.
20. His Holiness Pope John Paul II, *Crossing the Threshold of Hope*, pp. 225-228.
21. Ibid.
22. Rev. Peter M. J. Stravinskas, Ph.D., S.T.L., (ed.), *Our Sunday Visitor's Catholic Encyclopedia*, *Our Sunday Visitor Publishing Division*, Huntington, Indiana: 1991, pg. 864.
23. John Paul II, General Audience, September 3, 1986.
24. John Paul II, General Audience, September 3, 1986, September 10, 1986.
25. Dr. Ludwig Ott, *Fundamentals of Catholic Dogma,* 1974, pp. 110-111.
26. Ibid.
20. Ibid.
27. Ibid.
28. Ibid.
29. Ibid.
30. Ibid.
31. Ibid.
32. John Paul II, General Audience, October 1, 1986.
33. John Paul II, General Audience, October 8, 1986.
34. His Holiness Pope John Paul II, *Crossing the Threshold of Hope*, pp. 225-228.

35. Ibid.
36. Ibid.
37. John Paul II, General Audience, April 30, 1986.
38. His Holiness Pope John Paul II, *Crossing the Threshold of Hope*, pp. 225-228.
39. John Paul II, General Audience, August 27, 1986.
40. Dr. Ludwig Ott, *Fundamentals of Catholic Dogma*, pp. 110-111.
41. John Paul II, Encyclical Letter, *Dominum et Vivificantem* (18 May 1986), II, N. 33.
42. Ibid.
43. Ibid., N. 38.
44. Ibid.
45. Ibid.
46. John Paul II, General Audience, October 29, 1986.
47. His Holiness Pope John Paul II, *Crossing the Threshold of Hope*, pp. 225-228.

CHAPTER TWO – THE RAYS OF GOD'S FATHERHOOD

1. *Catechism of the Catholic Church*, N. 53, N. 54.
2. *Dogmatic Constitution of the Church, Lumen Gentium, The Mystery of the Church*, I, N. I, pg 350.
3. *Dogmatic Constitution of the Church, Lumen Gentium, The Mystery of the Church*, I, N. 1-8.
4. Eph 3:14.
5. Gen 6:22.
6. Gen. 15:4.
7. *Catechism of the Catholic Church*, N. 57.
8. *Dogmatic Constitution on Divine Revelation*, Boston, Mass: Daughters of St. Paul, November 18, 1965, I, N.3.
9. *Catechism of the Catholic Church*, N. 239.
10. Ibid., N. 53.
11. Ibid., N. 239.

CHAPTER THREE – ONE WITH THE FATHER

1. John Paul II, Encyclical Letter, *Dives en Misericordia*, (30 November 1980), I, N. 2.

CHAPTER FOUR – THE THRESHOLD OF THE FATHER

1. *Catechism of the Catholic Church*, N. 1327.
2. The Catholic Church, *Catechism of the Council of Trent*, Part IV (translated by John A. McHugh, O.P., S.T.M. Litt..D., and Charles J. Callan, O.P., S.T.M. Litt. D.), Rockford, Illinois, Tan Books and Publishers, Inc., 1982, II, pp. 162-163.
3. Ibid.
4. Ibid.
5. Ibid.
6. Ibid.
7. *Catechism of the Catholic Church*, N. 683.
8. Ibid, pg. 170.
9. His Holiness Pope John Paul II, *Crossing the Threshold of Hope*, pp. 225-229.
10. Ibid.
11. Ibid., pp. 4, 229.
12. John Paul II, Encyclical Letter, *Dives en Misericordia*, I, N. 2.
13. His Holiness Pope John Paul II, *Crossing the Threshold of Hope*, pp. 225-229.
14. John Paul II, Encyclical Letter, *Tertio Millennio Adveniente*, IV, N. 52.
15. Ibid., I, N. 7, N. 8.

PART II – NEAREST TO THE FATHER'S HEART

CHAPTER FIVE – NEAREST TO THE FATHER'S HEART

1. *The Jerusalem Bible – Reader's Edition* New York: Doubleday, 1966.
2. Jean Galot, SJ., *ABBA, Father, We Long to See Your Face – Theological Insights into the First Person of the Trinity*, pp. 1-3.
3. Ibid., pg. 8.
4. Ibid.

5. Ibid.
6. Joseph Ratzinger, Pope Benedict XVI, *Jesus of Nazareth, From the Baptism in the Jordan to the Transfiguration*, San Francisco: Ignatius Press, 2007, pp. 265-266.
7. Pope John Paul II, General Audience, June 3, 1987.
8. Joseph Ratzinger ,Pope Benedict XVI, *Jesus of Nazareth, From the Baptism in the Jordan to the Transfiguration*, pp. 340, 341.
9. John Paul II, General Audience, August 19, 1987.
10. John Paul II, General Audience, December 7, 1988.
11. John Paul II, General Audience, December 7, 1988, January 11, 1989.
12. Mariology: A Guide for Priests, Deacons, Seminarians and Consecrated Persons, *Mary, Mother and Model of the Church*, Fr. Enrique Llamas, O.C.D.,Goleta, California: Queenship Publishing, 2007, pg. 572.

CHAPTER SIX - THE MYSTERY OF THE FATHER'S HEART

1. John Paul II, Encyclical Letter, *Dives in Misericordia*,(30 November 1980), VIII, N. 15; Cf. Jn 14:9.
2. Ibid, I, N. 2
3. Ibid, V N. 7.
4. Dr. John Magee, D.D., *The Two Hearts in Papal Teaching*, pg. 5.
5. John Paul II, Encyclical Letter, *Redemptor Hominis*, (4 March 1979), N. 9; Ps 8:6; Cf. Gn 1:26; Cf. Gn 3:6-13; Cf. Eucharistic Prayer IV; . Cf. Vatican Council II: Pastoral Constitution on the Church in the Modern World *Gaudium et Spes*, 37:*AAS* 58 (1966) 1054-1055; Dogmatic Constitution on the Church *Lumen Gentium,* 48: *AAS* 57 (1965) 53-54.
6. Dr. John Magee, D.D., *The Two Hearts in Papal Teaching*, pg. 7.
7. Ibid., pp. 5-23.
8. John Paul II, General Audience, December 7, 1988.
9. John Paul II, General Audience, January 2, 1980.
10. John Paul II, General Audience, September 10, 1986.
11 John Paul II, *Tertio Millennio Adveniente*, I, N. 8.

12. Jean Galot, S.J., *ABBA, Father, We Long to See your Face – Theological Insights into the First Person of the Trinity*, pp.8-9.
13. Ibid.
14. Ibid.
15. Pope Benedict XVI, *Jesus of Nazareth, From the Baptism in the Jordan to the Transfiguration*, pg. 6.
16. Pius XII, *Haurietis Aquas*, N. 106.
17. John Paul II, *Tertio Millennio Adveniente*, I, N. 7.
18. *Catechism of the Catholic Church*, N. 759; LG 2.
19. Ibid., N. 758.
20. John Paul II, *Dives in Misericordia*, I, N.2.

CHAPTER SEVEN – A CRISIS OF CIVILIZATION

1. Pius XI, Encyclical Letter, *Caritate Christi Compulsi*, (3 May 1932), N. 32; Hebr. IV, 16.
2. John Paul II, *Redemptor Hominis*, N. 8, N. 15; Rom. 8:22
3. John Paul II, Apostolic Letter, *Letter to the Family from Pope John Paul II*, (2 February 1994), I, N. 2.
4. Ron Rosenbaum, *How the End Begins, The Road to a Nuclear World War III*, pp. 24-27.
5. Ibid., pg. 6.
6. Ibid., pg. 27.
7. John Paul II, *Act of Entrustment to Mary*, Rome, (8 October 2000), N. 3.
8. Ron Rosenbaum, *How the End Begins, the Road to a Nuclear World War III*, pp. 8-14.
9. Ibid.
10. Ibid., pp. 16-23
11. Ibid., pp. 23-27.
12. Ibid., pg. 26.
13. John Paul II, Encyclical Letter, *Evangelium Vitae*, (25 March 1995), I, N. 28.
14. Ibid., III, N. 66.
15. Ibid., I, N. 12.
16. Ibid., III, N. 66.

17. Ibid., IV, N. 101.; Message for the 1977 World Day of Peace: AAS 68 (1976), 711-712.
18. Ibid., I, 1; N.3; 12; 20; Pastoral Constitution on the Church in the Modern World *Gaudium et Spes*, 27.
19. Benedict XVI, *Caritas in Veritate*, II, N. 28.
20. Francis, General Audience, June 2, 2013.
21. Ibid.
22. John Paul II, General Audience, November 12, 1986.
23. John Paul II, *Redemptor Hominis*, N. 1.
24. Ibid., N. 13; 18.
25. John Paul II, *Tertio Millennio Adveniente*, IV, N. 52.
26. Ibid., IV, N. 49.
27. Ez 36.
28. John Paul II, General Audience, December 7, 1988.
29. John Paul II, *Tertio Millennio Adveniente*, IV, N. 39-49.
30. John Paul II, Encyclical Letter, *Dominum et Vivificantem* (18 May 1986), I, N. 7; Jn 16:15.
31. John Paul II, *Tertio Millennio Adveniente*, IV, N. 46.
32. Benedict XVI, Encyclical Letter, *Deus Caritas Est* (25 December 2005), I, N. 17.

PART III – THE HEART OF GOD IN SCRIPTURE AND THE CHURCH

CHAPTER EIGHT – A FATHERLY GOD

1. John Paul II, *Dives in Misericordia*, I, N. 1; III, N. 4; Jn 14:8-9.
2. John Paul II, Apostolic Letter, *Mulieris Dignitatem*, (15 August, 1988), III, N. 8.
3. Michael O'Carroll, , *Trinitas*, pg. 14.
4. The Catholic Church, *Catechism of the Council of Trent*, Part IV (translated by John A. McHugh, O.P., S.T.M. Litt..D., and Charles J. Callan, O.P., S.T.M. Litt. D.), IV, pg. 502.
5. *Catechism of the Catholic Church*, N. 200.
6. Ibid.
7. Ibid., N. 219.

8. Ibid., N. 238.
9. Ibid., N. 201; Dt 6:4-5.
10. Ibid., N. 219, 238; Cf. Dt 32:6; Mal 2:10.
11. Ibid., N. 238; Cf 2 Sm 7:14; Ps 68.6.
12. Ibid., N. 239; Cf. Is 66:13; Ps 131:2.
13. Ibid., Cf. Ps 27:10; Eph 3:14; Is 49:15.
14. Ibid.
15. Ibid., N. 257; Eph 1:4-5, 9; Rom 8:15, 29.

CHAPTER NINE – THE HEART OF GOD IN THE OLD TESTAMENT

1. Benedict XVI, *Jesus of Nazareth, From the Baptism in the Jordan to the Transfiguration*, pp. 206-207.
2. Pius XII, *Haurietis Aquas*, (15 May 1956), N. 38.
3. John Paul II, General Audience, December 4, 1985.
4. Michael O'Carroll, *Trinitas*, pp. 52-53.

CHAPTER TEN – THE PROPRIETY OF THE FATHER

1. Michael O'Carroll, *Trinitas*, pg. 61.
2. *Catechism of the Catholic Church*, N. 279.
3. Ibid., N. 288; Cf. Gn 15:5; Jer 33:19-26.
4. Ibid., N. 292.; Cf. Ps 33:6; 104:30; Gn 1:2-3
5. Ibid.; St. Irenaeus, *Adverse Haeresis*, 2, 30, 9; 4, 20, 1: PG 7/1, 822, 1032.
6. Michael O'Carroll, *Trinitas*, pg. 146.
7. Austin Flannery, O.P., Vatican Council II, Vol. I, pg. 350.
8. *Catechism of the Catholic Church*, N. 316.
9. Michael O'Carroll, *Trinitas*, pg. 14.
10. Ibid., pp. 42-45.
11. The Catholic Church, *Catechism of the Council of Trent*, Part IV, pg. 57.
12. Michael O'Carroll, *Trinitas*, pp. 42-45.
13. *Catechism of the Catholic Church*, N. 684; St. Gregory of Nazianzus, *Oratio Theol.*, 5, 26 (= Oratio 31, 26): PG 36, 161–163.
14. John Paul II, General Audience, October 16, 1985.

15. Benedict XVI, *Jesus of Nazareth, From the Baptism in the Jordan to the Transfiguration,* pp. 235-236.
16. Michael O'Carroll, *Trinitas,* pg. 14.

PART IV – THE DIVINE PATERNAL HEART OF GOD THE FATHER

CHAPTER ELEVEN – THE THEOLOGY OF THE FATHER

1. Jean Galot, S.J., *ABBA, Father, We Long to See your Face – Theolgical Insights into the First Person of the Trinity,* pg. 31.
2. Ibid., pg. 32.
3. Ibid.,
4. Ibid., pg. 33.
5. Ibid.
6. Ibid.
7. Ibid.
8. Ibid., pp. 39-40.
9. Ibid.
10. Ibid., pp. 48-50.
11. Ibid., pg. 34.
12. Ibid. pg. 35.
13. Ibid.
14. Ibid., pp. 35-53.

CHAPTER TWELVE – CHRIST REVEALS THE FATHER

1. Jean Galot, S.J., *ABBA, Father, We Long to See your Face – Theological Insights into the First Person of the Trinity,* pp. 50-55.
2. Edward D. O'Connor, C.S.C., *The Catholic Vision* from *Our Sunday Visitor,* Huntington, Indiana: Our Sunday Visitor Publishing Division, Inc., pp 135-138.
3. Ibid.
4. Ibid.
5. Ibid.
6. John Paul II, General Audience, July 24, 1985.
7. John Paul II, General Audience, December 4, 1985.

8. John Paul II, General Audience, October 2, 1985.
9. Ibid.
10. St. John Damascene, *An Exact Exposition of the Orthodox Faith*, Kindle Edition [2010-08-08], pg. 173.
11. St. Basil the Great, *On the Holy Spirit*, 3rd Printing, Westwood, NY: St. Ulandanirs, Seminary Press, 1997.
12. St. Athanasius, *On the Councils of Ariminum and Seleucia*, N. 26.
13. V. Lossky, *In the Image and Likeness of God*, Crestwood, New York: St. Vladimir's Seminary Press, 1974, pg. 34.
14. John Alexander (Gen. Ed.), *The Jerusalem Bible – Reader's Edition* New York, New York: Doubleday, A Division of Random House, Inc., 1966.
15. John Paul II, General Audience, August 19, 1987.
16. Benedict XVI, *Jesus of Nazareth, From the Baptism in the Jordan to the Transfiguration*, pp. 222-223.

CHAPTER THIRTEEN – THE HEART OF THE FATHER IN THE NEW TESTAMENT

1. Jean Galot, S.J., *ABBA, Father, We Long to See your Face – Theological Insights into the First Person of the Trinity*, pg. 211.
2. Ibid., pg. 9.
3. Ibid., pg. 8.
4. Ibid.
5. Ibid., pp. 8-9.
6. Ibid. pg. 8
7. John Paul II, General Audience, June 19, 1991.
8. John Paul II, General Audience, August 19, 1987.
9. Jean Galot, *ABBA, Father, We Long to See Your Face*, pg. 135.
10. Ibid.
11. Ibid.
12. Ibid.
13. Ibid. pp. 134-135.
14. Ibid., pg. 133.
15. Johannes Quasten, *Patrology, Vol II, The Anti Nicene Literature After Iraneius*, pg. 232.

16. Mariology: A Guide for Priests, Deacons, Seminarians and Consecrated Persons, *Mary, Mother and Model of the Church*, Fr. Enrique Llamas, O.C.D., pg. 572.
17. John Paul II, General Audience, August 19, 1987.
18. John Paul II, General Audience, December 7, 1988.
19. Francis, Encyclical Letter, *Lumen Fidei*, (29 June 2013), IV, N. 56.
20. Benedict XVI, *Jesus of Nazareth, From the Baptism in the Jordan to the Transfiguration*, pg. 266.

CHAPTER FOURTEEN – THE PATERNAL HEART AND THE BREAD OF LIFE

1. John Paul II, General Audience, December, 9, 1987.
2. John Paul II, General Audience, May, 27, 1987.
3. Ibid.
4. Ibid.
5. Michael O'Carroll, C.S.Sp. *Corpus Christi*, Collegville, Minnesota: The Liturgical Press, 1988, pg. 91.
6. John Paul II, *Dives in Misericordia*, V. 7.
7. John Paul II, General Audience, July, 13, 1988.
8. John Paul II, General Audience, December 9, 1987.

CHAPTER FIFTEEN – THE SACRED HEART OF JESUS

1. Matthew Bunson, *Our Sunday Visitor's Encyclopedia of Catholic History*, Huntington, Indiana: Our Sunday Visitor, Inc., 1995, pp. 740-741, J. Bainvel, (1910) *Devotion to the Sacred Heart of Jesus*, in *The Catholic Encyclopedia*, New York: Robert Appleton Company. Retrieved August 19, 2012, from New Advent: http://www.newadvent.org/catlen/071/163a.h+m.
2. James Kubicki, S.J., *A Heart on Fire, Rediscovering Devotion to the Sacred Heart of Jesus*, Notre Dame, Indiana: Ave Maria Press, 2012, pg. 40.
3. Ibid.
4. Ibid, pg. 42.
5. Dr. John Magee, *The Two Hearts in Papal Teaching*, pg. 8.
6. Ibid., pg. 8.

7. Ibid.
8. Ibid., pg. 10.
9. Ibid.
10. Ibid., pg. 12.
11. Ibid., pp. 8-9.
12. Ibid., pg. 8.
13. Ibid., pg. 14.
14. Ibid., pg. 16.
15. Ibid., pg. 19.
16. Ibid., pg. 20.
17. Ibid., pg. 21.
18. John Paul II, Homily at Paray-le-Monial, 5 October 1986, English translation *The Pope Speaks*, 1986, N. 11, pg. 329.
19. Dr. John Magee, *The Two Hearts in Papal Teaching*, pg. 22.
20. Ibid., pp. 21-23.
21. John Paul II, *Tertio Millennio Adveniente*, IV, N. 46.
22. J. Bainvel, (1910) *Devotion to the Sacred Heart of Jesus*, in *The Catholic Encyclopedia*, New York: Robert Appleton Company. Retrieved August 19, 2012, from New Advent: http://www.newadvent.org/catlen/071/163a.h+m.
23. Ibid.
24. Leo XIII, Encyclical Letter, *Annum Sacrum*, (25 March 1899), N. 8.
25. Pius XI, Encyclical Letter, *Miserentissimus Redemptor*, (8 May 1928), N. 18.
26. Pius XI, Encyclical Letter, *Caritate Christi Compulsi*, (3 May 1932), N. 30.
27. Pius XII, *Haurietis Aquas*, N. 69.
28. Ibid., N. 65; 106.

CHAPTER SIXTEEN – DIVINE HEARTS

1. Jean Galot, S.J., *ABBA, Father, We Long to See your Face – Insights into the First Person of the Trinity*, pg. XIII.
2. Ibid., pp. 51-56.
3. John Paul II, General Audience, March 8, 1989.
4. Michael O'Carroll, *Trinitas*, pp. 42-45.

5. Ibid., pg. 35.
6. St. John Damascene, *De Fide Orthodoxa,*1,8, PHSCIV.
7. Michael O'Carroll, *Trinitas*, pp. 210-212.
8. John Paul II, General Audience, November 20, 1985.
9. Ibid.
10. John Paul II, General Audience, November 27, 1985.
11. Johannes Quasten, *Patrology, Vol I, The Beginnings of Patristic Literature*, pg. 240.
12. John R. Willis, S.J., *The Teachings of the Church Fathers*, pg. 85.
13. Pope Pius XII, *Haurietis Aquas*, N. 106.; Jn 14:6.
14. Benedict XVI, *Jesus of Nazareth, From the Baptism in the Jordan to the Transfiguration*, pg. 340.

CHAPTER SEVENTEEN – THE RIGHT HAND OF THE FATHER

1. Benedict XVI, *Deus Caritas Est*, II, N. 19.
2. Dr. Ludwig Ott, *Fundamentals of Catholic Dogma*, pp. 52, 53, 57.
3. Ibid., pg. 59.
4. Ibid., pg. 194-195
5. The Catholic Church, *Catechism of the Council of Trent*, Article VI, pg. 75.
6. Ibid., pg. 74.
7. *Catechism of the Catholic Church*, N. 663; St. John Damascene, De Fide Orth., 4, 2: PG 94, 1104C.
8. St. John Damascene, *An Exact Exposition of the Orthodox Faith*, [2012-08-08], Kindle Edition, pg. 173.

CHAPTER EIGHTEEN – THE DIVINE PATERNAL HEART OF GOD OUR FATHER

1. John Paul II, *Tertio Millenio Adveniente*, IV, N. 54
2. John Paul II, *Dives in Misericordia*, I, N. 2.
3. Thomas W. Petrisko, *Fatima's Third Secret Explained*, McKees Rocks, Pennsylvania: St. Andrew's Productions, 2001, pp. 56-59.
4. John Paul II, *Dives in Misericordia*, IV, N. 5.

5. Jean Galot, S.J., *ABBA, Father, We Long to See your Face – Theological Insights into the First Person of the Trinity*, pp. 8-9.
6. John K. Ryan (ed.), *Introduction to the Devout Life – St. Francis de Sales*, pg. 85.
7. Gn 1:27, Sir 17:1.
8. Jean Galot, S.J., *ABBA, Father, We Long to See your Face, Theological Insights into the First Person of the Trinity*, pp. 82-83.
9. Ibid.
10. *Catechism of the Catholic Church*, N, 369, N. 370, N. 371, N. 372, N. 373.
11. *Divine Mercy in My Soul, The Diary of Sr. M. Faustina Kowalska*, Diary N. 603, pg. 253.
12. Benedict XVI, *Jesus of Nazareth, From the Baptism in the Jordan to the Transfiguration*, pp. 222-223.
13. Ibid.
14. Is 62:4.
15. Ez 36:26.
16. *Catechism of the Catholic Church*, N. 541, 542.
17. Benedict XVI, *Jesus of Nazareth, From the Baptism in the Jordan to the Transfiguration*, pg. 147.

CHAPTER NINETEEN – THE PATERNAL HEART OF LIFE

1, John Paul II, *Evangelium Vitae*, II, 61.; Hence the Prophet Jeremiah: "The word of the Lord came to me saying: 'Before I formed you in the womb I knew you, and before you were born I consecrated you; I appointed you a prophet to the nations'" (1:4-5). The Psalmist, for his part, addresses the Lord in these words: "Upon you I have leaned from my birth; you are he who took me from my mother's womb" (Ps 71:6; cf. *Is* 46:3; *Job* 10:8-12; *Ps* 22:10-11). So too the Evangelist Luke - in the magnificent episode of the meeting of the two mothers, Elizabeth and Mary, and their two sons, John the Baptist and Jesus, still hidden in their mothers' wombs (cf. 1:39-45) - emphasizes how even before their birth the two little ones are able to communicate: the child recognizes the coming of the Child and leaps for joy

2. Ibid., Int., 2.
3. Ibid., II, 44.

CHAPTER TWENTY – AN ATTACK ON GOD HIMSELF

1. John Paul II, *Evangelium Vitae*, II, N. 50.
2. Ibid., I, N. 9.
3. Ibid., I, 21.
4. Ibid., III, 12, 59
5. Ibid., I N. 22.
6. John Paul II, *Dominum et Vivificantem*, II, 38; *De Civitate Dei*, XIV, 28: CCL 48, p. 541.
7. Ibid., II, 38; Pastoral Constitution on the Church in the Modern World, *Gaudium et Spes*, N. 36.

CHAPTER TWENTY-ONE – THE GRANDEUR OF THE FATHER'S LOVE

1. John Paul II, *Evangelium Vitae*, I, 25.
2. *Catechism of the Catholic Church*, N. 700.

PART V – TRIUMPH OF THE LIVING FATHER

CHAPTER TWENTY-TWO – THE LIVING FATHER

1. John Paul II, General Audience, April 19, 1989.
2. John Paul II, Apostolic Letter, *Novo Millennio Inuente*, (6 January 2001), III, N. 33.
3. Jean Galot, *ABBA, Father, We Long to See Your Face, Theological Insights into the First Person of the Trinity*, pg. 2.
4. Ibid., pg. 2.
5. Ibid.
6. Ibid.
7. Ibid.
8. *Catechism of the Catholic Church*, N. 1439.

CHAPTER TWENTY-THREE – FAVORED DAUGHTER OF THE FATHER

1. Mariology: A Guide for Priests, Deacons, Seminarians and Consecrated Persons,
The Virgin Mary in the New Testament, Fr. Settimio Manelli, pg. 77.
2. Ibid., pg. 77.
3. Ibid..
4. Ibid., pp. 70-71.
5. Mariology: A Guide for Priests, Deacons, Seminarians and Consecrated Persons, *The Mother of God*, Fr. Manfred Hauke, pg. 185.
6. Ibid., pp. 185-186.
7. Ibid., pp. 185-187.
8. Mariology: A Guide for Priests, Deacons, Seminarians and Consecrated Persons, *Mary Co-Redemptrix: The Beloved Associate of Christ*, Msgr. Arthur Burton Calkins, pp. 349-409.
9. Ibid., pp. 349-409.
10. Mariology: A Guide for Priests, Deacons, Seminarians and Consecrated Persons, *The Virgin Mary in the New Testament*, Fr. Settimio Manelli, pg. 112.
11. Mariology: A Guide for Priests, Deacons, Seminarians and Consecrated Persons, *Mary Co-Redemptrix: The Beloved Associate of Christ*, Msgr. Arthur Burton Calkins, pg. 356.
12. Ibid., pp. 349-409.
13. Mariology: A Guide for Priests, Deacons, Seminarians and Consecrated Persons, *The Virgin Mary in the New Testament*, Fr. Settimio Manelli, pg. 51.
14. Ibid., pg. 63.
15. Ibid., pp. 67-68.
16. Mariology: A Guide for Priests, Deacons, Seminarians and Consecrated Persons, *The Mother of God*, Fr. Manfred Hauke, pp. 208-210.
17. Ibid.
18. Mariology: A Guide for Priests, Deacons, Seminarians and Consecrated Persons, *The Mother of God*, Fr. Manfred Hauke, pg. 208.
19. Ibid.

20. Ibid., pg. 209.
21. Ibid.
22. Ibid., pg. 212.
23. *Catechism of the Catholic Church*, N. 722.
24. Ibid.
25. Mariology: A Guide for Priests, Deacons, Seminarians and Consecrated Persons, *The Predestination of the Virgin Mother and Her Immaculate Conception of God*, Fr. Peter M. Fehlner, pp. 218-220.
26. Ibid., pp. 213-276.

CHAPTER TWENTY-FOUR – OUR LADY OF THE PATERNAL HEART

1. Mariology: A Guide for Priests, Deacons, Seminarians and Consecrated Persons, *The Predestination of the Virgin Mother and Her Immaculate Conception of God*, Fr. Peter M. Fehlner, pg. 272.
2. Ibid.
3. Mariology: A Guide for Priests, Deacons, Seminarians and Consecrated Persons, *The Mother of God in the Orthodox Church*, Fr. Vladimir Selinsky, pp. 788-789.
4. John Paul II, General Audience, July 8, 1987.
5. Ibid.
6. St. Francis de Sales, *Introduction to the Devout Life*, 2, N. 16.

CHAPTER TWENTY-FIVE – THE TRIUMPH OF THE IMMACULATE HEART

1. Thomas W. Petrisko, *The Fatima Prophecies; At the Doorstep of the World*, McKees Rocks, Pennsylvania, Saint Andrew's Productions, 1998, pp. IX-XII.
2. Ibid., pp. 93-109.
3. Pope John Paul II, *Crossing the Threshold of Hope*, pp. 225-228.
4. Thomas W. Petrisko, *The Last Crusade*, McKees Rocks, Pennsylvania: St. Andrew's Productions, 1996, pg. III.
5. Ibid., pg. 1.
6. Ibid.
7. Ibid.

8. Ibid., pg. 7.
9. Ibid.
10. Ibid.
11. Ibid.
12. Ibid., pp. 7-8.
13. Ibid.
14. Ibid.
15. Ibid.
16. Mariology: A Guide for Priests, Deacons, Seminarians and Consecrated Persons, *The Spiritual Maternity of the Blessed Virgin Mary*, Msgr. Charles M. Managan, pg. 523.
17. 1. Thomas W. Petrisko, *The Fatima Prophecies, at the Doorstep of the World*, pp. 359-408.

PART VI – TEMPLES OF GOD

CHAPTER TWENTY-SIX – DAVID: A MAN AFTER GOD'S OWN HEART

1. Rev. Peter M. J. Stravinskas, Ph.D., S.T.L., (ed.), *Our Sunday Visitor's Catholic Encyclopedia*, pg. 283.
2. Ibid.
3. The translation of this psalm is from an unknown source. It is held by some to be the original translation of the psalm from ancient texts no longer found in the bibles of the past century.

CHAPTER TWENTY-SEVEN – THE HEART OF SOLOMON

1. Kenneth Baker, S.J., *Inside the Bible*, San Francisco: Ignatius Press, 1998, pg. 80.
2. *Catholic Encyclopedia*, pg 921.
3. Ibid. pg. 921.

CHAPTER TWENTY-EIGHT – "MY HEART SHALL BE THERE"

1. Baker, *Inside the Bible*, pg, 149.

2. Ibid., pg. 155.
3. Ibid., pg. 167.

CHAPTER TWENTY-NINE – CHRIST: THE NEW TEMPLE

1. *Catechism of the Catholic Church*, N 583.
2. Ibid.
3. Ibid., N. 584.
4. Ibid.
5. Ibid.
6. Ibid.
7. Ibid.
8. Ibid., N. 586.
9. Ibid.
10. Ibid.

CHAPTER THIRTY – TEMPLES OF GOD

1. *Catechism of the Catholic Church*, N. 260.
2. Ibid., N. 2562
3. Ibid.
4. Ibid.
5. Ibid.
6. General Audience, December 3, 1980, Pope John Paul II.
7. Pope Benedict XVI, *Deus Caritas Est*, I, N. 18.

PART VII – THE COMING OF THE FATHER

CHAPTER THIRTY ONE – THE ARK OF THE FATHER

1. J. Bainvel, (1910) *Devotion to the Sacred Heart of Jesus*, in *The Catholic Encyclopedia*, New York: Robert Appleton Company. Retrieved August 19, 2012, from New Advent: http://www.newadvent.org/catlen/071/163a.h+m.
2. Ibid.
3. Ibid.
4. Ibid.

5. *Mystical City of God by Venerable Mary of Agreda*, Rockford, Illinois: Tan Books and Publishers, Inc., 1978, pg. 24.
6. Pius XII, *Haurietis Aquas*, N. 106.; Jn. 14:6.
7. Ibid.
8. John Paul II, Encyclical Letter, *Tertio Millennio Adveniente*, I, N. 7.
9. Ibid., III, N. 18.
10. Ibid., IV N. 46.

CHAPTER THIRTY-TWO – THE COMING OF THE FATHER

1. Dr. Rev. Joseph Iannuzzi, *Splendor of Creation*, McKees Rocks, Pennsylvania: St. Andrew's Productions, 2004, pp. 33-126.
2. Ibid. pp. 58-59.
3. Ibid.
4. Ibid.
5. Ibid, pg. 60.
6. Thomas W. Petrisko, *Fatima's Third Secret Explained*, McKees Rocks, Pennsylvania: St. Andrew's Productions, 2001, pp. 71-76.
7. Joseph Iannuzzi, *Splendor of Creation*, pp. 64-65.
8. *Catechism of the Catholic Church*, N. 676; Cf. DS 3839; Pius XI, *Divini Redemptoris*, condemning the "false mysticism" of this "counterfeit of the redemption of the lowly"; cf. GS 20-21.
9. John Paul II, *Tertio Millennio Adveniente*, IV, N. 46.
10. Joseph Iannuzzi, *Splendor of Creation*, pg. 23.
11. Benedict XVI, *Jesus of Nazareth, Holy Week, From the Entrance into Jerusalem to the Resurrection*, pp. 290-291.
12. Ibid.
13. Ibid., pg. 291.
14. Ibid.
15. Ibid., pp. 284-285.
16. Ibid.
17. Ibid., pg. 291.
18. Ibid., pp. 291, 292.
19. Ibid.

CHAPTER THIRTY-THREE – THE OUR FATHER

1. St. Thomas Aquinas, *Summa Theologica – Vol. I*, Warminster, Maryland: Christian Classics, 1981, pg. 175.
2. Ibid.
3. *Catechism of the Catholic Church*, N. 541, 542, 959.

PART VIII – TO KNOW, LOVE AND HONOR GOD OUR FATHER

CHAPTER THIRTY-FOUR – CONSECRATION TO OUR FATHER

1. *Catechism of the Catholic Church*, N. 541, 542, 959.
2. Ibid., N. 757, 758.
3. *Holy Octave of Consecration to God Our Father*, pp. III-IV.
4. Ibid.
5. Ibid. pg. 3.
6. Ibid.
7. Ibid.
8. Ibid.
9. Ibid.
10. Ibid.
11. Ibid.
12. Ibid.
13. Ibid.
14. Ibid.
15. Ibid.
16. Ibid.
17. Ibid.
18. Ibid.
19. Ibid.
20. Ibid.

CHAPTER THIRTY-FIVE – THE SOLEMNITY OF THE DIVINE PATERNAL HEART OF GOD OUR FATHER

1. Jean Galot, S.J., *ABBA, Father, We Long to See your Face – Theological Insights into the First Person of the Trinity*, pp. 83, 132.
2. Vatican Council II, *The Conciliar and Post Conciliar Documents*, (28) *The Dogmatic Constitution of the Church, Vatican II Lumen Gentium*, (21 November 1964), II, The People of God, pg. 369.

CHAPTER THIRTY-SIX – THE FEAST OF THE FATHER OF ALL MANKIND

1. Jean Galot, S.J., *ABBA, Father, We Long to See your Face – Theological Insights into the First Person of the Trinity*, pp. 203-205.
2. Ibid.
3. Ibid., pg 204.
4. Ibid.
5. *Catechism of the Catholic Church*, N. 1076, 1077, 1082.
6. Ibid., N. 1082.
7. Jean Galot, S.J., *ABBA, Father, We Long to See your Face – Theological Insights into the First Person of the Trinity*, pg. 206.
8. Ibid.
9. Leo XIII, Encyclical Letter, *Divinum Illud*, (4 May 1897).
10. Jean Galot S.J., *ABBA, Father, We Long to See your Face – Theological Insights into the First Person of the Trinity*, pp. 207-212.
11. Thomas W. Petrisko (Ed.), Queen of Peace Newspaper, *God the Father Edition*, McKees Rocks, Pennsylvania, St. Andrew's Productions, 1999.
12. Ibid.
13. Ibid.

CHAPTER THIRTY-SEVEN – THE CELEBRATION OF LIFE

1. Jean Galot, S.J., *ABBA, Father, We Long to See your Face – Theological Insights into the First Person of the Trinity*, pp. 203-232.
2. Ibid.
3. Ibid.
4. Ibid.

5. Ibid.
6. John Paul II, *Dives in Misericordia*, I, 2.
7. Jean Galot, S.J., *ABBA, Father, We Long to See your Face – Theological Insights into the First Person of the Trinity*, pp. 203-232.
8. Ibid.
9. Ibid.
10. Ibid.
11. John Paul II, *Letter to Families from Pope John Paul II*, I, N. 13.
12. Jean Galot, S.J., *ABBA, Father, We Long to See your Face – Theological Insights into the First Person of the Trinity*, pp. 203-232.
13. Ibid.
14. Ibid.
15. Ibid., pp. 207-232.
16. Ibid., pp. 215-232.
17. Ibid., pp. 206-232.
18. Benedict XVI, *Caritas in Veritate*, Conclusion, N. 79.
19. John Paul II, Apostolic Letter, *Euntes in Mundum*, (25 January 1988).
20. *The Holy Octave of Consecration to God Our Father*, McKees Rocks, Pennsylvania: St. Andrew's Productions, 1998.
21. Ibid.
22. Ricardo J. Cardinal Vidal, Chancery, Cardinal Rosales Pastoral Center, *Solemn Feast of the Father of All Mankind Newsletter and Homily*, (13 June 2006), 6000 Cebu City, Philippines.
23. John Paul II, Apostolic Letter, *Euntes in Mundum*, VI, N. 16.
24. John Paul II, *Dives in Misericordia*, VIII, N. 15.

CHAPTER THIRTY-EIGHT – ST. PHILIP AND THE APOSTLES OF THE FATHER

1. *The New American Bible, Fireside Family Edition* (1984-85),Witchita, Kansas: Catholic Bible Publishers, 1970, pp. 1071-1072.
2. Mt 17:5.
3. Michael O' Carroll,C.S.Sp., *Trinitas*, pp. 136-137.
4. Author's personal commentary of the *Last Discourse*.
5. *The New American Bible*, foonote commentary by editors of *The Gospel According to John*, Chapter 17:1-26, pg. 1075.

6. Ibid.
7. Ibid.
8. Ibid.
9. Ibid.
10. Ibid.

EPILOGUE – BACK TO THE GARDEN

1. John Paul II, General Audience, July 15, 1988.
2. Ibid.
3. Ibid.
4. Ibid.
5. Ibid.
6. Ibid.
7. Ibid.
8. Ibid.
9. Ibid.
10. Ibid.
11. John Paul II, General Audience, July 23, 1988.
12. Ibid.
13. John Paul II, General Audience, March 15, 1989.
14. John Paul II, General Audience, February 3, 1988.
15. *Catechism of the Catholic Church*, N. 541, 542.

Appendix A

GOD OUR FATHER

CONSECRATION AND FEAST DAY
FOR
THE FATHER OF ALL MANKIND

DEDICATION

TO GOD OUR FATHER

We pray that through The Holy Octave of Consecration and its solemn eighth day, The Feast of the Father of All Mankind, He may be known, loved, served, and honored by all His children.

Dearest God Our Father, we love You; we adore You; we worship You!

Copyright © 1998 Father of All Mankind Apostolate
All Rights Reserved

ISBN: 1-891903-07-1

Published by:
St. Andrew's Productions
5168 Campbells Run Road Ste. 203
Pittsburgh, PA 15205

Phone: (412) 787-9735
Fax: (412) 787-5204
Web: www.SaintAndrew.com

Front and Back Cover Illustrations:
Medal of The Holy Octave of Consecration to God Our Father.

Scriptural quotations are taken from *The Holy Bible*—RSV: Catholic Edition. Alternate translations from the Latin Vulgate Bible (*Douay Rheims Version—DV*) are indicated when used.

PRINTED IN THE UNITED STATES OF AMERICA

FOREWORD

GOD THE FATHER

by Fr. Michael O'Carroll C.S.SP.

The Holy Trinity is the centre of our faith: three Persons in one God. How do we express our belief in public worship and in private prayer? How do we initiate and continue a spiritual attitude towards each divine Person? In the western, that is the Latin, church there has been a very great emphasis on Christocentric spirituality. If that is designed to eliminate devotions which put others too heavily in focus, one saint or another, it is laudable. If it has the effect of minimizing our attention to the other two divine Persons it needs radical correction. At the end of the third session of the Second Vatican Council an Orthodox theologian Nikos Nissiotis, published an article in The Ecumenical Review of which he was editor, which said, in effect, that if the Council Documents did not say more about the Holy Spirit they would have little impact in the Orthodox Church.

Whether this article had any influence on things or not, there is much about the Holy Spirit in the conciliar texts which issued during the fourth session. Then Pope Paul VI publicly urged Catholic teachers and pastors to add to the theology of the Church and that of Our Lady that had come from the Council, a theology of the Holy Spirit. He led the way splendidly as Fr. Edward O'Connor has shown in his book, Pope Paul VI and the Holy Spirit. But no one has answered this appeal as fully as his successor in the See of Peter. John Paul II has, in public discourses and writings, taught more on the Holy Spirit than all his predecessors together. He is the first Pope to declare a Year of the Holy Spirit.

This leads logically to the question: What of God the Father? Here to, we have lived to witness an awakening of consciousness, and of conscience, in regard to His Person. For the first time in history churches have been built in His honour and a special feast is envisaged to God the Father.

Will this serve to diminish attention to God the Son incarnate? On the contrary it will enable us to come closer to the mystery of His Sonship. Anyone who doubts this will gain reassurance from the words of Jesus Himself: his first words recorded were "Did you not know that I must be in My Father's House?" (Lk 2:49); the last from His lips were "Father, into thy Hands I commit My Spirit" (Lk 23:46). All Jesus' prayers were directed to the Father; His words when near death, "My God, my God, why hast thou forsaken Me" were from a psalm (22:1), intended, some scholars think, as an invitation to His faithful friends to recite the psalm, which ends on a note of triumph.

The reader must especially ponder St. John's Gospel, chapters 14 to 17, delaying on the sensational assertion "He who has seen Me, has seen the Father; how can you say 'Show us the Father'? Do you not believe that I am in the Father and the Father in Me?" (Jn 14:9,10). Such reflection will enable us to appreciate why the only formal prayer given to us by Jesus is the "Our Father".

Thus Jesus, the mediator and sum-total of all revelation" (Vatican II) fulfilled the promise inherent in certain inspired intuitions of the Old Testament. As with the Spirit of God we have not therein an explicit theology of a divine Person and of relationship with the others. The Father is mentioned fourteen times, spoken of as creator, as a merciful One. As to relationship with humanity it is to Israel that his fatherhood shows itself: I am a Father to Israel and Ephraim is My first born" (Jer.31:9;cp. Deut. 14:2; Ex 4:22). In this context the great Lutheran biblical scholar, Joachim Jeremias, has convincingly maintained that the momentous innovation of prayer addressed to the Father by an individual was the achievement of Jesus. This is one more reason why a spirituality oriented to the Father enhances, amplifies, deepens intimacy with Jesus. We lose nothing by reflecting on the great find" of recent times: His Jewishness, with all that this connotes, for example in regard to the theology of the Heart.

There were three great civilizations around the ancient Mediterranean, Roman, based on law, Greek, based on the intellect, and the greatest, Jewish, based on the heart, as the statement of the living person: the word occurs 850 times in the sacred writings of this people, our spiritual ancestors. Their greatest gift to us was Jesus, the supreme Jew, Son of the Eternal Father, whom He disclosed to us and to whom He interceded with His very life for our salvation.

Once convinced of this consoling reality we may ask what means may we best employ to strengthen our faith and satisfy our need for meaningful prayer? The answer, an enlightened, highly acceptable one to this question is given in this book which I am recommending. The Holy Consecration to God the Father and its Feast day. I do not have to remind the reader that 1999 has been declared the Year of the Father by John Paul II. This explains the petition to the Pope for a feast which readers are invited to support. They may expect a favourable response, for John Paul II has emphasized his Trinitarian attitude in three Encyclicals: the Father in Dives in Misericordia, the Son in Redemptor Hominis, the Holy Spirit in Dominum et Vivificantem.

I shall not enter into the detail of this solidly constructed work. The Holy Octave of Consecration to God our Father is convincingly expounded; biblical reference is abundant. Note for interest how often the "eight" is significant in crucial saving events, modeled on the great revelation in the Bible. Here there is much that is profoundly theological and yet totally accessible. To those interested I say: Read, ponder, pray and benefit.

– Michael O'Carroll, C.S.Sp.
8 May, 1998
Feast of the Apparition of St. Michael

[Editor's note: Fr. Michael O'Carroll, C.S.Sp. was an Irish theologan and author of over 35 books. He lectured at Blackrock College in Dublin.]

+

A son honors his father, and a servant his master. If then I am a father, where is my honor?

—Mal 1:6

But the hour is coming, and now is, when the true worshipers will worship the Father in spirit and truth, for such the Father seeks to worship him. God is spirit, and those who worship him must worship in spirit and truth.

—Jn 4:23-24

And for their sake I consecrate myself, that they also may be consecrated in truth.

—Jn 17:19

+

INTRODUCTION

RETURNING TO THE HOUSE OF GOD OUR FATHER

The Catholic Church teaches us that God Our Father sent His Son Jesus to bring us back home to Him and that the Holy Spirit was sent to lead us on that journey. This is reflected in Pope John Paul II's preparation for the Jubilee 2000—1997, the Year of Jesus; 1998, the Year of the Holy Spirit; and 1999, the Year of the Father. Our spiritual journey, then, is intended to move us always in the direction of God Our Father. As Jesus tells us:

> *I came down from heaven, not to do my own will, but the will of him that sent me. Now this is the will of the Father who sent me: that of all that he hath given me, I should lose nothing; but should raise it up again in the last day. (Jn 6:38-39 DV)*
>
> *In my Father's house there are many mansions. If not, I would have told you: because I go to prepare a place for you. And if I shall go, and prepare a place for you, I will come again; and will take you to myself, that where I am, you also may be....I am the way, and the truth, and the life. No man cometh to the Father, but by me. (Jn 14:2-3,6 DV)*

Our Holy Father John Paul II writes in *Tertio Millenio Adveniente* [As the Third Millennium Draws Near] that "the whole of the Christian life is like a great pilgrimage to the house of the Father, whose unconditional love for every human creature, and in particular for the 'prodigal son' (Lk 15:11-32), we discover anew each day." In this same apostolic letter he also reminds us that during this time, Mary, our Mother, will be lovingly and urgently inviting "all the children of God so that they will return to the house of the Father when they hear her maternal voice: **'Do whatever Christ tells you'**" (Jn 2:5).

Our return to the house of our Father, then, is ordained by God as a "process." It is a process that begins with our Mother Mary who lovingly guides us to her Son. Jesus then mercifully lifts us up on His Cross to our Father. While comforting us on this journey home, the Holy Spirit purifies and refines us so God Our Father can come and dwell in us as living temples, and we, in turn, can dwell in Him. To do this, we must, unlike our first parents, Adam and Eve, offer our unconditional "Yes" to our Father's Will. For it was in saying "No" that mankind was exiled from Paradise and the intimate presence of God Our Father.

As children of God, we have been provided with a beautiful means to return to God Our Father, a progressive process that is described by St. Louis de Montfort in The Secret of Mary: "If the falsely enlightened, whom the devil has so miserably illusioned, even in prayer, had known how to find Mary, and through her to find Jesus, and through Jesus, God the Father, they would not have had such terrible falls. The saints tell us that when we have once found Mary, and through Mary, Jesus, and through Jesus, God the Father, we have found all good. He who says all, excepts nothing: all grace and all friendship with God, all safety from God's enemies, all truth to crush falsehoods, all facility to overcome difficulties in the way of salvation, all comfort and all joy amidst the bitterness of life" (21). Our spiritual journey, then, is a dynamic process which takes us through Mary to Jesus in union with the Holy Spirit back home to God Our Father. That is the reason for our existence.

If we could climb to the top of a mountain and look down on the panorama of Man's Salvation History, we would see that mankind was created solely for the purpose of returning to its Creator—God Our Father.

THE TRIUMPH OF OUR MOTHER MARY'S IMMACULATE HEART

In these times, **Mary's greatest Triumph will be her cooperative role in leading us back home and restoring us to God Our Father.** The first child of God to offer her "Yes" to our Father, Mary brought Jesus, our Savior, into the world. In this, and by guiding all her children to offer their "Yes," she truly "crushes the head" of the serpent—the serpent who seduced mankind into disobedience and exile (Gen 3:15 DV). Because of this "woman," the children of God Our Father will once again—as it was in the beginning—dwell with Him in the Paradise of His Divine Will. She is, indeed, the Mother of All Mankind—cooperating with God's Plan for our redemption, reconciling and uniting us with our Father, and acting as an intercessory helper for the children of God.

Like His mother, Jesus also offered his "fiat." In saying "Yes" to the Will of His Father, Jesus offered Himself for each and every one of us. His Passion, Death, and Resurrection defeated the sin and death which resulted from Adam and Eve's free-will choice to say "No" to our Father's Will. Through the "Yes" of Jesus and His mother Mary, we are no longer exiled. Jesus is the Way, the Truth, and the Life. Both He and His mother wait patiently to lead us back home to God Our Father. They wait for our "Yes!"

After the "fiats" of Mary and Jesus, the Holy Spirit was sent by our Father, at the request of Jesus, so that we would not be left as orphans. He comforts, guides, and purifies us on our journey back home to the Father. With our "Yes," He prepares us so that we can become consecrated temples of the Living God.

With God truly living "in" us, we, the exiled, prodigal children, will finally be restored to God Our Father. Our Mother Mary's Immaculate Heart will have triumphed—our Father's Kingdom will have truly come!

KNOWING, LOVING, AND HONORING GOD OUR FATHER

The Roman Catholic Church defines God as the three Persons of the Holy Trinity: Father, Son, and Holy Spirit. However, since the earliest beginnings of the Church, there has been a tendency to focus primarily on the Second Person of the Holy Trinity—Jesus, the Son of God. And to a lesser extent, there has been renewed interest in the Holy Spirit in the latter half of the 20th century. But what of the Father?

True, the Holy Sacrifice of the Mass is offered up to God Our Father and the "Our Father Prayer" is directed to Him. But do we "know" the Father? Do we believe that when Jesus came to earth as the Incarnation of God, that we no longer needed to know, love, serve, or honor the Father? Do we think that Jesus replaced the Father? Do we feel that God Our Father belongs to the Old Testament era and Jesus belongs to New Testament times? Do we perceive God Our Father as an ancient, mythic figure that is stern, aged, and unapproachable? Do we truly know Him? Love Him? Serve Him? Honor Him? The response to these questions by most Catholics would indicate that, indeed, something is seriously lacking in our perception and relationship with God Our Father.

Think for a moment. Do we typically see statues or paintings of the Father in our Catholic churches? Are any of our churches named in honor of Him? Does the Catholic Church have any special feasts that specifically honor Him?

The answer, unfortunately, is "No!"

THE HOLY OCTAVE OF CONSECRATION TO GOD OUR FATHER—AND THE FEAST OF THE FATHER OF ALL MANKIND

Why don't we honor our Creator, our Father—especially with a feast?

This is an unsettling question and a disturbing revelation, but it is also something we can easily remedy. As children of God Our Father, we can work towards establishing a feast for Him. The time has come to know, love, serve, and honor God Our Father through a special feast of consecration—a feast that would provide us with an opportunity to offer our fiat. Holy Scripture provides us with a blueprint for such a feast as was foreshadowed in the Feasts of Tabernacles [Booths] and Dedication (Lev 23:33-43; 2 Chron 7:1-9; 1 Mac 4:59; 2 Mac 2:1-18). Both eight-day feasts involved seven days of preparation and a solemn eighth day of prayer and assembly. This proposed feast would involve **honoring** and **consecrating** ourselves to God Our Father over an eight-day period, or **"octave."** It would be, then, **a Holy Octave of Consecration to God Our Father** with its solemn eighth day celebrated as **The Feast Day of the Father of All Mankind**.

The Holy Octave of Consecration to God Our Father and its Feast of the Father of All Mankind would integrate the purpose and meaning of both the previous Old Testament feasts in its focus on knowing, loving, serving, and honoring God our Father. Because of this, it would involve a commemoration of what God has done for His children and what we need to do for our Father. With this feast, God would not only be present as He was in the Ark of the Covenant, in a stone temple, or in the tabernacle of a church—He would be housed and present in those souls who were purified and dedicated to Him through consecration.

What exactly is The Holy Octave of Consecration to God Our Father and its Feast of the Father of All Mankind?

Its greatest significance in these times is that it provides us with an opportunity (1) to honor God Our Father, (2) to offer Him our "fiat," and (3) to consecrate ourselves to Him. In this way, we are truly cooperating with our Mother Mary in the Triumph of Her Immaculate Heart. We are returning to our Father; we are offering Him our unconditional "fiat" as Mary and Jesus did; and we are consecrating ourselves to Him—totally. As He so richly deserves, we are finally knowing, loving, serving, and honoring Him as God Our Father—The Father of All Mankind.

CONSECRATING OURSELVES TO GOD OUR FATHER

The most compelling precedent for consecrating ourselves to God Our Father over an eight-day feast, or octave, is found in John 10:22-39. This passage describes how Jesus, during the eight-day Feast of Dedication, revealed that He was consecrated to God Our Father.

Jesus further explains that He consecrated Himself to our Father so we, too, could be consecrated in truth (Jn 17:19-21). The concept of "Consecration to God Our Father" is crucial because, as Jesus tells us, "the hour is coming, and now is, when the true worshipers will worship the Father in spirit and truth, for such the Father seeks to worship him. God is a spirit, and those who worship him must worship in spirit and truth" (Jn 4:23-24). If we follow Jesus, if we model ourselves after Him, shouldn't we also consecrate ourselves to God Our Father during an eight-day feast, so that we, too, can adore Him "in spirit and in truth?"

If we choose to consecrate ourselves to God Our Father, how should this be done? The concept of an "octave," or 8-day feast, has been significant in our relationship with God since the beginning of our Salvation History. It is not by coincidence that Jesus chose to reveal His consecration to God Our Father on the eight-day Feast of Dedication. Clearly, the octave symbolizes a designated period of time when God's children grow and God's relationship with them changes or is transformed.

Unlike other feasts and consecration methods, The Holy Octave of Consecration to God Our Father views the "big picture" of our Salvation History. It involves the entire process of our spiritual journey which includes Mary, our Mother; Jesus, our God and our Savior; and the Holy Spirit, our God and our Sanctifier—with progression always toward God Our Father.

God's Word in both the Old and New Testaments provides us with extensive Scriptural support for an eight-day, or "octave," format. From the Book of Genesis to the Gospels and Epistles, the number "eight" is used to signify salvation, covenant, purification, and dedication. Perhaps, more importantly, it is used to indicate the end of one era and the beginning of another in which God is revealed, manifested, and present to His children in a new way.

The Holy Octave of Consecration to God Our Father, in its most powerful form, is intended as a formal eight-day feast for God Our Father culminating on the first Sunday of the "eighth" month, God Our Father's Month—August. The solemn eighth day of The Holy Octave of Consecration of God Our Father would be celebrated under the title of The Feast of the Father of All Mankind. However, consecration to God our Father using the eight-day formula of The Holy Octave of Consecration to God Our Father can be done informally at any time during the year.

A PERIOD OF TRANSFORMATION

Wouldn't it be appropriate to consecrate ourselves and the world to the One we were created to return to—God Our Father? Wouldn't it be equally appropriate to recite this consecration publicly and to renew it annually on a feast specifically celebrated for God Our Father—"The Father of All Mankind"? Isn't it time to cleanse, purify, and re-dedicate the Temple of God Our Father—individually and as the Body of Christ?

Are we entering a new period of transformation? Does the chaos, confusion, and darkness of our culture signal the need for change in our relationship with God Our Father? Does it signal the Mercy of God's Justice, so that in these times we are truly feeling the consequences and effects of our sins, our turning away from God, our refusal to do God's Will?

Instead of punishment, is the misery of our times really God Our Father's Mercy? Is He allowing us to feel the full brunt of our bad choices, our sin, so that we might clearly see what it is like to live outside His Will? Is He allowing this so that we can better make the choice to return to Him where we belong?

If so, Holy Scripture illustrates that in the past, these periods of transformation always involved a time of our turning away from God, a time of purification and cleansing, a time of re-dedication, and a time of regathering and renewal.

The octave or eight-day period is significant, then, in representing a divinely ordained process that involves a shifting from one period to the next. Often the process that propels us from one period into the next has involved seven days of praise, thanksgiving, offering, and repentance, followed by an eighth day of solemnity and assembly of God's children. This process can work on two levels to purify and dedicate us: individually and as a body. Therefore, The Holy Octave of Consecration to God Our Father, culminating in The Feast of the Father of All Mankind is necessary and much needed in these times—for each of us individually and for the Church as a whole.

To place the need for a consecration feast to God Our Father in proper perspective for the times we live in, we should remember that at the turn of the last century, Pope Leo XIII dedicated the world to the Sacred Heart of Jesus. Again in 1925, Pope Pius XI ordered a formal consecration of mankind to the Sacred Heart of Jesus, to be publicly recited and renewed annually on the Feast of Christ the King.

As we have now entered a new millennium, isn't it time that we know, love, and honor God Our Father through a formal feast day of consecration especially for Him?

If we say "yes" to God Our Father, cleanse and purify ourselves, consecrate and re-dedicate ourselves to Him, individually and collectively, what could possibly keep Him from coming to us—in a more powerful and glorious way than we could ever imagine!

"THY KINGDOM COME"

Like eight footlights guiding us home, like runway lights beckoning our Father to descend among us, The Holy Octave of Consecration to God Our Father would prepare us for His indwelling. And this indwelling represents one of the greatest gifts ever given to us—that God Our Father is with us always, actively and intimately. With this in mind, we need to say "Yes," Father, and become lights to the world, signaling the change to come. For, surely, a new time is coming, a time of renewal and transformation, when Mary's Immaculate Heart will finally Triumph—the era when our Father's Kingdom comes and His Will is done "on earth as it is in heaven."

May we approach God Our Father through The Holy Octave of Consecration and its eighth solemn day—the Feast of the Father of all Mankind—with anticipation, love, and confidence. For He is not the old, stern, and distant man we imagined. Rather, He is Divine, and as such, cannot age, for age is a sign of corruption and decay of "life." No, He is a healthy, vital God. He is the Creator—Life itself! He "is" Love and Mercy. And He is close, even now, tracing the smiles and tears upon our faces with His divine finger, sharing our every joy, our every sorrow. He is our Father and we are His children. We belong to Him and to Him we were created to return each and every one of us!

TIME LINE
OLD TESTAMENT

Eight people saved by God.	Noe's Ark (Gen 7:13)
Covenant sign eight days after birth.	Circumcision (Gen 17:12)
Eight-day period of Consecration and offering preceding the manifestation of God to His people	Manifestation of God to Moses and His People (Lev 8:33-36; 9:1-24)
Eight-day feast requested by God.	Feast of Tabernacles [Booths] (Lev 23:33-43)
Offerings accepted by God for purification on the final eighth day.	Purification Rituals (Lev 14:10-11;15:14-15,29-30)
David, the eighth son of Jesse, brought the Ark of the Covenant into the City of David amidst praises sung for the octave upon harps.	The Ark of the Covenant is Returned to the Hebrews (1 Sam 17:12-14) (1 Para 15:21 DV)
David's repentant cry played on an eight string harp.	(Ps 6 DV)
Solomon finishes building the House of the Lord in the eighth month of the year.	Solomon Completes the Temple (1 Kings 6:38)
Eight-day feast dedicating and preparing the Temple for God's presence.	Solomon's Feast of Dedication (2 Chron 7:1-9)
Dimensions for the New Temple based on number eight.	The New Temple as envisioned by Ezechial (Ezek 40:8,30,34,37,41 [40:49 DV])
Eight-day feast for cleansing and re-dedicating the Temple.	Maccabee's Feast of Dedication (1 Mac 4:59; 2 Mac 2:1-18)

TIME LINE

New Testament

Covenant sign on the eighth day	John the Baptist's Circumcision (Lk 1:59)
Covenant sign on the eighth day	Jesus' Circumcision (Lk 2:21)
Jesus reveals His union with God Our Father and His consecration on this eight-day feast.	Jesus walks on Solomon's' Porch at the Temple on the Feast of Dedication (Jn 10:22-38)
Jesus prophesies His Transfiguration to the Apostles eight days before the actual event.	The Transfiguration of Jesus - The Apostles Peter, James and John hear the voice of God Our Father say, "This is my beloved Son; hear Him." (Lk 9:35)
Jesus rose from the dead on the eighth day of His Week of Redemptive Passion.	The Resurrection of Jesus (Mt 28:1-8; Mk 16:9; Lk 24:1-5; Jn 20:1-17)
Jesus shows His wounds to unbelieving Thomas eight days after His Resurrection.	Jesus appears to Thomas (Jn 20:26-29)

THE HOLY OCTAVE OF CONSECRATION TO GOD OUR FATHER
Overview

The Holy Octave of Consecration to God Our Father involves eight days of prayer, scripture readings, and meditation, as well as participation in the Holy Mass, the Eucharist, and the Sacrament of Reconciliation. The first seven days serve as preparatory steps leading to the final day of assembly and solemn consecration—*The Feast of the Father of All Mankind.*

A chaplet, medal, and litany have been specially designed for the octave approach of this consecration and feast day. All God's children are invited to use the following spiritual practices and format to consecrate themselves to God Our Father. Although the consecration can be done at any time by setting aside an eight-day period (preferably Sunday to Sunday), it is suggested that (1) it be renewed formally each year on the proposed date (an octave ending on the first Sunday of August) and that (2) it be renewed informally each day by praying the chaplet. In addition, the short prayer, "I love You, Father, and I give myself to You" can be prayed throughout the day to help us live our consecration more fully.

Two publications are available for *The Holy Octave of Consecration to God Our Father: (1) God Our Father—Consecration and Feast Day for the Father of All Mankind* **(full-length book) and (2)** *God Our Father—Consecration and Feast Day for the Father of All Mankind* **(the booklet).** Both publications contain an introduction, the formal and daily chaplet, and litany. However, the full-length book contains sections that provide additional information and support for *The Holy Octave of Consecration to God Our Father:* "The Journey of God Our Father's Children" and "Scriptural Meditations on The Octave of God Our Father."

Daily Format: A relevant theme taken from Holy Scripture has been selected for each of the eight days of the consecration: praise, thanksgiving, offering, repentance, inheritance (acknowledging that God is truly our Father and we are truly His children), fiat (saying "Yes" unconditionally to God Our Father's Will), fidelity, and consecration. Therefore, general daily practice during this eight-day period involves meditation on the selected daily theme, scripture reading, and prayer. In addition, the chaplet and litany of the *Holy Octave of Consecration to God Our Father* are to be recited daily. Daily Mass and reception of the Holy Eucharist are recommended, as is the Sacrament of Reconciliation during this eight-day period.

The Chaplet: The chaplet is made up of the Medal of the *Holy Octave of Consecration to God Our Father* and 75 beads—11 gold and 64 red. The gold beads signify our precious goal, the Divine Treasure—God Our Father. The red beads signify the Blood of Jesus Christ which allows us to return to God Our Father.

To begin, *A Prayer Invoking the Presence of God Our Father* is recited. Then the Sign of the Cross and a preparatory prayer are said on the Holy Octave of Consecration Medal. Introductory prayers to Mary, Jesus, and the Holy Spirit are prayed on the three introductory gold beads that lead into the larger circle of beads.

The circle of beads is designed with major octaves (eight gold beads), each with it's own minor octave (eight red beads). The eight main themes of our journey as prodigal children of God Our Father are meditated on the eight gold Major Octave beads.

The eight daily themes of the consecration are recited on the eight red Minor Octave beads.

To finish the chaplet, the Holy Octave of Consecration Prayer to God the Father is then recited on the medal.

Both an extended version of the chaplet for formal consecration (with meditations) and a concise version for daily use (without meditations) are provided in this booklet.

The Medal: A special medal was designed to illustrate the process of this consecration (see book cover). Depicted on the front of the medal is the actual consecration process. God Our Father is seen in heaven reaching down to us on earth; man is seen on earth reaching up to God Our Father in heaven. The force of God's Love for us is shown in the rays that proceed down from His hand; the force of our love for Him is pictured in our "fiat" radiating up to Him. These rays intersect through the Cross of Jesus. This Cross is the bridge or link between God Our Father and His children. At one end, it is grounded in the earth through Mary, our Mother. It then proceeds up through the sanctifying power of the Holy Spirit into Heaven at the other end. Eight lights, signifying the Scripturally-supported Octave, are shown on the horizontal beam of the Cross. These eight lights serve to guide us on our journey back home to God Our Father.

The back of the medal displays the eight-stringed harp of David, as mentioned in Psalm 6. St. Augustine understood this mystically, as symbolizing the octave—seven days of this mortal life followed by the last resurrection and the world to come. And that during our mortal life, like David, we must also feel sorrow for our sins and repent of them while here on earth. On this eight-stringed harp we have placed the eight themes or steps of the Holy Octave of Consecration to God Our Father—praise, thanksgiving, offering, repentance, inheritance, fiat, fidelity, and consecration. Inside the bow of the harp are printed the words: "The rhythm and harmony of God's Will." This reminds us that when we pluck the eight strings or themes of this consecration to God Our Father, a beautiful music ascends to heaven—we are choosing to live in the rhythm and harmony of His Will.

The Scapular of God Our Father – "The Offering Cloth"; Whereas the medal shows God Our Father's love for us (a road-map back home to Him), the Offering Cloth shows our love for God Our Father (the total offering of ourselves). It is a small, white piece of linen embroidered around the edges for durability and worn by a cloth rope or pinned through two eyelets in the upper corners. Worn close to the heart (as a scapular), it is held in our open hand during our daily prayers of offering. This may occur during recitation of the chaplet or at anytime when we pray, "I love you, Father, and I give myself to You." Blessing of the Offering Cloth takes place during our formal consecration to God Our Father on the "Feast of the Father of All Mankind." However, it may be done by a priest at any time.

The Offering Cloth is a visual aid to remind us of what our souls should be like before God – clean and pure. Because of this, the Offering Cloth should be kept clean and may be laundered. It serves a concrete symbol of our souls given in offering to our Father. Not only does it remind us of the need to be purified, but it also helps us understand that purification is not a punishment, but rather a preparation for the indwelling presence of God. When we offer ourselves to God Our Father, He purifies us so that He May come to dwell in us personally.

The Litany: This litany for God Our Father was composed specifically for the Holy Octave of Consecration. It lists all the major passages in Holy Scripture that cite the octave or number "eight." Each citation is followed by the phrase, "Have mercy on us, O Loving Father."

The Feast of the Father of All Mankind: This crowning feast day of the *Holy Octave of Consecration to God Our Father* serves to solemnly assemble the children of God, the ultimate purpose of which is to **honor God Our Father** (1) by recognizing that He is truly our Father and we are truly His children, (2) by offering Him our unconditional "fiat," and (3) by consecrating ourselves to Him totally. Having prepared for this solemn day and our consecration by exercising and offering the Holy Octave themes of praise, thanksgiving, offering, repentance, inheritance, fiat, and fidelity, we now ask Mary, our Mother; Jesus, our God and our Savior; and The Holy Spirit, our God and our Sanctifier, to guide and prepare us so that through our total consecration, we can become living temples of the indwelling Presence of God.

We also ask God Our Father on this special day (1) to allow us to cultivate and maintain a close and intimate relationship with Him, (2) to have Mercy on all His children—past, present, and future, (3) to bring His peace to the world, (4) to gather all His children to Himself, and (5) and that His Kingdom comes and His Will is done on earth as it is in heaven.

Liturgically, this day should include a Holy Mass with Scripture readings and a homily that specifically honor God Our Father as "The Father of All Mankind." Blessed palms should also be provided for praising our Lord and Father.

After the Celebration of Holy Mass, medals, chaplets, and Offering Cloths may be blessed. The children of God should be invited to collectively pray the chaplet, litany, and the daily theme prayer for the eighth day of the consecration.

THE EIGHT DAYS OF THE HOLY OCTAVE OF CONSECRATION TO GOD OUR FATHER

DAY ONE

Suggested Daily Devotional Practices:
1. Holy Mass (Recommended)
2. The Formal Holy Octave of Consecration to God Our Father Chaplet
3. The Litany of The Holy Octave of Consecration to God Our Father
4. Daily Meditation on a Minor Octave Theme (See Below)

DAILY THEME: PRAISE

"I will praise the Lord as long as I live; I will sing praises to my God while I have being."—Ps 146:2

Glory to You, God my Father!
You, Who made the universe and all that is in it.
You, Who made the brightest star and the darkest ocean depth.
You, Who made the fiercest storm and the gentlest summer breeze.
You, Who made the heavenly angels, as well as the beasts, birds, and fishes of the earth.
You, Who made me, created in Your image.
I praise you, God my Father—now and forever! Amen.

[Meditate on the wonders God Our Father has created, and praise Him in your own thoughts and words.]

END OF DAY ONE DEVOTION

DAY TWO

Suggested Daily Devotional Practices:
1. Holy Mass (Recommended)
2. The Formal Holy Octave of Consecration to God Our Father Chaplet
3. The Litany of The Holy Octave of Consecration to God Our Father
4. Daily Meditation on a Minor Octave Theme (See Below)

DAILY THEME: THANKSGIVING

"Bless the Lord, O my soul, and forget not all His benefits."—Ps 103:2

Thank You, my dearest Father, for loving me into existence.
Thank You for this body, mind, and soul that You fashioned specially for me.
Thank You for the people and circumstances of my life.
Thank You for opening my eyes, ears, and heart so that I may see, hear, and love You.
Thank You for taking me by the hand and leading me back home through all the dangers and difficulties of my life.
Thank You for loving me. Amen.

[Meditate on all that God Our Father has given you. Thank Him in your own words.]

END OF DAY TWO DEVOTION

DAY THREE

Suggested Daily Devotional Practices:
1. Holy Mass (Recommended)
2. The Formal Holy Octave of Consecration to God Our Father Chaplet
3. The Litany of The Holy Octave of Consecration to God Our Father
4. Daily Meditation on a Minor Octave Theme (See Below)

DAILY THEME: OFFERING

"And like living stones be yourselves built into a spiritual house, to be a holy priesthood, to offer spiritual sacrifices acceptable to God through Jesus Christ."

—1 Pet 2:5

You have given me everything, Father.
You have given me Yourself!
What can I possibly offer You?
Let me offer you the first fruits, the best fruits, of all I do or receive.
Let all Your children offer themselves as the fruit of Your Tree of Life,
Ripened on the sacrifices, sufferings, and crosses of their earthly journeys,
So that the worldwide effects of Your children's "No"—darkness, discord, and disorder—
May be transformed and made new through Your Light and Love.
I raise my arms in offering to You, Father.
Receive all You have given me into Your Paternal Heart.
Amen.

[Meditate on what you can offer up to God Our Father. Offer back to Him all that He has given you—the blessings and the crosses—so that all may be transformed in His Love.]

END OF DAY THREE DEVOTION

DAY FOUR

Suggested Daily Devotional Practices:
1. Holy Mass (Recommended)
2. The Formal Holy Octave of Consecration to God Our Father Chaplet
3. The Litany of The Holy Octave of Consecration to God Our Father
4. Daily Meditation on a Minor Octave Theme (See Below)

DAILY THEME: REPENTANCE

"Blessed be the God and Father of our Lord Jesus Christ, the Father of mercies and God of all comfort."—2 Corinthians 1:3

My Good Father, You are all loving,
But You are also Just.
How can Your children ever make reparation for all their sins?
How can they ever hope to balance Your Scales of Justice—especially in these times:
These times when so many of Your children say "No" to You,
These times when so many of Your children reject Your Will,
These times when so many of Your children no longer believe in You and have enthroned themselves as "gods,"
These times when so many of Your children embrace the fruit of the Tree of Knowledge of Good and Evil.
They have embraced the lie; they have embraced death.
Shower us with Your Grace and Mercy, Father.
Cleanse us in your tears,
Allow us to be compassionate warriors of Your Mercy on earth,
So that Your Sword of Justice may be transformed into a loving means of Your Mercy. Amen.

[Meditate on all the many ways you have hurt or offended God Our Father. Ask for His forgiveness and mercy. Ask for the grace to know, love, serve, and honor Him and to do His Will in all things.]

END OF DAY FOUR DEVOTION

DAY FIVE

Suggested Daily Devotional Practices:
1. Holy Mass (Recommended)
2. The Formal Holy Octave of Consecration to God Our Father Chaplet
3. The Litany of The Holy Octave of Consecration to God Our Father
4. Daily Meditation on a Minor Octave Theme (See Below)

DAILY THEME: INHERITANCE

For all who are led by the Spirit of God are sons of God. For you did not receive the spirit of slavery to fall back into fear, but you have received the spirit of sonship. When we cry, Abba! Father! it is the Spirit himself bearing witness with our spirit that we are children of God, and if children, then heirs, heirs of God and fellow heirs with Christ, provided we suffer with him in order that we may also be glorified with him."—Rom 8:14-17

Dearest God My Father:

With awe and wonder, I have learned to praise You and all Your creation, With sincere gratefulness, I have learned to thank you for Your unboundless generosity.

With humility and love, I have learned to offer up to You all that You have given me.

With a sorrowful but hopeful heart, I have learned to ask for Your forgiveness and tender mercy. And now that I can fully appreciate that You exist, that You are God, that You created this entire universe, that You created me, I now learn, that in addition to these wonders, You are truly my Father and I am truly Your child.

How can my heart contain the excitement—I am not only Your creature, but I am actually Your child. You created me in Your own image so that I could spend eternity with You. You loved me that much. But even though You have told me this in Holy Scripture and through the teachings of the Church, my ears have not heard the words, my heart was hardened. I had wandered far away—from Your voice, Your Heart, Your Love for me.

But now the veil is lifted, the fog has cleared. I see, I hear, I understand—

You are truly my Father and I am truly Your child!

I am Your prodigal child, running back to You, into Your waiting arms.

I am coming home, to You, my Father, where I belong.

God Our Father: Consecration and Feast Day for the Father of All Mankind   405

Please hold me tightly to Your Heart and never let me go—now and forever. Amen.

[Meditate on what it means to have God as your true Father and for you to be His true child. What does this legacy mean? Think about the tremendous joy and responsibilities that this involves.]

END OF DAY FIVE DEVOTION

DAY SIX

Suggested Daily Devotional Practices:
1. Holy Mass (Recommended)
2. The Formal Holy Octave of Consecration to God Our Father Chaplet
3. The Litany of The Holy Octave of Consecration to God Our Father
4. Daily Meditation on a Minor Octave Theme (See Below)

DAILY THEME: FIAT
(SAYING "YES" TO GOD OUR FATHER)

"Behold, I am the handmaid of the Lord; let it be to me according to your word."—Lk 1:38
"My Father, if it be possible, let this cup pass from me; nevertheless, not as I will but as thou wilt."—Mt 26:39

My Good and Loving Father:

Please allow me the privilege of saying my "Yes" to You! I say "Yes" to You, Father, in all things. Not a conditional "Yes" that involves doing only those things that are comfortable or easy. Not a conditional "Yes" that means doing only those things that benefit me. No, I give you my "Yes" in all things, Father, Because I know You are pure Love and as pure Love You can transform all things.

Doing Your Will can never hurt me. Doing Your Will can never harm another.

Doing Your Will can never separate me from You. Doing Your Will can only bring about the rhythm and harmony of Your Will here on earth. Doing Your Will can only spread Your Light and Love. Doing Your Will can only help bring me to You. Doing Your Will can only help me bring others to You. When I step inside Your Will, I am dancing with You in the order, rhythm, and harmony of Your Divine Will. When I step outside Your Will, I am stumbling alone in the chaos, disorder, and discord of darkness. Let me listen to Your gentle, loving voice beckoning me, inviting me into Your Divine Will. I am yours, Lord, do with me what You will. Because I know that Your Will is Love. Even when Your Will may seem painful or unfair, I know that Your ways are not always man's ways. Only You can see the grand scheme of things. Only You know the "why's" of my crosses. But despite what may sometimes appear to be unjust, I trust You totally. Why? Because You are my Father…and You love me. You want only what is good for me. You want me to come home—to You. There's nothing in heaven or on earth that I want more. So I say "Yes," Father! I say "Yes" to You! I say "Yes" to the rhythm and harmony of Your Divine Will. Amen.

[Meditate on what it means to give your fiat, your "Yes" to God Our Father. How will this change your life? How will this change your relationship with God, with others?]

END OF DAY SIX DEVOTION

DAY SEVEN

Suggested Daily Devotional Practices:
1. Holy Mass (Recommended)
2. The Formal Holy Octave of Consecration to God Our Father Chaplet
3. The Litany of The Holy Octave of Consecration to God Our Father
4. Daily Meditation on a Minor Octave Theme (See Below)

DAILY THEME: FIDELITY

"I have fought the good fight, I have finished the race, I have kept the faith."—2 Tim 4:7

Dearest Father, my Love and my Life:

I pledge my faith, hope, and love,
As a precious gift, a promise, of my unconditional fidelity to You.
Know that I trust in Your love for me.
Give me the strength, courage, and perseverance to never doubt, never stray, never despair.
Please bless this vow and make of me a gentle warrior,
Battling the darkness with Your Sweet Sword of Love and Mercy.
As You will never abandon me,
I pray I will never abandon You.
Please press me tenderly to Your heart, and never let me go.
In You, Father, I trust! Amen.

[Meditate on pledging your fidelity to God Our Father. What does it mean to be loyal and committed to God? Do you feel committed to returning to your Father? Do you want to help others return, too? What does it mean to be a "gentle warrior" of God Our Father's Love and Mercy here on earth? Like St. Paul, when you die, will you feel as though you've fought a good fight?]

END OF DAY SEVEN DEVOTION

DAY EIGHT

Suggested Daily Devotional Practices:
1. Holy Mass (Recommended)
2. The Formal Holy Octave of Consecration to God Our Father Chaplet
3. The Litany of The Holy Octave of Consecration to God Our Father
4. Daily Meditation on a Minor Octave Theme (See Below)

The Offering Cloth – held in an open hand during recitation of the Day Eight Daily Theme and, thereafter, during a prayer of daily offering: the chaplet or the short prayer, "I love you, Father, and I give myself to You." Ideally, Offering Cloths should be blessed before the formal consecration on "The Feast of the Father of All Mankind." However, this can be done by a priest at any time.

DAILY THEME: CONSECRATION

"For we are the temple of the living God; as God said, 'I will live in them and move among them, and I will be their God, and they shall be my people.'"

—2 Cor. 6:16

Dearest God My Father:

I call upon You to witness and participate in my solemn consecration to You. After seven days of preparation, I come to You now as one who is still learning how to know and love You, how to praise and thank You, how to offer up to You all the blessings and crosses You have given me, and how to ask for Your forgiveness and mercy. I also come to You as a warrior, strong in my resolve to serve and honor You. But most importantly, I come to You as a wide-eyed child, filled with awe and wonder in the knowledge that I am truly Your child and that You—Creator of the vast universe—are truly my Father.

Although I have wandered far from You in my lifetime, I choose now to return, for I long to be with You in Your house forever.

In Your Divine Presence, with full knowledge and free will, I consecrate myself to You on this day. Like a small child, I approach You; I lay tenderly against Your Fatherly Heart, and I ask that You hold me tightly and never let me go. Let me be a temple for You to dwell in, Father. And with the greatest love and tenderness, may I be Your gentle and loyal companion, carrying You within me all the days of my life. May I bring You to my family and friends, to strangers I have yet to meet, so that they might also see Your Light and feel your tender Love. When You dwell in us, there is a blessed connection between heaven and earth. May more and more of Your children consecrate themselves to You. As Jesus taught us to pray, may "Thy Kingdom come. Thy Will be done on earth as it is in heaven." Amen.

[Meditate on what it means to be "consecrated" to God Our Father. The word consecration means to "make holy" or "to give oneself for a holy purpose." How does this change your life? How does this change your relationship with God Our Father? How can you "live" your consecration everyday?]

END OF DAY EIGHT DEVOTION

THE FORMAL CHAPLET

Extended Version With Meditations

A Preparatory Prayer Invoking the Presence of God Our Father:

Dearest Father—my Creator and my God:

You promised that in every place where we honor Your name, You would come to us and bless us.

O Father, arise and come to rest in us, Your children. Clothe us in Your Salvation and let us rejoice in Your goodness. Please do not turn away our faces from Your loving presence.

If we have found favor in Your sight, show us Your face so that we may know You and find grace before Your eyes. Please speak to us now as You spoke to Moses—as a man speaks to his friend.

Let it be known this day that You are the "Father of All Mankind" Who can turn all hearts back to Yourself, and that we are Your children who desire only to do Your Will in all things. Answer us, Lord; answer us—so all Your children may know that You are mankind's one true God and Father.

As Your prodigal children, we want only to return home to You. As we approach You, Father, please run to meet us. And in Your unconditional love and compassion, embrace and kiss us.

Like Mary, Your handmaid, and Jesus, Your Son, we love You, Father, and we give ourselves to You. Following those You sent to bring us back home, we now freely consecrate ourselves to You, saying:

(With Mary, our Mother)— "Be it done to me according to Your Will."

(Through Jesus, our God and Savior)—"Not as I will but as You will."

(In the Holy Spirit, our God and Sanctifier)— "Abba, Father!"

Jesus promised, when two or three are gathered together in His name, He is in the midst of us. So as Jesus is in You and You in Jesus—and Jesus is the vine and we are the branches—be with us now, and through Your Holy Spirit, dwell in us always as Your living temples.

Bless us, Father, and walk among us, Your children. And may Your Glory descend upon us as the transforming fire of Your tender love and mercy—now and forever. Amen.

On the Medal of *The Holy Octave of Consecration to God Our Father*:

In the name of the Father, and of the Son, and of the Holy Spirit. Amen.

Dearest God Our Father, I humbly ask that on my journey home to You, Your Holy Angels protect and guide me; that Your Blessed Saints in Heaven intercede for me; and that Your suffering souls in Purgatory pray for me, as I pray for them now. Amen.

On the three gold beads:

> **Bead 1**—Hail Mary full of grace, the Lord is with Thee, Blessed art Thou among women and Blessed is the Fruit of thy womb, Jesus. Holy Mary, Mother of God, pray for us sinners now, and at the hour of our death. Amen.
>
> **Bead 2**—Jesus, my God and my Savior, You loved me so much, You died for me on the Cross, so that I, too, could return to our Father in Heaven. You are the Way, the Truth, and the Life. Through Your Holy Eucharist, please sustain me and be present with me always on my journey home. Amen.
>
> **Bead 3**—Holy Spirit, my God and my Sanctifier, Jesus sent You to me for my journey back home to the Father. Please purify and refine me. Fill me with Your Divine Light and Love so that the Presence of God may dwell in me. Amen.

On the eight gold beads of the *MAJOR OCTAVE*:

FIRST MAJOR OCTAVE: (gold bead):
THE DISOBEDIENCE AND EXILE OF GOD OUR FATHER'S CHILDREN

> Let us Meditate on (1) Adam and Eve's choice not to do God Our Father's Will, (2) their exile from the Paradise He created for them, and (3) Our Father's promise that "the woman" (Mary)

would someday Triumph by "crushing the head" of the serpent that seduced them into disobedience.

God Our Father was with us at the beginning in the Paradise He created for us—the Paradise of His Divine Will. Seduced by Satan, Adam and Eve chose not to do the Will of God and were, therefore, expelled from this Paradise and denied God's intimate presence. However, Our Father promised that "the woman" would ultimately defeat the evil that had caused this separation—the evil of saying "No" to God's Will. (Gen 2:8-3:24)

Our Father Prayer

Minor Octave (eight red beads):

Bead 1: In *praise* ~ I love You, Father, and I give myself to You!
Bead 2: In *thanksgiving* ~ I love You, Father, and I give myself to You!
Bead 3: In *offering* ~ I love You, Father, and I give myself to You!
Bead 4: In *repentance* ~ I love You, Father, and I give myself to You!
Bead 5: In my *inheritance* ~ I love You, Father, and I give myself to You!
Bead 6: In saying my *"Yes"* ~ I love You, Father, and I give myself to You!
Bead 7: In *fidelity* ~ I love You, Father, and I give myself to You!
Bead 8: In *consecration* ~ I love You, Father, and I give myself to You!

SECOND MAJOR OCTAVE: THE PRESENCE OF GOD OUR FATHER IN THE OLD TESTAMENT ERA

Let us meditate on God Our Father's Presence Among Us During the Old Testament era:

Although God's children were expelled from Paradise by their choice not to do God's Will, God never abandoned them. He was present with them from the beginning. In Old Testament times, He manifested His presence through His own voice, the words of His Prophets, in the burning bush, in a pillar of smoke, and in the Ark of the Covenant.

After God rescued His children from the bondage of Egypt, He requested that they celebrate the Feast of Tabernacles for eight days each year. He wanted them to remember that He loved them, He saved them, and He was present with them. Later when God was present in the Ark of the Covenant, Solomon built a magnificent Temple to house it. He then celebrated an eight-day Feast of Dedication in preparation for God's presence in the Temple. And God responded by manifesting His presence in a tangible and powerful way.

At the close of the Old Testament, the Maccabee's re-instituted this eight-day feast to purify and re-dedicate the Temple that had been defiled through Pagan influence, so the Presence of God would dwell with them once more. (Lev 8:33-36-9:1-24; 23:33-43; 2 Chron 7:1-9; 2 Mac 2:1-12)

Our Father Prayer

Minor Octave (eight red beads):

Bead 1: In *praise* ~ I love You, Father, and I give myself to You!
Bead 2: In *thanksgiving* ~ I love You, Father, and I give myself to You!
Bead 3: In *offering* ~ I love You, Father, and I give myself to You!
Bead 4: In *repentance* ~ I love You, Father, and I give myself to You!
Bead 5: In my *inheritance* ~ I love You, Father, and I give myself to You!
Bead 6: In saying my *"Yes"* ~ I love You, Father, and I give myself to You!
Bead 7: In *fidelity* ~ I love You, Father, and I give myself to You!
Bead 8: In *consecration* ~ I love You, Father, and I give myself to You!

THIRD MAJOR OCTAVE: THE FIAT OF MARY, OUR MOTHER

Let us meditate on (1) Mary's "Triumphant" Fiat, her "Yes" to God's Will, and (2) how she became the "New Ark," a living tabernacle for the newly manifested presence of God: Jesus, the Second Person of the Holy Trinity—Savior of God Our Father's children:

Mary gave her "Yes" when the angel Gabriel came to her and asked her to be the mother of the Son of God. The Holy Spirit came upon her and the power of God Our Father overshadowed her. In saying "Yes" to God's Will, Mary "the woman") allowed God to be present with His children in a new way. She actually became the "New Ark," a living tabernacle of Jesus, the Second Person of the Holy Trinity—mankind's Savior—who with His Mother's cooperation, would restore the exiled children of God to their Father. (Lk 1:26-35)

Our Father Prayer

Minor Octave (eight red beads):

Bead 1: In *praise* ~ I love You, Father, and I give myself to You!
Bead 2: In *thanksgiving* ~ I love You, Father, and I give myself to You!
Bead 3: In *offering* ~ I love You, Father, and I give myself to You!
Bead 4: In *repentance* ~ I love You, Father, and I give myself to You!
Bead 5: In my *inheritance* ~ I love You, Father, and I give myself to You!
Bead 6: In saying my *"Yes"* ~ I love You, Father, and I give myself to You!

Bead 7: In *fidelity* ~ I love You, Father, and I give myself to You!
Bead 8: In *consecration* ~ I love You, Father, and I give myself to You!

FOURTH MAJOR OCTAVE: THE FIAT OF JESUS, OUR SAVIOR—SON OF GOD, AND SECOND PERSON OF THE HOLY TRINITY

Let us meditate on (1) Jesus' Fiat, His "Yes" to God's Will, and (2) how God Our Father sent Jesus to save us and to bring us back home to Him:

Jesus offered His "fiat" to God Our Father during His Passion in the Garden of Gethsemani. "My Father, if it be possible, let this cup pass from me; nevertheless, not as I will, but as thou wilt" (Mt 26:39). Through His Passion, Death, and Resurrection, Jesus redeemed us, defeating the sin (saying "No" to God's Will) and death (separation and exile from God) which Satan introduced into the world. Through Jesus, His Church, and His Sacraments, we could now return to God Our Father and have eternal life.

Our Father Prayer

Minor Octave (eight red beads):

Bead 1: In *praise* ~ I love You, Father, and I give myself to You!
Bead 2: In *thanksgiving* ~ I love You, Father, and I give myself to You!
Bead 3: In *offering* ~ I love You, Father, and I give myself to You!
Bead 4: In *repentance* ~ I love You, Father, and I give myself to You!
Bead 5: In my *inheritance* ~ I love You, Father, and I give myself to You!
Bead 6: In saying my *"Yes"* ~ I love You, Father, and I give myself to You!
Bead 7: In *fidelity* ~ I love You, Father, and I give myself to You!
Bead 8: In *consecration* ~ I love You, Father, and I give myself to You!

FIFTH MAJOR OCTAVE: THE SENDING OF THE HOLY SPIRIT, OUR SANCTIFIER—SPIRIT OF GOD AND THE THIRD PERSON OF THE HOLY TRINITY

Let us meditate on how Jesus, after completing His Mission for God Our Father, asked Him to send the Holy Spirit, a newly revealed manifestation of God—the Third Person of the Holy Trinity. The Holy Spirit was sent (1) to lead us on our journey back home to Our Father and (2) to purify and refine us so that we could become living tabernacles of the indwelling presence of God:

Before ascending to His Father, Jesus promised that He would not leave us orphans. He asked God Our Father to send the Holy Spirit. In doing this, God could again be present with us in a new way. It was now "possible" for God, not only to be "with" us (as in Old Testament times), but "in" us (Jn 14:16-17).

Our Father Prayer

Minor Octave (eight red beads):

Bead 1: In *praise* ~ I love You, Father, and I give myself to You!
Bead 2: In *thanksgiving* ~ I love You, Father, and I give myself to You!
Bead 3: In *offering* ~ I love You, Father, and I give myself to You!
Bead 4: In *repentance* ~ I love You, Father, and I give myself to You!
Bead 5: In my *inheritance* ~ I love You, Father, and I give myself to You!
Bead 6: In saying my *"Yes"* ~ I love You, Father, and I give myself to You!
Bead 7: In *fidelity* ~ I love You, Father, and I give myself to You!
Bead 8: In *consecration* ~ I love You, Father, and I give myself to You!

SIXTH MAJOR OCTAVE: THE CHOICE OF GOD'S PRODIGAL CHILDREN TO RETURN TO THEIR FATHER

Let us meditate on (1) how we are all prodigal children of God Our Father and (2) how He has provided every one of us with the opportunity to make a free-will choice to return to Him:

As prodigal children of God Our Father, we are given the opportunity (individually and collectively) to make a sincere, free-will decision to return to our Father's House. This means deciding to turn away from our own will, our own sinfulness, our own worldliness, and "convert" or turn back towards the presence of God Our Father (Lk 15:11-24).

Our Father Prayer

Minor Octave (eight red beads):

Bead 1: In *praise* ~ I love You, Father, and I give myself to You!
Bead 2: In *thanksgiving* ~ I love You, Father, and I give myself to You!
Bead 3: In *offering* ~ I love You, Father, and I give myself to You!
Bead 4: In *repentance* ~ I love You, Father, and I give myself to You!
Bead 5: In my *inheritance* ~ I love You, Father, and I give myself to You!
Bead 6: In saying my *"Yes"* ~ I love You, Father, and I give myself to You!
Bead 7: In *fidelity* ~ I love You, Father, and I give myself to You!
Bead 8: In *consecration* ~ I love You, Father, and I give myself to You!

SEVENTH MAJOR OCTAVE: THE FIAT OF GOD OUR FATHER'S CHILDREN—INDIVIDUALLY AND AS THE BODY OF CHRIST

Let us meditate on how, in consecrating ourselves to God Our Father and saying "Yes," unconditionally, to His Will, we find our way home to Him—we become living tabernacles of the indwelling presence of God:

In giving our "Yes" to God Our Father, in agreeing to do His Will in all things, in giving ourselves completely to Him, He comes to dwell in us and we dwell in Him—we are home with our Father. We become temples of the Living God (2 Cor 6:16). In a sense, heaven and earth are joined: "Thy kingdom come. Thy will be done on earth as it is in heaven" (Mt 6:10).

Our Father Prayer

Minor Octave (eight red beads):

Bead 1: In *praise* ~ I love You, Father, and I give myself to You!
Bead 2: In *thanksgiving* ~ I love You, Father, and I give myself to You!
Bead 3: In *offering* ~ I love You, Father, and I give myself to You!
Bead 4: In *repentance* ~ I love You, Father, and I give myself to You!
Bead 5: In my *inheritance* ~ I love You, Father, and I give myself to You!
Bead 6: In saying my *"Yes"* ~ I love You, Father, and I give myself to You!
Bead 7: In *fidelity* ~ I love You, Father, and I give myself to You!
Bead 8: In *consecration* ~ I love You, Father, and I give myself to You!

EIGHTH MAJOR OCTAVE: THE COMING OF THE NEW JERUSALEM

Let us meditate on the eventual conclusion of our Salvation History—the New Jerusalem promised in the Book of Revelation—when heaven and earth will be transformed, when mankind will finally be fully restored to God our Father, and when God will manifest His presence and dwell with His children forever in a new way:

Then I saw a new heaven and a new earth; for the first heaven and the first earth had passed away, and the sea was no more.

And I saw the holy city, new Jerusalem, coming down out of heaven from God, prepared as a bride adorned for her husband; and I heard a great voice from the throne saying, "Behold, the dwelling of God is with men. He will dwell with them, and they shall be his people, and God himself will be with them; he will wipe away every tear from their eyes, and death shall be no more, neither shall there be mourning nor crying nor pain any more, for the former things have passed away.

And he who sat upon the throne said, "Behold, I make all things new." Also he said, "Write this, for these words are trustworthy and true." And he said to me, "It is done! I am the Alpha and the Omega, the beginning and the end. To the thirsty I will give water without price from the fountain of the water of life. He who conquers shall have this heritage, and I will be his God and he shall be my son. (Rev 21:1-7)

Our Father Prayer

Minor Octave (eight red beads):

Bead 1: In *praise* ~ I love You, Father, and I give myself to You!
Bead 2: In *thanksgiving* ~ I love You, Father, and I give myself to You!
Bead 3: In *offering* ~ I love You, Father, and I give myself to You!
Bead 4: In *repentance* ~ I love You, Father, and I give myself to You!
Bead 5: In my *inheritance* ~ I love You, Father, and I give myself to You!
Bead 6: In saying my *"Yes"* ~ I love You, Father, and I give myself to You!
Bead 7: In *fidelity* ~ I love You, Father, and I give myself to You!
Bead 8: In *consecration* ~ I love You, Father, and I give myself to You!

On the Medal of *The Holy Octave of Consecration to God Our Father*:

CONSECRATION PRAYER OF *THE HOLY OCTAVE OF CONSECRATION TO GOD OUR FATHER*

My Dearest Father, please accept this offering of myself—my body, mind, and soul:

I *praise* You for Your Creation—all Your works and wonders.
I *thank* You for giving me life and for all that You have done for me.
I *offer* up to You all that You have so generously given me.
I am sincerely *sorry* for not knowing, loving, serving, and honoring You as I should.
I embrace my *inheritance* as Your child, both the joy and the responsibilities.
I give you my *"Yes"* so that I may be an instrument of Your Will.
I pledge my *fidelity* and I ask for the grace of steadfastness and perseverance in my Faith.

Most loving, caring, and merciful of Fathers, in Your Divine Presence, I sincerely proclaim my love for You; I give myself (and my family) to You; and I solemnly *consecrate* myself (and my family) to You—now and forever.

Dearest Father, as Your child, I ask—

That You send Mary to guide me to Jesus, and that Jesus sends me the Holy Spirit so that they may all bring me to You.
That You dwell with me and in me—a living temple prepared by Mary, dedicated by Jesus, and purified by Your Holy Spirit. And may I always be with You and in You.
That You permit me, as Your child, to be Your true and intimate friend—one who loves You above all things.
And that You come for me when I die, to bring me home to You.

I further ask You, Father, for the sake of all mankind:

To have mercy on all Your children—past, present, and future.
To bring peace to the world and to gather all Your children to Yourself.
And that Your Kingdom comes and Your Will is done on earth as it is in heaven.
Amen.

[NOW PROCEED TO THE LITANY]

LITANY

The Holy Octave of Consecration to God Our Father

Lord, have mercy. **Lord, have mercy.**
Christ, have mercy. **Christ, have mercy.**
Lord, have mercy. **Lord, have mercy.**
Christ, hear us. **Christ, graciously hear us.**

God, the Father of Heaven. **Have mercy on us.**
God, the Son, Redeemer of the World. **Have mercy on us.**
God, the Holy Spirit. **Have mercy on us.**
Holy Trinity, one God. **Have mercy on us.**

God Our Father saved eight people on Noe's Ark.
—Have mercy on us, O Loving Father.

God Our Father decreed that all male babies be circumcised on the eighth day as a sign of His Covenant with us.
—Have mercy on us, O Loving Father.

God Our Father manifested Himself to Moses and His children after they completed an eight-day period of consecration and offering to Him.
—Have mercy on us, O Loving Father.

God Our Father instituted the eight-day Feast of Tabernacles to remind His children that He was with them, loved them, and brought them out of the bondage of Egypt.
—Have mercy on us, O Loving Father.

God Our Father accepted purification offerings from His children on the final eighth day of ritual cleansing.
—Have mercy on us, O Loving Father.

God Our Father was glorified when David, the eighth son of Jesse, brought the Ark of the Covenant into the City of David amidst praises sung for the octave upon harps.
—Have mercy on us, O Loving Father.

God Our Father heard David's repentant cry played on an eight-stringed harp.
—Have mercy on us, O Loving Father.

God Our Father: Consecration and Feast Day for the Father of All Mankind

God Our Father was glorified when Solomon completed the House of the Lord in the eighth month of the year.
—Have mercy on us, O Loving Father.

God Our Father filled the Temple with His majesty and came to dwell with His children on the eighth day of Solomon's Feast of the Dedication.
—Have mercy on us, O Loving Father.

The Presence of God Our Father was to be approached by eight steps in the new Temple envisioned by His prophet Ezekial.
—Have mercy on us, O Loving Father.

God Our Father was glorified when His defiled Temple was purified and re-dedicated by the Maccabee's during the eight-day Feast of the Dedication.
—Have mercy on us, O Loving Father.

God Our Father made a new covenant with His children, through Jesus, His Son, Who was circumcised on the eighth day.
—Have mercy on us, O Loving Father.

God Our Father revealed His Son Jesus during the Transfiguration, eight days after Jesus fed the multitudes.
—Have mercy on us, O Loving Father.

God Our Father was glorified when, from Solomon's Porch in the Temple, on the eight-day Feast of the Dedication, His Son, Jesus, revealed that He was consecrated to God Our Father and that He and the Father were one.
—Have mercy on us, O Loving Father.

God Our Father was glorified after His Son, Jesus, rose from the dead on the eighth day of His week of Passion and Redemption for our sins.
—Have mercy on us, O Loving Father.

God Our Father was glorified when Jesus showed His wounds to unbelieving Thomas eight days after His Resurrection.
—Have mercy on us, O Loving Father.

Let us pray:

Dearest God Our Father, let us know, love, and honor You through eight days of purification and dedication, as You willed it throughout our Salvation History. And may The Holy Octave of Consecration to God Our Father and its eighth solemn day, The Feast of the Father of All Mankind, serve to bring all Your children back home to You.

May this be granted through Your Love and the Love of Jesus, our God and Savior; the Holy Spirit, our God and Sanctifier; and Mary, our Mother. Amen.

[NOW PROCEED WITH THE DAILY THEME]

THE DAILY CHAPLET

For Daily Prayer After Formal Consecration

This concise version of the chaplet is provided at the end of the booklet for easy reference. In contrast to the extended version which is provided for the formal eight-day consecration, this concise version is easily memorized and may conveniently be used on a daily basis—especially after completion of the formal eight-day consecration. As was mentioned previously, we strongly recommend that the formal consecration be renewed yearly during The Holy Octave of Consecration to God Our Father, culminating on The Feast of the Father of All Mankind, and that the chaplet (either the formal or daily version) be prayed on a daily basis.

The Holy Octave of Consecration to God Our Father

On the Medal of *The Holy Octave of Consecration to God Our Father:*

In the name of the Father, and of the Son, and of the Holy Spirit. Amen.

Dearest God Our Father, I humbly ask that on my journey home to You, Your Holy Angels protect and guide me; that Your Blessed Saints in Heaven intercede for me; and that Your Suffering Souls in Purgatory pray for me, as I pray for them now. Amen.

On the three gold beads:

> **Bead 1**—Hail Mary full of grace, the Lord is with Thee, Blessed art Thou among women and Blessed is the Fruit of thy womb, Jesus. Holy Mary, Mother of God, pray for us sinners now, and at the hour of our death. Amen.
>
> **Bead 2**—Jesus, my God and my Savior, You loved me so much, You died for me on the Cross, so that I, too, could return to our Father in Heaven. You are the Way, the Truth, and the Life. Through Your Holy Eucharist, please sustain me and be present with me always on my journey home. Amen.
>
> **Bead 3**—Holy Spirit, my God and my Sanctifier, Jesus sent You to me for my journey back home to the Father. Please purify and refine me. Fill me with Your Divine Light and Love so that the Presence of God may dwell in me. Amen.

Now continue with Major Octaves on the following page.

The Our Father Prayer

Our Father, who art in heaven, hallowed be thy name, thy kingdom come, thy will be done on earth as it is in heaven. Give us this day our daily bread and forgive us our trespasses, as we forgive those who trespass against us, and lead us not into temptation, but deliver us from evil. Amen.

GOLD BEADS:
Major Octaves

1st MAJOR OCTAVE
The Disobedience and Exile of God's Children
Our Father Prayer
Minor Octave

2ND MAJOR OCTAVE
The Presence of God Our Father in the Old Testament Era
Our Father Prayer
Minor Octave

3rd MAJOR OCTAVE
The Fiat of Mary, Our Mother
Our Father Prayer
Minor Octave

4th MAJOR OCTAVE
The Fiat of Jesus, Our Savior
Our Father Prayer
Minor Octave

5th MAJOR OCTAVE
The Sending of the Holy Spirit, Our Sanctifier
Our Father Prayer
Minor Octave

6th MAJOR OCTAVE
The Choice of God's Prodigal Children to Return to Their Father
Our Father Prayer
Minor Octave

7th MAJOR OCTAVE
The Fiat of God Our Father's Children
Our Father Prayer
Minor Octave

8th MAJOR OCTAVE
The Coming of the New Jerusalem
Our Father Prayer
Minor Octave

RED BEADS:
Minor Octave

Bead 1: In *Praise*
I love You, Father, and I give myself to You!

Bead 2: In *Thanksgiving*
I love You, Father, and I give myself to You!

Bead 3: In *Offering*
I love You, Father, and I give myself to You!

Bead 4: In *Repentence*
I love You, Father, and I give myself to You!

Bead 5: In my *Inheritance*
I love You, Father, and I give myself to You!

Bead 6: In *Saying My "Yes,"*
I love You, Father, and I give myself to You!

Bead 7: In *Fidelity*
I love You, Father, and I give myself to You!

Bead 8: In *Consecration*
I love You, Father, and I give myself to You!

MEDAL: CLOSING PRAYER

Dearest God Our Father, I love You; I adore You; I worship You! Amen.

Advancing THE FEAST OF THE FATHER OF ALL MANKIND, the Eighth Solemn Day of THE HOLY OCTAVE OF CONSECRATION TO GOD OUR FATHER

If after reading this book, you support the institution of a yearly solemn feast for God Our Father to be celebrated on the first Sunday of August under the title of **The Feast of the Father of All Mankind**, please fill out and mail the following petition. Petitions will be collected and presented to the appropriate Church officials. While we await formal approval, you might also contact your local bishop and parish priest, asking them for permission to celebrate this beautiful consecration feast for God Our Father in your diocese and local churches.

The format for the seven days of preparation is outlined in this book and can easily be adapted for communal preparation in your diocese or local church. The eighth day of solemn consecration (*The Feast of the Father of All Mankind*) should be celebrated with a Mass and appropriate readings and homily. This would be followed by the litany, the formal chaplet, and by the meditative theme for the eighth day of consecration.

May the Grace of God Our Father be with us in our efforts to know, love, serve, and honor Him better—especially in the formal recognition and approval of this eight-day consecration and feast day.

To obtain additional petition forms, please write, call, or FAX the *Feast of the Father of All Mankind Petition Center:*

St. Andrew's Productions
5168 Campbells Run Road Ste. 203
Pittsburgh, PA 15205

Phone: 412-787-9735   Fax: 412-787-5204
Web: www.SaintAndrew.com   Email: standrewsproductions@yahoo.com

Appendix B

PETITION FOR:

The Solemnity of the Divine Paternal Heart
The Feast of the Father of All Mankind

Your Holiness:

With humility and love, we, the children of God, petition you, the Vicar of Christ, to approve a Feast for God Our Father. We ask that this Feast be entitled **The Solemnity of the Divine Paternal Heart – The Feast of the Father of all Mankind,** the eighth solemn day of the holy octave of consecration to God Our Father. We ask that it be celebrated annually on the first Sunday of August. We believe that it is our privilege and responsibility to know, love, serve and honor God Our Father through such a yearly Feast. We pray that Jesus Our God and Savior, The Holy Spirit Our God and Sanctifier, and Mary, Our Mother, guide you in approving this octave Feast so that all mankind may offer their "fiat" to God Our Father, and so that "His Kingdom comes and His Will is done on Earth as it is in Heaven."

Respectfully Submitted:

NAME (Signature)   **ADDRESS**

1._____ _____

2._____ _____

3._____ _____

4._____ _____

5._____ _____

6._____ _____

7._____ _____

8._____ _____

9._____ _____

10._____ _____

11._____ _____

12._____ _____

13._____ _____

14._____ _____

15._____ _____

PLEASE COPY AND DISTRIBUTE THIS PETITION
Mail all petitions to the following address:

St. Andrew's Productions
5168 Campbells Run Road, Ste 203
Pittsburgh, PA 15205

Phone: 412-787-9735   Fax 412-787-5204

Available now:

Jesus came to reveal that the God who "so loved the world that he gave his only Son" (Jn 3:16) had a Heart – a Divine Paternal Heart – the Heart of a Father who existed from eternity. Yes, the Divine Paternal Heart of the Father is the treasure of Heaven that desires to 'beat in unison' with our hearts through shared love in order that "Your kingdom come, your will be done, on earth as [it is] in heaven" (Mt 6:10).

Now, Dr. Thomas Petrisko sheds light on this infinite mystery of the Father to be known, loved and honored by each of his children, in this grace-filled 'era of time.' He also calls for a Feast Day in honor of the Divine Paternal Heart of God the Father. This Feast Day will help us to see with 'the eyes of our souls' – to experience the love of our Father in the depths of our spiritual heart and to return to Him as His prodigal children, to return to the "God and Father of all, who is over all and through all and in all" (Eph 4:4-6).

Father David Tourville
Feast of Christ the King
November 25, 2013

ABOUT THE AUTHOR

Dr. Thomas W. Petrisko was the President of the Pittsburgh Center for Peace from 1990 to 1998 and he served as the editor of the Center's ten special edition *Queen of Peace* newspapers. These papers, primarily featuring the apparitions and revelations of the Virgin Mary, were published in many millions and distributed throughout the world. He is the author of over 20 books, including: **The Fatima Prophecies**, *At the Doorstep of the World;* **The Face of the Father**, *An Exclusive interview with Barbara Centilli Concerning Her Revelations and Visions of God the Father;* **Glory to the Father**, *A look at the Mystical Life of Georgette Faniel;* **For the Soul of the Family**; *The Story of the Apparitions of the Virgin Mary to Estela Ruiz,* **The Sorrow, the Sacrifice and the Triumph**; *The Visions, Apparitions and Prophecies of Christina Gallagher,* **Call of the Ages**, **The Prophecy of Daniel**, **In God's Hands**; *The Miraculous Story of Little Audrey Santo,* **Mother of The Secret, False Prophets of Today, St. Joseph and The Triumph of the Saints, The Last Crusade, The Kingdom of Our Father, Inside Heaven and Hell, Inside Purgatory, The Miracle of the Illumination, Fatima's Third Secret Explained, Living in the Heart of the Father, The Mystery of the Divine Paternal Heart of God Our Father,** and **Honor Thy Father**.

Dr. Petrisko, along with his wife Emily, have four daughters, Maria, Sarah, Natasha, Dominique and two sons, Joshua and Jesse.

www.ingramcontent.com/pod-product-compliance
Lightning Source LLC
Chambersburg PA
CBHW071644160426
43195CB00012B/1354